Happy 50th!

Donald

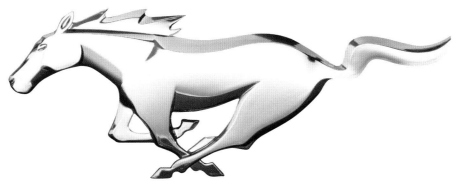

# MUSTANG
## FIFTY YEARS
CELEBRATING AMERICA'S **ONLY TRUE PONY CAR**

**DONALD FARR**
FOREWORD BY EDSEL B. FORD II

First published in 2013 by Motorbooks, an imprint of MBI Publishing Company,
400 First Avenue North, Suite 400, Minneapolis, MN 55401 USA

Motorbooks titles are also available at discounts in bulk quantity for industrial or sales-promotional
use. For details, write to Special Sales Manager at MBI Publishing Company,
400 First Avenue North, Suite 400, Minneapolis, MN 55401 USA.

To find out more about our books, visit us online at www.motorbooks.com.

ISBN-13: 978-0-7603-4396-8

Library of Congress Cataloging-in-Publication Data:

Farr, Donald N.
  Mustang, fifty years : celebrating America's only true pony car / by Donald Farr.
     pages cm
  Summary: "Mustang: fifty years is the first official Ford-licensed fiftieth anniversary celebration of
the iconic Mustang sports car.  Featuring historic photos from Ford's archives, this book follows the
vehicle's lineage from birth to include the Mustang GT, Shelby GT350, Shelby GT500, Super Cobra
Jet, Boss 302, and Boss 429"-- Provided by publisher.
  Includes bibliographical references and index.
  ISBN 978-0-7603-4396-8 (hardback)
  1.  Mustang automobile--History.  I. Title.
  TL215.M8F373 2013
  629.222'2--dc23
                                    2013011840

Editors: Darwin Holmstrom, Jordan Wiklund
Design manager: Cindy Samargia Laun
Cover design: Karl Laun
Design: Simon Larkin
Layout: John Sticha


Printed in China

10 9 8 7 6 5 4 3

# CONTENTS

# ACKNOWLEDGMENTS

On a chilly afternoon in February 1966, I arrived home from junior high and spotted a brand-new Mustang GT in my grandparent's driveway on the other side of Highway 49. At the time, I had no way of knowing that the little red hardtop would change my life forever. As an impressionable and car-crazed 13-year-old, I would never forget the pride of being seen around town in a Mustang—even with my grandparents in the front seats. When the time came to purchase my first car, I chose a Mustang, a new 1970 SportsRoof that led me into the Mustang hobby and launched my career as an automotive journalist specializing in—you guessed it—Mustangs.

Fifty years ago, Lee Iacocca had the right idea—a practical, affordable four-seat car with sporty styling and youthful appeal. Although music, fashion, and hairstyles have changed drastically since April 17, 1964, the Mustang has endured as everyman's sports car, whether as an economical commuter, a powerful muscle car, or top-down weekend convertible. Many car lines don't last a decade; the Mustang has prevailed every model year for the past 50 years, something no other American car can claim.

While assembling this book, the most difficult task involved choosing the highlights that chronicle the Mustang's history. After 50 years and over nine million sold, there are many stories to tell, many special editions to cover, and many people at Ford who fought to keep the Mustang alive in spite of fuel shortages, emerging technology, and engineering budgets. In *Mustang: 50 Years*, I have attempted to relate how the Mustang progressed from its beginnings as a Falcon-based compact to today's world-class automobile. Along the way, it generated a fan following, entered America's popular culture, and won many racing championships.

There are many great Mustang books with outstanding photography, but for *Mustang: 50 Years*, I wanted to illustrate the Mustang's history with period photography (warning to restorers: many photos show prototype or pre-production cars, so don't rely on them for concours detailing!). Over 30 years ago, I visited librarian Bill Buffa at what was then called Ford PhotoMedia to dig out photos from the rows of file cabinets in Ford World Headquarters' basement. Today, Ford's tremendous photo history is preserved at the Ford Motor Company Archives, where I spent several days in white gloves sifting through thousands of old negatives and transparencies in an effort to find unpublished photos, a difficult task for a car that has likely had more books and magazines published about it than any other vehicle. I found a few, thanks to help from Dean Weber, Jamie Myler, Leslie Armbruster, Courtney McAlpine, Aimee Bastion, and Caryl Woods. Contracted archivist Bill Bozgan also pointed me in the right directions or, in some cases, amazingly reached into a box of negatives to locate a specific image.

I am also fortunate to work for Source Interlink Media, a company rich in automotive publishing history with its stable of magazines from the former Petersen Publishing. SIM vice-president Doug Evans and *Mustang Monthly* publisher Sandy Patterson graciously allowed me to use photos from the company's archives, including vintage shots from original *Hot Rod* and *Motor Trend* road tests along with more recent photography from our *Mustang* titles.

As with any book of this magnitude, there are many people to thank. First, I am grateful to Motorbook's Zack Miller for recommending me for this project and to Regina Watson from Ford Licensing for adding her stamp of approval. My friends at Ford, Large and Performance Car Marketing Manager Steve Ling and Shelby/Mustang 50 Year Marketing Manager Jim Owens, offered encouragement, advice, and information. Many thanks as well to Edsel Ford II for writing the Foreword.

I must also thank two long-time friends and associates. Whenever I was unable to locate a specific photo or piece of information, Mustang historian Jim Smart came to my rescue. Photojournalist Jerry Heasley, my cohort in crime throughout much of my career, allowed me to use photos from his vast archives. Another long-time pal, Keith Keplinger, loaned his PhotoShop skills to help clean up old photos.

Hundreds of books have been written about the Mustang and I used many of them for research, including *Mustang: The Complete History of America's Pioneer Ponycar* (Witzenburg), *Mustang Recognition Guide* (Dobbs/Farr/Heasley/Kopec), *Standard Catalog of Mustang: 1964-2004* (Bowling), *Mustang Red Book* (Sessler), *Fox-body Mustang Recognition Guide 1979-1993* (Shreiner/Sessler), *The Mustang Destiny* (Clor), *Mustang Genesis* (Fria), *Mustang: The Next Generation* (McClurg), *The Saleen Book* (Bowling), *Iron Fist, Lead Foot: John Coletti and Ford's Terminator* (Moriarty), *Ford Drag Team* (Morris), *Mustang Boss 302: From Racing Legend to Modern Muscle Car* (Farr), *Boss 429: Performance Mustang Style* (Strange), *Shelby American Registry* (Kopec), *Fast Mustangs* (Gabbard), and *Mustang…By the Numbers* (Marti). I highly recommend these books for anyone in search of specific Mustang information. Although *An Autobiography: Lee Iacocca* (Iacocca) and *Carroll Shelby: The Authorized Biography* (Mills) touch briefly on Mustangs, they provide excellent accounts of two men who are most famously associated with Mustang history.

For proofreading and fact-checking, I relied on Austin Craig, Bob Fria, Mark Houlahan, Jim Smart, and Steve Turner. I can't thank them enough for taking the time to read chapter manuscripts.

There is not enough space here to thank everyone who has provided me with nuggets of Mustang information over the years, but I do need to mention those who specifically helped for this book, in alphabetical order: Marc Christ, John Clor, Scott Halseth, Rick Kirk, Rick Kopec, Matt Lasziac, Kevin Marti, Mickey Matus, Liz Saleen, Jim Wicks, Jeff Yergovich, and a few others that I know I am overlooking. Additional photo assistance came from Drew Alcazar, Dale Amy, Josh Bolger, Bill Bozgan, Francis Butler, Bob Cloutier, Denice Halicki, Jeremy Henrie, Michael Leone, Bob McClurg, Ron Sessions, Evan Smith, Bob Tasca Jr., Tom Wilson, and Jerry Winker.

Thanks also to Judene and Rick Barry for the weekends of peace and solitude in Boca Grande and Winter Haven, and to former colleague Howard Buck for Wednesday evening encouragement sessions.

Finally, I must thank my parents, Ned and Laura Farr, for instilling the confidence to chase my dreams and my wife, Pam, for once again giving up her social life while her husband pecked away on a keyboard.

# FOREWORD

# *"What was your favorite Mustang?"*

By Edsel B. Ford II

You hear people say that all the time. Everyone has a favorite Mustang.

Whether it was the first Mustang you owned, the classic Mustang that you always wanted, or the Mustang that roared by you as you sat amazed in the grandstand, there are as many favorite Mustang stories as there were cars built over the last 50 years.

Now it's time to get personal. On December 27, 1964, my father pulled up to the front door of our home. When I looked outside, there was a pearlescent white 1965 Mustang GT fastback. I was speechless!

For you, the memory may be just as vivid.

After all, what other car has captured the imagination of the American public? From songs like "Mustang Sally" and "First Gear" to movies like *Bullitt*, *Diamonds Are Forever*, *Bull Durham*, and *Gone in 60 Seconds*, to two U.S. postage stamps, Mustang has become ingrained, not just in American car culture, but in American culture itself.

I think about the legendary names that have been part of Mustang's history. Our cars: the Bosses, King Cobra, SVT Cobra, SVO, Bullitt, Mach I, FR500, GT500, Cobra Jet. The Shelby cars: GT350, GT500-H, GT500-KR, Roush, Steeda, Saleen.

Legendary racing names . . . close friends like Carroll Shelby, Mickey Thompson, Jack Roush, Bud Moore, and Bob Tasca, along with legendary race drivers Parnelli Jones, George Follmer, Scott Pruett, Tommy Kendall, John Force, Bob Glidden, Dan Gurney, Jerry Titus, and so many more.

Since its stunning debut at the New York World's Fair in April 1964 to the latest models Ford Motor Company produces today, Mustang has been a car for all people: men and women, young and old, collector or cruiser, racer or restorer.

I've been fortunate in my life to attend many great Mustang events and have loved to talk about this great car with so many of you. We share a wonderful passion for a great car, and although this book celebrates the 50th anniversary of the Mustang, I know we will be able to share many more Mustang memories in the decades to come.

Enjoy!

*Edsel B. Ford II*

# MUSTANG **ENTERS** THE MARKET

**THE EDSEL NEARLY DOOMED THE MUSTANG** from the start.

Just before the dawn of the 1960s, on November 19, 1959, Ford announced it was discontinuing its Edsel line of automobiles after only three years of production. Introduced as a medium-priced 1958 model to compete against General Motors' midlevel Oldsmobile, the Edsel was doomed by a conflagration of an ill-timed U.S. recession, internal Ford politics, unpopular styling (think "horse collar" front grille), and a name that failed to resonate with the car-buying public.

Over a three-year lifespan, Ford sold fewer than 120,000 Edsels, compared to nearly three million Fords sold during the same time period. The company reportedly lost $350 million on the Edsel program. The name itself became a synonym for failure and remains so even today. It was a debacle and an embarrassment for Ford Motor Company—something not lost on Ford president Henry Ford II.

So when Ford Division president Lee Iacocca proposed a new sporty four-seat car in 1961, Henry, still smarting from the Edsel fiasco, walked out of the meeting. He was not interested.

Undeterred, Iacocca treated the snub as an opportunity to prepare for a second presentation, one that was craftily designed to target Ford's lack of product in the up-and-coming sporty youth market. This time, Henry liked what he saw.

Don Frey (left) and Lee Iacocca spearheaded the effort to transform the economical Falcon into the sporty Mustang. *Ford Motor Company*

The Ford brothers—William Clay, Benson, and Henry II—had high hopes for the Edsel when it was introduced for the 1958 model year. *Ford Motor Company*

## YOUTH MOVEMENT

At the end of World War II in 1945, American soldiers returned from the European and Pacific Theaters with an optimistic outlook for the future. With the conflict over, factories dismantled their war-making machine and began hiring workers for domestic production, including automakers who resumed building cars after four years of tanks and airplanes.

And American families began having babies. Lots of them. In 1946, nearly 3.5 million births were recorded in the United States, up from 2.8 million in 1945. By 1964, some 79 million "baby boomers" entered the population.

On September 20, 1945, an ailing Henry Ford called his grandson, Henry Ford II, to his home to inform him that he was ready to step aside so the 28-year-old could take over the presidency of Ford Motor Company. Within months, the younger Henry had surrounded himself with a group of 10 former U.S. Air Force officers known for their management skills while overseeing the Air Force Office of Statistical Control. At Ford, the Harvard-trained ex-officers became known as The Whiz Kids. Two of them—Robert S. McNamara and Arjay Miller—would eventually become presidents of Ford Motor Company.

To bring Ford out of the war doldrums, The Whiz Kids looked outside the company for talent. They hired new engineers and designers, including a contracted stylist named

Joe Oros. Oros's bold approach to the 1949 Ford helped rocket the vehicle to more than one million units sold. As a whole, the U.S. automotive industry had a banner year in 1949. But it would soon learn that American consumers were looking for something more than just sedans and coupes.

American servicemen had discovered European sports car during World War II. Yet U.S. automakers offered nothing like the Jaguar, MG, and Alfa Romeo with their floor shifts and bucket seats. Chevrolet soon quenched the thirst for an American sports car with the 1953 Corvette, a two-seat roadster with a fiberglass body. It was not an immediate success, selling just 315 cars in its first year. The Corvette generated a tremendous amount of publicity, however, and earned Chevrolet a reputation as a performance car company, especially when the new 265 cubic-inch small-block V-8 engine was added to the Corvette's option list in 1955.

Unwilling to cede the sports car market to Chevrolet, Henry Ford II issued a directive to proceed with the development of a two-seater Ford. In October 1954, the Thunderbird debuted at Ford dealers around the country, pulling in orders for 4,000 cars on its first day. More than 16,000 Thunderbirds were sold for 1955, compared to less than 5,000 Corvettes over its first three model years, 1953–1955. Chevrolet even entertained thoughts about discontinuing its slow-selling sports car; instead, the Thunderbird's success convinced

Henry Ford II was 26 years old and the executive vice president of Ford Motor Company when this photo was taken in 1944 with his grandfather, an 80-year-old Henry Ford, as they look over a scale model of the River Rouge industrial complex, which incorporated the Dearborn assembly plant. In 1945, Henry Ford would hand over the presidency to Henry II. *Ford Motor Company*

The 1955 Thunderbird was Ford's response to Chevrolet's Corvette. During its three-year run as a two-seater, Ford's first entry in the youth market outsold the Corvette five-to-one before becoming a larger four-seater in 1958. *Ford Motor Company*

# THE COMPACT REVOLUTION

By the late 1950s, American cars had ballooned into large, heavy vehicles. However, Volkswagen's inroads into the American market had not gone unnoticed, even though most Americans viewed the Volkswagen as too small and cheaply built. Market research indicated that American families—especially those in search of a second car—wanted something smaller and less expensive. In October 1959, all three of the major U.S. automakers responded with smaller, lower-priced vehicles.

At Ford, assistant general manager and "Whiz Kid" Robert McNamara had initiated a marketing study to find out why Americans were purchasing Volkswagens. The research indicated that a 2,400-pound compact car with a six-cylinder engine would be the ideal economy car for Americans. Championed by McNamara, the Falcon debuted as no-frills two-door and four-door sedans, selling more than 400,000 units in its first year. The Falcon's unibody chassis also proved versatile, spawning station wagon, Ranchero, sedan delivery, and Econoline van models by 1961. Three years later, yet another variant exploited an even more lucrative market for Ford.

Chrysler felt so strongly about the new compact market that it introduced the 1960 Valiant as a separate car line. Powered by an unconventional slant-six engine and supported by a new unit-body chassis, the radical appearance came from Virgil Exner, who was known for his forward-look designs with fins. In 1961, the Valiant was merged into the Plymouth line, then restyled for 1963 before adding a fastback model in April 1964.

General Motors took a different approach for its compact car. While the Valiant and Falcon were traditional water-cooled, front-engine cars, Chevrolet's Corvair entered the market with an air-cooled, rear-mounted engine, similar to Volkswagen's Beetle. The rear-engine design allowed a lower, albeit stodgy, profile, and the Quadri-Flex independent suspension resembled the design used in European sports cars, attracting the attention of car enthusiasts. However, the Corvair's erratic handling, blamed on cost savings, garnered an "unsafest car" title by Ralph Nader in his 1965 book, *Unsafe at Any Speed*. Regardless, a new model, the Monza, introduced in the spring of 1960 with bucket seats and a more powerful engine option, earned the reputation as a "poor man's Porsche." It also sold well, making up more than half of Corvair sales by 1962 with help from a new Corsa option with a 150-horsepower turbocharged engine. Although total Corvair sales never reached Falcon levels during 1960–1962, Ford executives took note of the Monza's appeal.

Chevrolet added a sportier Monza model to the Corvair line-up in the spring of 1960. With bucket seats and more powerful engine options, it was promoted as "the poor man's Porsche." The Monza sold well and garnered *Motor Trend*'s 1960 Car of the Year award. Ford took notice. *Source Interlink Media*

Chevy to proceed with a scheduled redesign for 1956. Oddly enough, the Thunderbird saved the Corvette.

Over the next three years, the Thunderbird continued to outsell the Corvette, reaching 21,380 units for 1957. However, Ford assistant general manager Robert McNamara felt that a four-seater would add appeal to a wider base of buyers. The result was the larger 1958 Thunderbird. Although still a two-door design, the size and heft took it out of the sports car category. Once again, Corvette was America's only sports car.

## LEE IACOCCA

Just one month after the introduction of the Valiant, Falcon, and Corvair in October 1959, Lee Iacocca was named vice president and general manager of Ford Division.

Born Lido Anthony Iacocca on October 15, 1924, he was the son of Italian immigrant Nicola Iacocca, who came to the United States at age 12 and eventually parlayed his first car, a Ford Model T, into a successful rental car business followed by more success in real estate around Allentown, Pennsylvania. Nicola had returned to Italy to marry Antonietta Perrotta, and they named their son Lido after the Lido district of Venice. In the northeast tradition of shortening names to one syllable, Lido became known as Lee as he grew up in Allentown.

Early on, Iacocca wanted to work for Ford Motor Company. "I suppose it was partly because my father had always been interested in automobiles," he told *Time* magazine in 1964. "And because I was influenced by family friends who were Ford dealers."

Iacocca prepared for his future career choice by securing a degree in industrial engineering from Lehigh University and a master's in mechanical engineering from Princeton before breezing through Ford's 18-month training course in just nine months. He turned down a job as a Ford automatic transmission engineer, electing instead to pursue sales, explaining, "I learned at Princeton that pure research did not fascinate me. I wanted to get into the people side of the business."

In 1946, Iacocca landed his first sales job at Ford's assembly plant in Chester, Pennsylvania, and made no secret that his goal was to become a company vice president by age 35. He quickly advanced into a sales manager position for the East Coast. As assistant district manager in Philadelphia by 1956, Iacocca attracted the attention of Ford's corporate offices with his "$56 a month for the '56 Ford" promotion. Ford Division General Manager Robert McNamara eventually adopted the program for the entire United States. As a reward for his proactive and clever sales tactic, McNamara brought Iacocca to Detroit to manage Ford's truck marketing. When truck sales climbed to record numbers, Iacocca was moved into car marketing, where promotions eventually placed him on Henry Ford II's radar. In November 1960, the Henry Ford II promoted Iacocca to Ford vice president and general manager of Ford Division. Five weeks later, McNamara resigned as Ford president to join the Kennedy administration as Secretary of Defense. Iacocca took his place. He was 36 years old.

"For my colleagues and me, this was fire-in-the-belly time," Iacocca said in his 1984 book, *Iacocca: An Autobiography.* "We were high from smoking our own brand—a combination of hard work and big dreams. We were young and cocky. We saw ourselves as artists, about to produce the finest masterpieces the world had ever seen."

Henry Ford II promoted Lee Iacocca (foreground) to Ford Motor Company vice president and general manager of Ford Division in late 1960, setting in motion a series of events that would lead to the development of the 1965 Mustang. *Ford Motor Company*

## THE FAIRLANE COMMITTEE

The idea for a car to satisfy the emerging youth market was already churning in Iacocca's head. With his new position at Ford, he now had the horsepower to move on his hunch. But first he needed research. And he needed help. Realizing that Henry Ford II was still reeling from the Edsel failure and would likely not be receptive to investing time and funds into a new car line, Iacocca put together a skunkworks group of executives to brainstorm how Ford should prepare for the predicted onslaught of younger buyers coming into the market over the next decade. The first meetings were held at the Fairlane Inn, providing the group with a name: the Fairlane Committee.

"We met at the Fairlane motel at night," Iacocca told Jim Smart in a 2004 *Mustang Monthly* interview. "No one [at Ford] believed we needed to come in with another brand. They were just recovering from the Edsel, which became synonymous with lemons and duds. And here I say I'd like to come out with a new concept for an all-new car. So we got everyone off-campus. It was like doing a prototype and not telling anyone!"

Headed by Iacocca, the group included representatives from various Ford departments—product planning, marketing, research, engineering, and styling. Product planning manager Don Frey was on board with Iacocca's thinking. In 2004, he told *Northwestern Magazine*, "I clearly remember sitting around the dining room table and my kids saying, 'Dad, your cars stink. They're terrible. There's no pizzazz.' That started the whole thing."

Iacocca's think tank also included special projects assistant Hal Sperlich; marketing executive Frank Zimmerman; public relations manager Walter Murphy; ad copywriter Sid Olsen from Ford's advertising agency, J. Walter Thompson; market research manager

For the short term, Iacocca's Fairlane Committee recommended a sportier version of the Falcon, resulting in the Sprint, shown here after the Falcon's restyling for 1964. The Sprint package added a V-8 engine, floor shift, and bucket seats to appeal to a younger demographic. *Source Interlink Media*

As Iacocca's idea for a sporty four-seat car jelled in 1961, Ford styling chief Gene Bordinat brought out a styling effort called the Allegro. Iacocca didn't care for the design but felt that the long hood, short deck package with a compact rear seat was on the right track. *Ford Motor Company*

Clay modelers from the Lincoln-Mercury studio work on their entry for Iacocca's sporty car design competition. It had a full-width front grille, rear fins, and quad exhaust tips protruding through the rear valance, but it failed to meet Iacocca's expectations. *Ford Motor Company*

During the design competition in Ford's styling courtyard on August 16, 1962, Iacocca immediately liked the Ford studio's clay model, named Cougar, as designed by Dave Ash under Joe Oros's supervision. *Ford Motor Company*

Robert Eggert; Ford car marketing manager Chase Morsey; Ford racing director Jacque Passino; and Ford advertising manager John Bowers.

For several months, the Fairlane Committee hashed out ideas to better identify the youth market, determining that, in the short-term, the Falcon needed a sportier image, resulting in Futura and Sprint models with bucket seats and floor shift to counter the Corvair Monza. Passino was given a bigger role in developing Ford's racing image; by 1963, Ford's new Total Performance campaign would be in full swing.

More importantly, the Fairlane Committee outlined the parameters for a new car, one that would appeal to a younger customer. Chase Morsey's research confirmed that the 20–24-year-old age group would increase by more than 50 percent during the 1960s, and that 18–34-year-olds would account for at least half of the increase in car sales over the same time period. The research also indicated a growth in two-car families and women buyers, who preferred small cars for their better handling.

By late 1961, the research and work by the Fairlane Committee had evolved into a set of goals for the ideal new sporty car:

- Four-passenger with a sizable trunk
- 2,500-pound target weight
- Retail price under $2,500

- Long hood, short rear deck styling
- One basic car with many available options
- Target introduction date: New York World's Fair, April 1964

Iacocca and the Fairlane Committee realized that everything the emerging youth market wanted in a car was already available—the sporty four-seater appeal of the Thunderbird, the sports car look of the Ferrari, and the economy of the Volkswagen. Yet something told Iacocca that there may be a market for car that combined all of those attributes in a compact yet sporty design.

At the time, developing a completely new car cost up to $400 million, and Iacocca knew better than to approach Henry Ford II with that scenario. Sperlich recommended using the Falcon chassis. "We spent six months trying to concept it," Sperlich told *Motor Trend*, "first trying to make it off the original two-seat Thunderbird, which was a dumb idea. I knew Charlie Baldwin, who had done the Falcon, which was probably the most boring car on the planet. But it was a good car on a great platform. So I said, 'Why don't we make it off the Falcon?'"

Iacocca concurred. "The answer lay in using components that were already in the system," Iacocca said. "The engines, transmissions, and axles for the Falcon already existed, so if we could adapt them, we wouldn't have to start from scratch. We could piggyback the new car onto the Falcon and save a fortune."

The project was given the code name T-5. Iacocca and his team had less than 28 months to engineer a new car. But first they needed a design—and Henry Ford II's blessing.

## SPORTY BY DESIGN

During the first half of 1962, Ford's styling staff presented no less than 18 clay models to Iacocca. None of them impressed.

The Ash-Oros clay model was two-sided, with a different type of rear brake cooling scoop on the opposite side. The tri-bar taillights would survive to become a styling cue for many years to come. *Ford Motor Company*

By December 1962, the front end styling of the Cougar still had its catlike grille emblem, but the headlight buckets had evolved into a more production-friendly shape with standard-size round headlights. *Ford Motor Company*

Most American cars in the 1960s were available in a variety of body styles, so it's no surprise that Ford designers explored different body styles in addition to hardtop and convertible. This four-door didn't meet expectations for a sporty car, so the idea was shelved. *Ford Motor Company*

"By now, I was growing impatient," Iacocca said in his autobiography. "If our new car was going to be ready in April 1964, we needed a design right away. There were 21 months left in which to get the idea approved, buy equipment, locate supply sources, and arrange for dealers to sell the finished product. We were well into the summer of 1962, and the only way we could still have a shot at the World's Fair was to come up with a fully approved clay model by September 1."

To speed up the process, Iacocca conceived a design competition. On July 27, styling director Gene Bordinat instructed his three styling departments—Ford, Lincoln-Mercury, and Advance Projects—to have designs ready within the month.

Chief Ford stylist Joe Oros was out of town for a weeklong seminar when he learned about the competition. "I was in touch daily with the Ford studio," Oros told *Mustang Monthly* in 1987. "One day when I called, I was told that we had been asked to come up with a proposal for the sporty car project. I finished my week at the conference, but I could barely keep my mind on the lectures because I was totally absorbed by the new assignment."

Less than three weeks later, on August 16, six clay models—three from Advance Projects, two from Lincoln-Mercury, and one with different treatments on each side from the Ford studio—were assembled in the styling courtyard for review by Iacocca and other executives. For Iacocca, the clear winner was the Cougar from the Ford studio, designed by Gale Halderman, Dave Ash, and Charlie Phaneuf under Joe Oros's supervision. Iacocca had seen it before and liked the design from the start.

Iacocca immediately liked Gale Halderman's Fastback design, as proposed in May 1962. However, it would have to wait until the beginning of the regular 1965 model year. *Ford Motor Company*

By September 1963, stylists were working with real sheetmetal stampings. Just six months before Job One, it still had the Cougar grille emblem. *Ford Motor Company*

"When it was about half done, Joe invited me down to have a look," Iacocca recalls. "As soon as I saw it, one thing hit me instantly: although it was just sitting there on the studio floor, the brown clay model looked like it was moving."

As Oros tells it, a clay model had already been started when he returned from his seminar. Oros had his own ideas, so he had the partially completed model covered with a tarp and called Ash, along with manager Gale Halderman and John Foster, into his office. "I had a discussion with them," Oros said, "and later extended the dialogue with all the designers from the Ford studio. We spent a day talking about the design for this sporty car. We reorganized our thinking and used a management problem-solving technique that I had picked up at the previous week's conference."

The group made lists of what the car should and shouldn't look like, and spent several days relaying their ideas to the designers in the studio.

"I asked them to give consideration to three design elements," Oros said. "Number one was a Ferrari-type mouthy air intake and a Maserati-like die-cast center motif for the grille. Number two was that we give serious thought to having an air intake just forward of the rear axle that might direct air to the rear brakes. And three was to have consideration for a personal Thunderbird-like greenhouse in a sporty four-seater configuration."

The design also incorporated the long hood, short rear deck design preferred by Iacocca, who admittedly admired the looks of Lincoln's 1956 Continental Mark II. As someone else explained, "A long hood indicates there's a lot of engine under there."

With the design selected, there was still the matter of getting Henry Ford II's approval. Subsequent to the August 16 viewing, Iacocca brought HFII to the styling courtyard to see the Cougar clay model. He was enthused, according to Halderman, although Iacocca also remembers a comment made in reference to the Edsel. HFII had not forgotten the Edsel's failure.

Still lacking a commitment, Iacocca visited Henry Ford II at his 12th-floor office in Ford World Headquarters for a private meeting. Obviously tiring of Iacocca's relentless pursuit

# FROM THE NEWS BUREAU

Ford Division of Ford Motor Company
Rotunda Drive at Southfield Road
Monday, April 13, 1964

Styling and features of expensive European road cars are combined with an American mass-production price, compact economy, and traditional Ford quality in the Mustang—a new line of cars from Ford Division of Ford Motor Company.

Aimed at the fastest-growing dimension in American motoring—driving for pleasure—the Mustang offers the practicality of a back seat and adequate trunk space in a car comparable in size to the classic two-passenger Thunderbird.

Standard equipment of Mustang hardtop and convertible models include sports and luxury features such as bucket seats, molded nylon carpeting, floor-mounted shift for manual and automatic transmissions, all-vinyl interior, padded instrument panel, and full wheel covers. "In the Mustang, Ford actually has created three cars in one," according to Lee A. Iacocca, Ford Motor Company vice president and Ford Division general manager. "Starting with the economical, fun-to-drive basic Mustang, the buyer may select options to give him a sports car for street or competition use, or a luxury car geared to either economy or performance."

Mustang options available to the performance-minded include a selection of three V-8 engines with up to 271 horsepower, four-speed transmission, quick-ratio steering, Rally-Pac with tachometer and clock, limited-slip differential, and a special handling suspension, and sports tires.

Luxury options include a center console, power brakes and steering, automatic transmission, power convertible top, rear-seat radio speaker, remote control trunk release, vinyl-covered hardtop, and air conditioning.

"We believe Mustang represents a new dimension in American motoring at a time when new and old generations of car lovers alike have come full circle to an appreciation of the automobile for its own sake," says Mr. Iacocca. "It offers a combination of driving fun, roominess, and style that permits the Mustang buyer to make of the car almost anything he desires—all at a low initial cost."

of his new sporty car, HFII reportedly said, "I'll approve the damn thing. But once I approve it, you've got to sell it, and it's your ass if you don't."

During a September 10 product approval meeting, Henry Ford II officially approved the project with one modification—he wanted an extra inch of leg room for rear seat passengers.

"Unfortunately, adding even an inch to the interior of a car can be a very expensive proposition," said Iacocca. "But we also knew that Henry's decisions were not open to debate. As he liked to remind us, his name was on the building."

With Henry Ford II's signoff, Iacocca had corporate approval and $45 million—not the $75 million he had requested—to develop and tool-up for a new Ford vehicle. He was also looking at less than 18 months to complete it compared to the typical three years required to build a new car.

## TIME TO ENGINEER

With HFII's approval on September 10, 1962, there was increased urgency to expand the development of the "Special Falcon," as the project was called by many. Although the exterior design was mostly established, Ford's engineering department needed to create sheetmetal stampings, design the interior, and adapt the new body to the Falcon chassis. It would

In late 1963, the name was chosen—Mustang—and the running horse forever replaced the Cougar in the grille emblem. *Ford Motor Company*

involve mostly body engineering because the basic chassis, engines, driveline, and suspension came from the Falcon.

By early 1963, the decision had been made to offer a hardtop and convertible, yet the styling department continued to explore other body-style options, including a four-door and station wagon. These ideas were quickly dismissed because they did not conform to the car's mission as a sporty vehicle. However, Halderman had an idea. Many European sports cars came with fastback styling, plus he had noticed the popularity of the 1963½ Galaxie 500 fastback.

"I did the fastback design and didn't tell anyone about it until it was finished and ready to show to Iacocca," Halderman said in a 1984 *Mustang Monthly* article. "Its appearance was startling, but well-received." Iacocca liked it immediately.

But with barely a year left, the decision was made to pursue the hardtop and convertible for the introduction on April 17, 1964, five months before the typical fall model year intros. The fastback would be delayed five months until September.

Throughout 1963, work continued on the Special Falcon. There were styling issues to be resolved, subcontractors and parts suppliers to choose, and details to iron out, like shifter and door handle designs. Stylist John Najjar came up with cowhide-grain imprints in the inner door sheet metal, something that would give the Mustang's interior more of a luxurious appearance. By April 1963, just one year before introduction, the first sheetmetal stampings were available, allowing engineers to work with real metal bodies instead of clay. Six months later, in late 1963, pilot cars were being assembled and assembly plant supervisors began training to learn how to incorporate Mustang builds on the assembly line.

Plymouth attempted to upstage Ford's pony car arrival by adding a fastback roof to the Valiant and calling it the Barracuda, introducing it on April 1, 1964, just two weeks before the Mustang's arrival. It was too little too late; the Barracuda never came close to matching the Mustang's sales success. *Source Interlink Media*

On April 3, 1964, the Dearborn assembly plant was turning out Mustangs by the thousands in preparation for the official April 17 introduction date. *Ford Motor Company*

At the same time, marketing research revealed that Iacocca's hunch about the youth market was not only on target, but that he may have even underestimated its impact. The original estimate of 85,000 units for the first year was increased to more than 200,000, more than the Dearborn assembly plant could handle. Iacocca gambled by preparing to convert a second assembly plant for his new car's production.

## COUGAR, TORINO OR MUSTANG?

As the styling and engineering departments ironed out the complicated details to roll completed cars off the assembly lines, there was much debate over the all-important process of naming the new car. "The name is often the toughest part of the car to get right," Iacocca said. "It's easier to design doors and roofs."

After approval, the new car took on the Cougar name of the Dave Ash and Joe Oros winning design. At a May product strategy meeting, Cougar was among the four names chosen, along with Monte Carlo, Monaco, and Torino. It was quickly determined that the first two had already been registered by other auto manufacturers, so the list was narrowed to Torino and Cougar. Henry Ford II suggested Thunderbird II, but as Iacocca recalls, "Nobody else liked that one."

Torino, the Italian spelling for the city of Turin, was initially selected because it made a connection to European sports cars. However, Charlie Moore in public relations soon pointed out that Henry Ford II was having an affair with a jet-setting Italian divorcee. Coming out with a new car with an Italian name could lead to negative publicity.

That left Cougar, the name preferred by design winners Ash and Oros. They even sent

Presenting the unexpected...
New Ford Mustang!

This is the car you never expected from Detroit. It is so distinctively beautiful it has received the Tiffany Award for Excellence in American Design, the first automobile ever to be so honored by Tiffany & Co. Mustang has the look, the fire, the flavor of one of the great European road cars. Yet it is as American as its name . . . and as practical as its price. Because Mustang is an amazingly versatile car and can be inexpensively tailored to the widest variety of individual tastes, many very different people will find it surprisingly easy to say: "This is the ideal car for me." Turn the page and you'll see why.

Iacocca called it the *Mona Lisa* look. The Mustang's initial advertising campaign showed off the new car's profile to illustrate its long hood, short deck proportions. Sid Olsen from the Fairlane Committee wrote much of the advertising copy. *Ford Motor Company*

Henry Ford II introduces the 1965 Mustang to the press at the New York World's Fair unveiling on April 13, 1964. The well-planned and elaborate launch campaign was officially under way. *Ford Motor Company*

Iacocca a die-cast Cougar emblem with a note: "Don't name it anything but Cougar." Iacocca wasn't convinced.

J. Walter Thompson's name specialist, John Conley, who had researched previous Ford nameplates, including Thunderbird and Falcon, was dispatched to the Detroit Public Library to compile a list of possible animal names. From his list, the choices were narrowed to Bronco, Puma, Cheetah, Colt, Cougar, and Mustang.

Around the same time, a two-seater styling concept, created to test the waters for a possible Ford sports car, was making the show car rounds. It debuted as the Ford Mustang Experimental Sports Car on October 7, 1962, at the U.S. Grand Prix race at Watkins Glen, New York, with designer John Najjar taking credit for the name, admitting that he borrowed it from the P-51 World War II fighter plane. However, when the aviation connection was rejected, he grabbed a dictionary and learned that the Mustang horse was defined as a "hardy, wild horse of the American plains." At that point, the Mustang concept car took on an equestrian identity. Designer Phil Clark was asked to pen a running horse logo. Later, a red, white, and blue tri-bar was added behind the horse to confirm the all-American heritage.

As late as midyear 1963, the name Torino was still the leading candidate. J. Walter Thompson even produced a film, *Torino*, to introduce the new car to the press, and sample newspaper and magazine advertisements touted "Torino by Ford." Personally, Iacocca felt the name sounded too European. Ford's J. Walter Thompson ad agency preferred Mustang because "it had the excitement of the wide-open spaces and was American as all hell." It also scored at the top of marketing surveys.

In a fall 1963 column for the *Des Moines Register* newspaper, sports writer Maury White recalled Iacocca visiting the Southern Methodist University football team's locker room after the SMU Mustangs had played an inspired, albeit losing, effort against the Michigan

Wolverines in the fall of 1963. Iacocca had attended the game in Ann Arbor, Michigan, and afterwards asked to speak to the SMU players. White recounted Iacocca's speech in the locker room: "Gentleman, Ford is coming out with a new sports car and we have been considering names. It will be light, like your team. It will be quick, like your team. It will be sporty, like your team. Today, watching Southern Methodist's Mustangs play with such flair, we reached a decision. We will call our new car the Mustang."

Likely, the decision had already been reached and Iacocca used the occasion as opportunistic publicity. Regardless, his description of light, quick, and sporty was right on target.

## WHEN STARS ALIGN

On January 1, 1964, Americans shook off their hangovers and woke up to a New Year filled with uncertainty. Less than two months earlier, on November 22, 1963, President John F. Kennedy had been assassinated in Dallas. As the youngest man to ever hold the office, the younger generation felt connected to the handsome, charismatic president. Also

Ford Pavilion visitors ride the moving sidewalk past a Mustang hardtop as they make their way to the entrance to the Magic Skyway. *Ford Motor Company*

Seven contestants from the 1964 Miss Smile contest, sponsored by Jantzen, got to take one of the 1965 Mustang convertibles for a spin on the Ford Pavilion's Magic Skyway ride at the New York World's Fair. *Ford Motor Company*

troubling was the threat of nuclear war and an escalating conflict in Vietnam. Kennedy had stood up to Russia's Nikita Khrushchev to end the Cuban Missile Crisis in 1962, yet baby boomers couldn't shake the memories of hiding under desks at school to prepare for nuclear holocaust. Perhaps more certain was the fact that most young men would be drafted into military service at 18 for a few weeks of basic training before being airlifted to the rice paddies of southeast Asia.

On February 9, American youth began to pull out of the doldrums when the Beatles appeared on *The Ed Sullivan Show*. Forced to suffer through manufactured teen music after Elvis's induction into military service in 1958, the youth market quickly embraced the four

Henry Ford II poses with a Mustang convertible display car in front of the Ford Pavilion at the 1964 New York World's Fair. Behind him is the Magic Skyway that wrapped around the replica of the Ford Wonder Rotunda before entering the building to take riders on a journey created by Disney. *Ford Motor Company*

lads from England. When *Billboard* magazine issued its Top 100 records on April 4, singles from the Beatles took the top five spots. The youth movement had begun.

There was more good news on the business front. Auto sales were on target for an all-time high during the first quarter of 1964. Disposable household income was also up, and Congress had just approved an income tax cut.

It was the perfect storm for a new kind of youthful car from Ford.

At the Dearborn assembly plant, workers returned on Monday, February 10—right after watching the Beatles' Ed Sullivan debut on Sunday night—to begin building the first preproduction Mustangs. Over the weekend, the plant had shut down so the assembly line could be prepared to simultaneously produce Fairlanes and Mustangs. By the end of February, 150 Mustangs had been built to familiarize workers with the assembly process. The target date of March 9 for Job One was on schedule.

## Radio Commercial
Hometown Mustang #1
1964 Ford Car Radio Commercial
60 second live

ANNOUNCER: Next time you're in the neighborhood of (ADDRESS), why not stop off at (HOMETOWN MOTORS) and see something really new and different? The new Ford Mustang! The Mustang features the styling you'd expect in a European import, but the Mustang is an American product, manufactured right here in Detroit. And that's not all—the new Ford Mustang comes with a long list of standard features . . . such as bucket seats . . . that are included at its unbelievably low price of $0000, excluding state and local taxes. And at (HOMETOWN), you can tailor the Mustang to your own personal needs and tastes with a choice of options previously unprecedented in a car of this low price. So your Mustang can be either a practical, sensible family car . . . or a sports car, eager for competition. See the versatile, low-priced Mustang now at (HOMETOWN MOTORS, ADDRESS).

## MADE TO BE MADE BY YOU

Ford was ready with its marketing campaign for the new Mustang, which would go down as one of the most expensive launches in American auto history. The PR machine cranked up in late 1963 when Ford invited a number of national magazine writers to Dearborn to make them aware of the emerging youth market. Several weeks before the April 17, 1964, introduction date, 200 of the nation's top radio disc jockeys visited Dearborn to drive Mustangs and college newspaper editors were also invited behind the wheel.

Two years earlier, Iacocca and his Fairlane Committee had visualized a gala introduction at the World's Fair in New York City. Four days before the Mustang's official debut at Ford dealerships, on April 13, 1964, Ford staged a Mustang press introduction at the Ford Pavilion, which featured a Disney-themed Magic Skyway ride where visitors rode in a variety of Ford convertibles, including 12 new Mustangs mounted to the unique conveyor system. Afterwards, selected members of the press were delivered to the nearby Westchester Country Club, where 70 Mustangs waited so the press could drive them on a 750-mile trek through Canada and into Dearborn.

On Thursday night, April 16, Ford purchased simultaneous commercial slots for all prime-time TV programming between 9:30 and 10 p.m.. Viewers who tuned in to watch popular shows *Hazel*, *Perry Mason*, and the *Jimmy Dean Show* could not miss the Mustang promotions. On introduction day, April 17, 2,600 major newspapers carried full-

During the World's Fair introduction festivities, Tiffany & Co. chairman Walter Hoving presented the Tiffany Award to Henry Ford II for "Excellence in American Design." *Ford Motor Company*

# THE WINDSOR SMALL-BLOCK

It's hard to say which is more synonymous with the other—the 289 in the Mustang or the Mustang powered by the 289. Initially produced in 1962 at the Windsor, Ontario, engine plant, Ford's new small-block became famously known as the Windsor family of engines and found its way into Mustangs in 260, 289, 302, and 351 displacements. With the exception of 1974, the Windsor small-block would be used in Mustangs through 1995.

Ford debuted its new small-block in 221-cubic-inch form in 1962 as a replacement for the Y-block, a heavy and bulky V-8 that had powered Ford vehicles in a variety of displacements since 1954. With the trend toward compact cars such as the Fairlane and Falcon, Ford developed the new V-8 with an advanced thin-wall casting, making the 221 much smaller and lighter, at 470 pounds, than its predecessor. With its wedge heads and a two-barrel carburetor for 145 horsepower, the 221 was originally used in the Ford Fairlane and Mercury Meteor.

In mid-1962, the 221's bore was increased to 3.80 inches to create a larger 260-cubic-inch version with 164 horsepower for full-size Fords and eventually the Falcon and Mercury Comet. At the Mustang's introduction in April 1964, the two-barrel 260 became the base V-8.

The Windsor small-block reached its most famous displacement for the 1963 model year when the bore was increased to 4.0 inches for 289 cubic inches. In both two-barrel and four-barrel form, the 289 found its way into most Fords, including optionally in the Mustang for the first four months of production as a D code with an Autolite four-barrel carburetor for 210 horsepower. During 1965 and 1966, the 289 was offered as a two-barrel with 200 horsepower and a four-barrel with 225 horsepower.

The 289 High Performance engine debuted late in the 1963 model year as an option for the Fairlane. Due to high demand for 289s, it was not available in the Mustang until June 1964. Also known as the Hi-Po or K-code for its engine designation in the VIN, the Mustang's 289 High Performance was rated at 271 horsepower thanks to a solid-lifter cam, 10.5:1 compression, 595-cfm four-barrel carburetor, dual-point distributor, open-element air cleaner, and low-restriction exhaust manifolds. Designed to make power at high rpm, the Hi-Po was also equipped with cast-in spring cups and screw-in rocker arm studs, thicker main caps and larger rod bolts, hardness-tested crankshaft, revised balancer, larger generator/alternator pulley, and five-blade fan.

Fittingly, Shelby utilized the 289 Hi-Po for the GT350, increasing output to 306 horsepower with a Holley four-barrel carburetor, Cobra aluminum intake, and Tri-Y tubular headers. A larger aluminum oil pan also reduced the chances of oil starvation during hard cornering.

Through 1965, Mustang engines followed Ford's engine identification system, with short-blocks painted black while air cleaners and valve cover finish identified the specific engine—260 with light blue, 289 with gold, and 289 High Performance with chrome. In 1966, all Ford engines were painted Corporate Blue with decal identification on the air cleaner.

From its humble beginnings as a lightweight, compact small-block, the Windsor engine would become the foundation for most Mustang V-8 engines, including the Boss 302 and 351W, for the next 30 years.

page Mustang advertisements; 24 national magazines were on the newsstands with full-page or double-truck ads featuring what Iacocca called the *Mona Lisa* look—a profile of a white hardtop along with the Mustang's "$2,368 F.O.B." price and the simple statement, "The Unexpected."

Iacocca credits Sid Olsen, from the Fairlane Committee, with the advertising campaign. "He was the guy who wrote all the copy," Iacocca told *Mustang Monthly*. "He was a genius on copy, headlines, and writing ads. He was the original three-martini guy. He couldn't drink

Ford went to great heights to promote the Mustang. In New York City, a Mustang was disassembled, placed on the elevator, then reassembled on top of the Empire State Building for this photo opportunity. *Ford Motor Company*

## PACE CAR

Just one month after its introduction, Mustang mania continued into May with the Mustang's selection as the pace car for the Indianapolis 500. Three Mustang convertibles were prepared for the duty with 289 High

Performance engines built by Ford's racing arm, Holman-Moody. Benson Ford drove the actual pace car during the Indy 500, which was won by A. J. Foyt, who turned down the pace car as a prize and took a highly optioned Wimbledon White convertible instead.

Ford took advantage of the Indy pace car publicity by creating a dealer sales contest that resulted in some 230 Indy 500 pace car replicas, all hardtops with the special Pace Car White paint and Indianapolis 500 Pace Car decals.

Mustangs were loaded by the train carload at the Dearborn assembly plant to make their way to dealers. *Ford Motor Company*

When first introduced, the Mustang was available in two body styles: hardtop and convertible. A fastback would join the lineup later. *Ford Motor Company*

With its selection as the pace car for the 1964 Indianapolis 500, a specially prepared Mustang convertible led the Indy race cars to the starting line for the greatest spectacle in racing. *Source Interlink Media*

at the Ford Division building, so he'd go to the Dearborn Inn, have a couple of martinis, and work from about 3:00 to 6:00. He couldn't do anything in the morning, but once he had those drinks, he was fantastic."

Walter Murphy in public relations scored the biggest coup of the campaign when both *Time* and *Newsweek* magazines featured Iacocca and the Mustang on their covers, a first for an auto executive. "This was outstanding publicity for a new commercial product," Iacocca said. "Both magazines sensed we had a winner, and their added publicity during the very week of the Mustang's introduction helped make their prediction a self-fulfilling prophecy. I'm convinced that *Time* and *Newsweek* alone led to the sale of an extra 100,000 cars."

In addition to the TV, newspaper, and magazine coverage, Mustangs were displayed in 200 Holiday Inn lobbies and in 15 of the country's busiest airports. Millions of pieces of direct mail were sent to owners of compact cars. It was the largest and most comprehensive vehicle launch in American automotive history. But would it work?

## MUSTANG MANIA

Ford dealers around the United States and Canada weren't prepared for the onslaught. After slyly off-loading new Mustangs and hiding them in shops or outbuildings, dealerships opened their doors on Friday morning, April 17, and were overwhelmed by just how many car-crazed drivers wanted their first glimpse at Ford's new Mustang. The stories have become Mustang lore:

In Texas, a dealer reported that 15 people were bidding on his last Mustang.

In Pittsburgh, a dealer was unable to bring a Mustang down off the wash rack because so many people were crowded underneath.

In Chicago, a dealer locked his doors for fear that the mobs endangered themselves and his employees.

One buyer slept in his car at the dealership until his check cleared the next day.

In Seattle, a concrete truck driver was so mesmerized by the Mustangs on display that he crashed into the dealership's showroom window.

The hysteria continued over the weekend as Ford dominated TV airwaves with Mustang commercials on Saturday and Sunday nights. According to Iacocca, more than four million people visited Ford showrooms over the April 17–19 weekend. Most dealerships sold out of their allotted Mustangs; salesmen wrote orders for 22,000 cars, creating a two-month backlog.

During the Mustang launch, a photograph was distributed to dealers with Iacocca and Frey standing with a red Mustang. On the front was a license plate with: "417 by 4-17," which stressed Iacocca's sales goal of beating the Falcon's record of 417,000 sales in its first year. By the evening of April 16, 1965, one day before the Mustang's first anniversary, Ford dealers had sold 418,812 Mustangs, a new record. *Ford Motor Company*

Ford took advantage of the Mustang's selection as the Indianapolis 500 pace car by readying replica hardtops for national sales contests. Winner of the Checkered Flag promotion traveled to Dearborn for a key presentation by Lee Iacocca. *Ford Motor Company*

Although Ford had directed dealers to keep at least one Mustang in their showroom until the end of April, most could not turn down the sales opportunities. A few jumped the gun and sold Mustangs before the official introduction. In Chicago, 22-year-old Gail Brown celebrated her first job by visiting Johnson Ford on April 15. She was looking for a convertible; the salesman told her, "Come back here, I have something you might like." In the garage area, under wraps, was a light blue Mustang convertible. Gail bought it on the spot and picked it up the next morning. For one day, Gail was driving the only Mustang on the road in the Chicago area. "I felt like a movie star," she said.

Within weeks of the April 17 introduction date, it was obvious that Ford had a runaway sales success on its hands. With that came the challenge of keeping up with demand. A third assembly plant, in Metuchen, New Jersey, was quickly overhauled to build Mustangs.

## THREE CARS IN ONE

The Mustang that arrived at dealers on April 17, 1964, was very similar to the Joe Oros and Dave Ash design. Stylists broke 78 inhouse styling rules to accomplish the original design, which included the long hood, short rear deck, mouthy grille opening, side sculpturing that led to a simulated rear quarter panel scoop, and tri-bar taillights. Although the 1965 Mustang would be 1½ inches longer and 108 pounds heavier than originally planned, it retailed for $2,368, well under the targeted $2,500 sticker price.

The curious who flocked into Ford dealerships in April 1964 were greeted by Mustangs in two body styles—hardtop and convertible. As initially planned, the base Mustang

*Continued on page 36*

Many early Mustang buyers were women, just as designer Joe Oros had envisioned. *Ford Motor Company*

Inside the 1965 Mustang, a twin eyebrow instrument panel gave the interior a cockpit feel. The Mustang came only with a floor shifter between the bucket seats; a steering column shifter, as found on many cars of the day, was not available. No rubber floor covering for the Mustang either—carpet was standard equipment—but the instrument cluster was straight out of the Falcon. *Ford Motor Company*

# FROM THE NEWS BUREAU

Ford Motor Company
Ford Pavilion
New York World's Fair

IMMEDIATE RELEASE
WORLD'S FAIR, NY—Convertibles cruising the "Magic Skyway" at the Ford Pavilion have traveled a combined distance equal to 34 times around the world in the first season of the New York World's Fair.

Part of the "magic" is that the 146 Ford-built convertibles are still going strong after 806,400 miles. Their doors still close with a solid click after 3,276,000 slams. Their seats still spring back after more than 6,500,000 passengers.

Ford engineers estimate the "Magic Skyway" cars have absorbed the equivalent of 15 years normal usage in the space of six months. They represent every convertible line built by Ford—Lincoln Continental, Mercury, Comet, Thunderbird, Mustang, Falcon, and Ford.

All are scheduled to be replaced by new 1965 convertibles during the winter. Ford's "changeover" to new models will be one of the most extensive modifications made to any World's Fair Pavilion.

The Ford Pavilion, one of the great hits of the fair, offered something unique in entertainment history by transporting its audience in moving cars through a Walt Disney-animated show.

The sight of new convertibles entering "time tunnels" in full sight of fairground crowds was magnetic.

Fairgoers moved constantly in line at the Ford Wonder Rotunda. Some waited over an hour to enter.

They boarded the "Magic Skyway" from a moving rubber belt that made the automobiles seem to stand still. Pushbuttons on car radios offered a narration in four languages.

Families invariably let the youngest member "drive." Young feet pushed energetically on brake and accelerator. Young arms turned steering wheels endlessly—and "steered" a true course.

One of the youngest and most enthusiastic "drivers" was John F. Kennedy Jr., not yet four years old when he took the wheel of a full-sized Ford, humming to supply the sound of the missing motor.

All but compact cars on the "Magic Skyway" had their motors removed to lessen dead weight. Other modifications were necessary to allow cars to be driven by a unique system devised by Disney's WED Enterprises Inc.

When the fair closes October 18, this year's convertibles will be returned to Detroit for reconditioning. With motors reinstalled, unused brakes and lights and steering mechanisms reconnected, they will be offered for sale as used cars through Ford and Lincoln-Mercury dealers.

Ordinary traffic and normal family use will be just a breeze for the "Magic Skyway" cars.

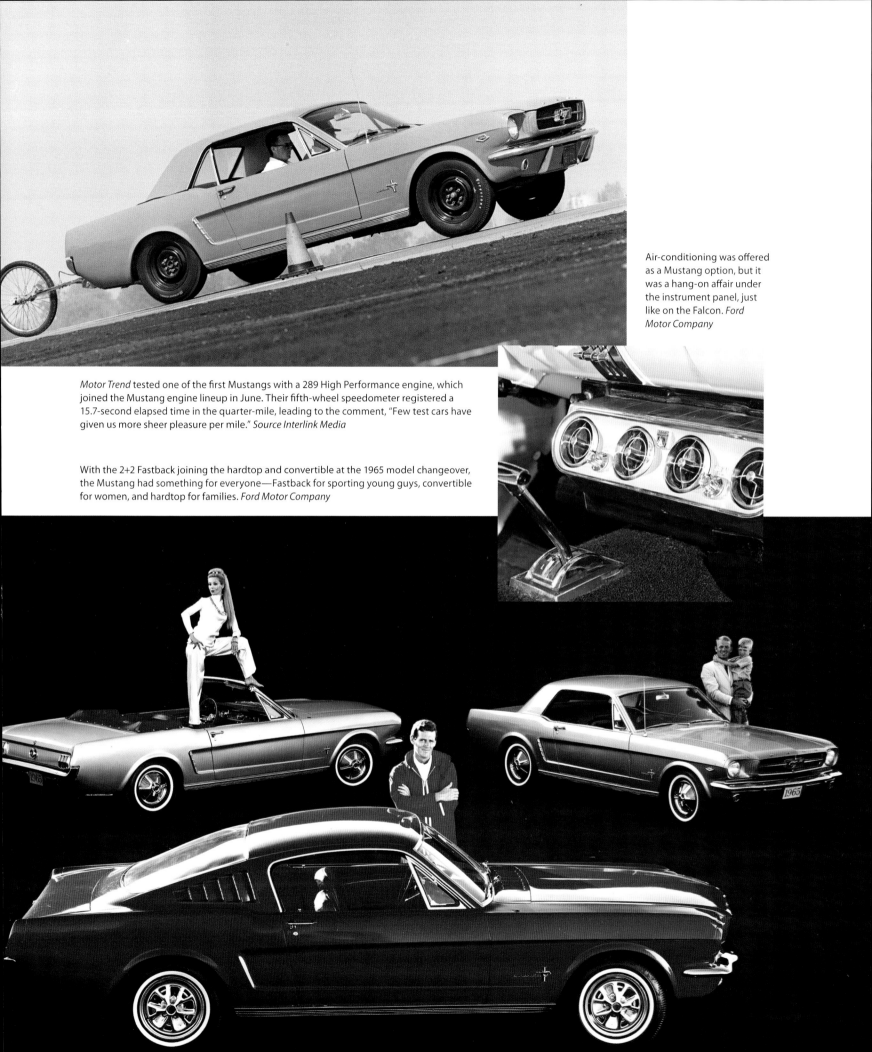

Air-conditioning was offered as a Mustang option, but it was a hang-on affair under the instrument panel, just like on the Falcon. *Ford Motor Company*

*Motor Trend* tested one of the first Mustangs with a 289 High Performance engine, which joined the Mustang engine lineup in June. Their fifth-wheel speedometer registered a 15.7-second elapsed time in the quarter-mile, leading to the comment, "Few test cars have given us more sheer pleasure per mile." *Source Interlink Media*

With the 2+2 Fastback joining the hardtop and convertible at the 1965 model changeover, the Mustang had something for everyone—Fastback for sporting young guys, convertible for women, and hardtop for families. *Ford Motor Company*

In addition to a sportier appearance, the 2+2 Fastback also added practicality with a fold-down rear seat. The pass-through from the trunk to the interior allowed storage of long items such as snow skis. *Ford Motor Company*

*Continued from page 33*
included items that were optional on other cars, like carpet, vinyl upholstery, and full wheel covers. Whether manual or automatic, the shifter was located on the floor between front bucket seats; a column shift, as found on most American cars at the time, was not available.

The base drivetrain was a 170-cubic-inch six-cylinder engine backed by a three-speed manual transmission. But many buyers ordered one of the available small-block V-8s, either the 260 two-barrel or the 289 four-barrel. The 271-horsepower 289 High Performance engine from the Fairlane was also listed in the sales brochure, but the demand for V-8s—over 70 percent of orders—delayed the more powerful engine until June.

With the low base price, buyers felt free to add options. Eighty percent ordered whitewall tires and push-button AM radio. Other popular options included a four-speed or automatic transmission, full-length console, power brakes and steering, and a vinyl roof for hardtops. Air conditioning was also offered, but it was a hang-on affair under the instrument panel,

# 1,000,001 FOR NUMBER ONE

During all the excitement and hoopla over the Mustang's introduction in April 1964, Ford somehow lost track of the historic first production Mustang. Although preproduction versions had been built earlier, Ford considered the white convertible with serial number 100001 as the ceremonial "first Mustang." As one of the first cars built, it was shipped to the far reaches of eastern Canada to serve as a promotional model.

However, when Capt. Stanley Tucker stopped at George Parsons Ford in St. Johns, Newfoundland, on April 17 to see why a large crowd had gathered, the 34-year-old airline pilot was smitten by the Wimbledon White Mustang convertible. He convinced dealership owner George Parsons to sell the car and unknowingly drove away in Mustang 100001.

"For a long time, I was the only Mustang owner in Newfoundland," Tucker said for a Ford press release. "It was quite an experience. Many times other motorists would force me to the side of the road to ask me about the car."

Two years later, Ford tracked down Tucker in Canada and offered him Mustang number 1,000,001 in trade for the return for 100,001. In a ceremony in Dearborn, Tucker received a Silver Frost convertible loaded with options.

Unknowingly, airline pilot Capt. Stanley Tucker purchased the ceremonial first production Mustang, VIN 100001, when he stopped at a Canadian Ford dealer on April 17 to check out the commotion. It was not the first Mustang built; a number of preproduction cars were assembled previously. *Ford Motor Company*

# TIFFANY AWARD

In early 1964 ads and TV commercials, Ford touted the fact that the Mustang had received the prestigious Tiffany Gold Medal Award, presented by the famous diamond company for "Excellence in American Design." Tiffany and Company's chairman, Walter Hoving, presented the award to Henry Ford II during the Mustang's introduction at the April 13, 1964, New York World's Fair. It was the first time the Tiffany Award had been bestowed on an automobile.

To the world, it appeared that Tiffany had given the honor in admiration of the Mustang's design. However, years later, product planner Hal Sperlich admitted that Ford first approached Tiffany, realizing that such a prestigious award would add appeal to the Mustang as a luxury car.

Many early Mustang owners received this miniature version of the Mustang's Tiffany Award for their key chains. *Donald Farr*

To celebrate the Mustang's first birthday in April 1965, Ford rolled out a pair of new option packages. The GT Equipment Group enhanced the Mustang's sporting image with fog lamps, side stripes, trumpet-style exhaust tips, handling package, front disc brakes, and a new five-gauge instrument cluster. The Interior Decor Group provided a more luxurious look with woodgrain trim, five-gauge instrument cluster, and molded door panels. Because the upholstery included embossed running horses in the seat backs, the option became known as the pony interior. *Donald Farr*

### Should a man in his 50's be allowed out in a Mustang?

Let's consider what might happen. To begin with, he'll go around with a mysterious little smile on his face, new spring in his walk. Mustang acts on a man that way, what with standard equipment like bucket seats, husky 200 cubic-inch Six, all-vinyl interiors, floor-shift, wall-to-wall carpeting, the works. Driving a Mustang can be like finding the Fountain of Youth! Then there's this: Mustang might give a man an incurable taste for luxury. Options include Stereo Tape System, air-conditioning, front disc brakes, power steering, big smooth 289 cubic-inch V-8. Finally, remember Mustang's low price. It will give a man a sense of spending power he's never had before. Do you know a man in his 50's who'd like all this to happen to him? *You do!* Well, welcome him to 1966—and tell him to get into a Mustang fast!

America's Favorite Fun Car
**MUSTANG**
**MUSTANG**
**MUSTANG**

Although created to appeal to the youth market, the Mustang was also marketed to older drivers. "Like finding the Fountain of Youth!" Ford proclaimed in this advertisement that ran in many popular magazines of the day. *Ford Motor Company*

just like the Falcon. Ford's "Made to be made by you" marketing campaign worked to the tune of an average of $1,000 per car in extras.

In 1964, safety wasn't as important an issue as it was destined to become. Braking on the first Mustangs was drums all around; front disc brakes were not offered. Backup lamps, two-speed wipers, and even seat belts were optional.

The first Mustangs, built between March 9 and mid-August 1964, were assembled during Ford's 1964 production cycle. As such, they included 1964 characteristics, primarily the generator charging system. Although legally titled as 1965 models, these early cars became identified as 1964½ models.

With its early introduction, the Mustang had been available for nearly five months when the rest of the 1965 Fords hit dealer showrooms in September 1964. Like all 1965 Fords, the Mustang was updated with an alternator charging system. Front disc brakes also became available as an option. But the bigger news was the introduction of the 2+2 Fastback, as proposed by Gale Halderman in 1963. It provided an even sportier look, along with functionality like C-pillar vents for interior ventilation and a fold-down rear seat with a pass-through into the trunk.

Reaching 250,000 sales in just a few months was noteworthy, so Ford illustrated the accomplishment with the office lights at world headquarters. *Ford Motor Company*

With Mustang fever running high, Ford dealers got creative with their local promotions. In Ohio, potential customers could register to win a Mustang—the four legged kind—at Johnny Parsons Ford. *Ford Motor Company*

Mustang sales topped the one million mark in February 1966, less than two years after its introduction. Iacocca noted that the 1965–1966 Mustang earned $1.1 billion in net profits. *Ford Motor Company*

Engine choices also changed for 1965. The 170-cubic-inch six was replaced by a sturdier and more powerful 200-cubic-inch inline six, while the 260 two-barrel V-8 gave way to a 289 version, offering Mustang buyers a trio of 289s—two-barrel, four-barrel, and Hi-Po.

To mark the Mustang's first birthday on April 17, 1965, Ford rolled out a pair of new option packages: the GT Equipment Group and Interior Decor Group.

By the end of the extended 17-month 1965 model year, Ford had sold 680,989 Mustangs.

With an obvious winner on its hands, Ford saw no reason to change the formula for 1966. The Mustang that went on sale on September 16, 1965, was merely updated with a new horizontal bar grille with a floating running horse emblem, three-finger side scoop ornamentation, and updated base wheel covers. The five-gauge instrument cluster from the 1965 GT and Interior Decor packages replaced the horizontal cluster on all models, eliminating one of the Mustang's most visible vestiges of its Falcon heritage. Seat belts, backup lights, and emergency flashers became standard safety equipment, and a Stereo-sonic AM radio with eight-track tape player was added to the option list.

In the spring of 1966, Ford launched the first Mustang special edition as a sales promotion. The Mustang Sprint came with the 200-cubic-inch six-cylinder and packaged select options, including pinstripes and wire wheel covers, for a special price. The Sprint springtime theme would be repeated for the next several years.

If anyone thought the Mustang couldn't improve on its sales success, they were wrong. During the usual 12-month sales period for 1966, 607,568 were sold. Mustang had topped one million sales in its first two years on the market.

The Mustang changed very little for 1966. Horizontal grille bars with a floating horse corral and a revised side emblem with fingers differentiate the second-year model from the first. *Ford Motor Company*

Mustang mania was even available to kids too young to possess a driver's license. This battery-powered "motorized Mustang" was sold through Ford dealerships. *Ford Motor Company*

Captain Tucker (seated) returned 100001 to Ford in trade for the One Millionth Mustang. Ford executives on hand for the swap presentation were, left to right, director of styling Gene Bordinat, vice president Lee Iacocca, executive vice president C. H. Patterson, and general manager Don Frey. *Ford Motor Company*

## SHELBY: MUSTANG "SPORTS CAR"

When Carroll Shelby first heard about the Mustang, he knew it was inevitable that Ford would eventually ask him and his team of California hot rodders to turn it into a real sports car for racing. Just a few years earlier, Shelby had been little more than a former racing champion with a 1959 Le Mans championship under his belt. Forced to hang up his helmet in 1960 due to a heart condition, Shelby desired to build his own race car with an American V-8 engine–could he equip a Ferrari, Maserati, or Aston-Martin with Yankee muscle under the hood? First he heard that AC Cars in England had lost its engine supplier; then he heard about Ford's new small-block V-8. Shelby put the two together to create the Cobra in 1962, and by 1963 the Ford-powered sports car was dominating Corvettes at racetracks around the country. By early 1964, Shelby and his company, Shelby American, had become an extension of Ford's road racing program.

With the Total Performance marketing campaign in full swing, Ford needed to improve the Mustang's racing and performance image. However, Shelby didn't need another project. In late 1964, his Venice, California, facility was bursting at the seams with projects, including phasing out the original 289 Cobra, the development of the replacement 427 Cobra, campaigning Cobra Daytona Coupes in the World Manufacturers Championship, and taking on the task of rebuilding the Ford GTs into Ferrari beaters.

Carroll Shelby reluctantly accepted the challenge to turn the Mustang into a sports car. "I never wanted to do it," he told *Mustang Monthly*. "Ray Geddes from Ford said, 'Iacocca

Already well known for his Cobra sports car and racing championships, Carroll Shelby added his magic to the Mustang by creating the GT350. *Shelby American*

# THE BUZZ:
## WHAT THE PRESS HAD TO SAY (THE BEGINNING OF MUSTANG)

"This week Ford's new Mustang sports car, one of the most heralded and attention-drawing cars in autodom's history, drives into showrooms all over the U.S. In it rides a big bundle of Ford's future and the reputation of the man who daily test-drives a different Mustang between Bloomfield Hills and Dearborn. The man is Lido Anthony Iacocca, general manager of Ford's Ford Division."

—*Time*, 1964

"It's easily the best thing to come out of Detroit since the 1932 V-8 Model B roadster."

—*Car & Driver*, 1964

"In the Mustang, the 289 in stock form gives bushy-tailed performance and encourages enterprising driving methods, greatly aided by the precise gate and well-chosen ratios and excellent synchromesh of the four-speed transmission."

—*Car & Driver*, 1964

"Ford aims to sell about a quarter-of-a-million Mustangs in its first 12-month period on the market. With the versatility of this design and the plentiful options, the demand might even exceed that figure."

—*Car & Driver*, 1964

"There isn't likely to be another Edsel, or ill-conceived Edsel promotion, in the Ford Motor Company's future. Their latest new car, the Mustang, was much more carefully planned as a car and has been launched with a promotion campaign that is, if all-out, no more given to superlatives than most new-car launchings."

—*Consumer Reports*, 1964

"All in all, CU finds the Mustang, on short acquaintance, an agreeable car—one in which an individual appearance is achieved in a compact package with minimum handicaps (except perhaps for the low seating) and without over-elaboration of detail and 'luxury' items that often make this type of car expensive rather than useful and efficient. If it's individuality or flair you are looking for in an American-made automobile, you can get the genuine article in the Mustang."

—*Consumer Reports*, 1964

"With its long hood and short rear deck, its Ferrari flare, and openmouthed air scoop, the Mustang resembles the European racing cars that American sports-car buffs find so appealing."

—*Time*, 1964

"If any new model deserved a 'car of the year' title, it was Ford's Mustang. From the day of its off-season introduction on April 17, until year's end, Ford had turned out 303,275 of the sporty models."

—*World Book Encyclopedia*, 1965 edition

"The new car, called the Mustang GT350, and known familiarly as the Shelby Mustang, will not have the mass appeal of the original, but by all that is sacred to us enthusiast-types, it certainly is a lot more interesting"

—*Car & Driver*, 1965

In early 1965, Shelby American moved into a pair of hangars adjacent to the Los Angeles airport where Mustangs rolled along an assembly line with an underground pit so they could be converted into GT350s. *Shelby American*

wants it and we're going to do it.' So we put a budget together to build a prototype. I went to John Bishop at the Sports Car Club of America and said, 'John, the people at Ford want to make this a sport car. Help me, will you?' He said to take the rear seat out, change the suspension, put bigger brakes on it, and put 300 horsepower in the engine. And that's what we did."

With Chuck Cantwell hired as project manager and Ken Miles handling much of the development work, Shelby American took Mustang fastbacks equipped with 289 High Performance engines and turned them into sports cars with a deleted back seat, competition

The street Shelby GT350 didn't look much different from the standard Mustang Fastback. This magazine test car is equipped with optional over-the-top Le Mans stripes and Cragar wheels. All 1965 Shelbys were painted Wimbledon White with blue side stripes. *Ford Motor Company*

For 1966, side scoops and C-pillar glass in place of the standard 2+2 Fastback's vents visually differentiated the Shelby GT350. *Source Interlink Media*

Hertz ordered 1,000 GT350H models for its Hertz Sports Car Club. As Carroll Shelby noted, "People would park them next to their standard Mustang, swap the engines, and return them to Hertz with the regular 289." *Source Interlink Media*

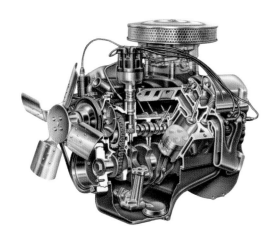

Several versions of Ford's lightweight and compact 90-degree Fairlane small-block, seen here in 1966 289 High Performance form, were used in Mustangs from 1965 to 1994. *Ford Motor Company*

seat belts, suspension upgrades, 15-inch wheels with Goodyear Blue Dot tires, a fiberglass hood with scoop, a locking rear axle, and a modified 289 High Performance engine. A competition version added a more powerful engine, a special front valance for improved cooling, and a plexiglass rear window with a vent for extracting interior air.

As for the name, Shelby told *Mustang Monthly*: "We had five or six meetings [with Ford]. A plane-load of people came from Detroit trying to decide what to call it. And after about the third meeting, I said, 'A name doesn't make a car; a car makes a name.' So we were all sitting around and I said to one of our guys, 'How far is it to that building over there?' And he said, 'What the hell you talking about?' And I said, 'Step it off.' He came back and said 'It's 348 paces.' I said, 'We're going to call it the GT350 and you guys can go back to Detroit.'"

To build GT350s, Ford's San Jose assembly plant provided stripped-down Wimbledon White Mustang fastbacks. The first ones were built in Shelby American's Venice facility, but by early 1965 the company had moved into a pair of hangars adjacent to the Los Angeles airport. There, GT350 project engineer Chuck Cantwell designed an assembly line with an underground pit so the fastbacks could be converted as they rolled along.

Shelby American built 562 GT350s for 1965, including 36 competition models, which racked up numerous wins in SCCA B-Production competition. All were white with blue rocker panel stripes. Most were equipped with silver 15-inch steel wheels, although special

For 1965, the standard Mustang V-8 engine was a 260-cubic-inch two-barrel. *Ford Motor Company*

five-spoke Cragars were an option. Another option, the over-the-top Le Mans stripes in Guardsman Blue, would become a Shelby trademark.

For 1966, Ford wanted to tame the GT350 to appeal to a wider base of potential buyers. The loud side-exit exhaust and locking rear end disappeared, the back seat stayed in, and more available colors were added. Plexiglass windows replaced the grille work in the C-pillar and functional side scoops were added to aid rear brake cooling.

When Shelby American general manager Peyton Cramer approached Hertz Rental Car about adding the GT350 to its Sports Car Club fleet, the company ordered 200 cars, all in the Hertz colors of black with gold stripes. Later, Hertz upped the order to 1,000 cars, some with white, blue, and red exteriors. The Hertz program helped Shelby production reach 2,378 for 1966, including four convertibles at the end of the production run. In some cases, GT350Hs were rented specifically for weekend track competition, then returned on Monday. Carroll Shelby noted more radical uses: "People would park them next to their standard Mustangs, swap the engines, and return them to Hertz with the regular 289."

Shelby utilized the 289 Hi-Po for the 1965–1967 GT350s, increasing output to 306 horsepower with a Holley four-barrel carburetor, Cobra aluminum intake, and tri-Y tubular headers. A larger aluminum oil pan also reduced the chances of oil starvation during hard cornering. Finned aluminum valve covers were part of the makeover. *Source Interlink Media*

# BIG-BLOCKS, MACHS AND BOSSES

ON OCTOBER 2, 1967, Lee Iacocca issued a memo; he wanted to know, "What are we going to do about the performance image problem?"

The November issue of *Hot Rod Magazine* had just landed on Iacocca's desk and he was not pleased with writer Eric Dahlquist's critique of Ford's performance image—or lack thereof. During a visit to Tasca Ford, Dahlquist took notes from his conversation with owner Bob Tasca, who complained about Ford's 1968 performance offerings compared to GM and Chrysler. Tasca griped that Ford's top performance engine for 1967, the 320-horsepower 390, was no match for Chevy's 375-horse 396, Pontiac's 360-horse 400 HO, or Chrysler's 375-horse 440 Magnum and 425-horse 426 Hemi. The other manufacturers also marketed a performance image with names such as Super Sport, GTO, and Road Runner.

During Dahlquist's visit, Tasca demonstrated his personal KR-8 (King of the Road 1968) Mustang, a 1967 GT hardtop that Tasca technicians had modified with performance parts readily available from Ford dealerships.

Vice president Don Frey's memo responded to Iacocca, stating that there were three pieces to the problem: "The first is sheer performance—I believe we are now on the road to recovery in this area. The second involves image models to dramaticize the power. We are working on this with [design chief] Gene Bordinat. The third is advertising, promotion, and public relations. The tone of this article, and others like it, suggest we will have a tough rebuilding job in this area once we get the product fixed."

Ford's quest for an improved performance image led to Mustangs such as the Mach 1 with 428 Cobra Jet power and Shaker hood scoop. *Ford Motor Company*

The big Mustang news for 1967 was the addition of a big-block option. With 320 horsepower, the FE passenger-car engine was not the right answer for the Camaro's optional 375-horsepower 396. *Source Interlink Media*

Ford Motor Company chairman Henry Ford II (left) changed the course of Mustang performance on February 6, 1968, when he announced that Semon E. "Bunkie" Knudsen (center) was leaving General Motors to take over as president of Ford. At the same time, he promoted Arjay Miller (right), one of the original "Whiz Kids" from the 1950s, to vice chairman. *Ford Motor Company*

Frey went on to say that Ford's street image needed to become a priority. His recommendations instigated a new urgency at Ford to develop performance cars along with a marketing program to support them.

In February 1968, just three months after Frey's memo to Iacocca, Henry Ford II surprised the automotive industry by hiring Bunkie Knudsen away from General Motors. As the new president, Knudsen wasted little time stirring up Ford personnel. He practically moved into the styling center to make changes to the soon-to-be-released 1969 models, scheduled styling shows for 7:30 a.m., and even set up his own personal studio to work on the 1971 Mustang.

Knudsen also recognized the need for performance Mustangs. At GM, he saw firsthand how models like the SS and Z/28 added appeal to the rest of the Camaro line. Knudsen explained the Mustang's position: "The Mustang was certainly a good-looking automobile. But there were people who wanted good-looking automobiles with performance."

It wouldn't take long for Knudsen to make his mark.

## PONY CAR COMPETITION

During its first two years, the Mustang enjoyed a fresh, new market unbridled by serious competition. While Ford sold more than one million Mustangs during 1965 and 1966, Corvair Monza sales dropped to 213,000 and the Valiant-based Barracuda fared even worse; Plymouth barely sold 100,000 in the model's first two years.

Mustang's coming out party officially ended on September 26, 1966, when General Motors countered with its Chevrolet Camaro. Early on, GM's corporate line stated that Chevrolet already had a suitable competitor to the Mustang—the rear-engined Corvair Monza. But as Mustang sales zoomed, Chevrolet was forced to develop the new Camaro based on the Nova II's F-body chassis. Like the Mustang, the base engine was an economical six-cylinder. However, the Camaro hit the highway with an available 375-horsepower 396-cubic-inch big-block, far out-muscling the 1967 Mustang's top-rated 320-horsepower 390. Mustang had the GT; Chevrolet offered two performance packages for the Camaro—the Rally Sport (RS) with hideaway headlights and the Super Sport (SS) with either the 350 or 396 V-8. In December, yet another performance package, the Z/28, legalized a special 290-horsepower 302 small-block for the SCCA's up-and-coming Trans-Am series.

In early 1967, Pontiac introduced the Firebird, built on the same chassis as the Camaro but with a more traditional Pontiac look. Like the Camaro, the Firebird debuted with an available big-block engine, the 325-horsepower 400 from the GTO. The Mustang also faced competition from its corporate sibling, Mercury, which grabbed one of the Mustang's earliest proposed names—Cougar—for its 1967 pony car.

Chevrolet's 1967 Camaro not only rivaled the Mustang for pony car sales, but it also raised the bar for performance. Right out of the box, the Camaro was available with a big-block engine as the SS396. *Source Interlink Media*

Like most Mercury vehicles, the 1967 Cougar was more upscale than its Ford counterpart, featuring additional sound deadening, more luxurious interior design, and European styling, including the popular hideaway headlights of the day and full-length taillights with sequential operation. *Source Interlink Media*

Styling for the 1967 Mustang was well under way by December 1964, just nine months after the 1965 Mustang's introduction. *Ford Motor Company*

Pontiac triggered the muscle car market with its GTO option for the 1964 Tempest, powered by a 389 V-8 with available Tri-Power induction. Identified as a compact or intermediate car with a big V-8 engine, the muscle car would power the American performance car industry for the next seven years. *Source Interlink Media*

## BIGGER EQUALS BETTER?

Even before the 1965 Mustang's introduction in April 1964, the stone was already carved that the Mustang would be restyled for 1967. In the 1960s, American cars were updated every two years, like it or not, so Ford began designing the next Mustang before the 1965 models hit the street.

"The plan was to change the styling after two model years," said George Schumaker, who took over the newly formed Mustang/Falcon design studio in July 1964. "The feeling at Ford was that the 1965–1966 Mustangs were really worked-over Falcons. When they became so successful, it was felt that the Mustang image should be expanded and made into more of its own car."

The second-generation Mustang gave Ford a chance to improve on the original. The challenge: to change the Mustang without changing it, yet also respond to GM's Camaro and Firebird.

The 1967 Mustang's styling reflected the emerging muscle car market, as launched by the Pontiac GTO in 1964. "The original Mustang was a smash hit," said Ford product planner Donald Petersen. "But one criticism people leveled at the car was that it wasn't muscular enough. So there was pressure from the start for a bolder, more powerful-looking design."

The decision to offer a big-block engine influenced the course of the Mustang for the foreseeable future. To shoehorn Ford's bulky passenger-car 390, the Mustang grew two inches wider and two and a half inches longer. Chassis and suspension refinements were also required to adapt to the heavier weight, which reached nearly 3,500 pounds as a convertible equipped with the big-block. The interior also received a much-needed overhaul, becoming more Mustang and less Falcon.

For 1967, the Mustang's interior shook off its Falcon lineage with a design of its own, including a new five-gauge instrument cluster and optional in-dash air-conditioning, unlike the hang-on A/C from the previous generation. The deluxe interior (pictured) added brushed aluminum panels and upgraded door panels. Available console and tilt-steering options added luxury and convenience. *Ford Motor Company*

The Swinging Sixties were in full swing when the larger and more muscular second-generation Mustang arrived for 1967. The 2+2 Fastback's roofline extended all the way to the concave rear end, which was available with an optional louvered panel, seen here in prototype form. *Ford Motor Company*

The larger 1967 Mustang, introduced on September 30, 1966, solved some of the complaints about the original, like front and rear seat legroom. The styling was bolder, with deeper side sculpturing and a concave rear panel with triple-lens taillights, leaving no doubt that it was a Mustang. While the hardtop and convertible models retained their basic profiles, the Fastback's roofline extended all the way to the end of the trunk lid. Braking was upgraded significantly with a dual hydraulic system with separate master cylinder chambers for front and rear. At last, optional air conditioning was incorporated into the instrument panel instead of the hang-on afterthought like in 1965 and 1966.

In late 1965, Ralph Nader's book, *Unsafe At Any Speed*, heightened public awareness about auto safety, leading to the establishment of the Department of Transportation in October 1966. The DOT then established the National Highway and Traffic Safety Administration, which had a large role in demanding mandatory

Ford advertising did not overlook the huge female market for the pony car segment. The Mustang Pledge campaign encouraged female customers to swear their allegiance by stating, "I *will not* sell tickets to the people who want to ride in my 1967 Mustang; I *will* keep the 'helpless female' look by shifting manually only when I'm alone." *Ford Motor Company*

Ford continued building Mustangs at three assembly plants for 1967. More than 470,000 were built, not as many as in 1965 or 1966 but still a successful model year, ranking number three in all-time best sales over the Mustang's 50-year history. *Ford Motor Company*

# BIG-BLOCK SHELBY

With the 390 big-block in the 1967 Mustang, Carroll Shelby saw an opening to one-up the competition. Like the GT350, the name didn't indicate horsepower or cubic inches; GT500 simply sounded bigger than anything else on the market. Instead of hopping up the Mustang's 390, Shelby realized that Ford's passenger car 428, also an FE big-block, would add both cubic inches and marketing appeal as Cobra Le Mans power. To top it off, an impressive-looking dual Holley four-barrel induction system with oval air cleaner sat between the finned aluminum valve covers.

For 1967, the Shelby as both the GT350 and GT500 looked much different than the Mustang it was based on. Fiberglass was used extensively for an extended front end and ducktail rear spoiler. The deep-set grille with driving lights, mounted inboard or outboard depending on state laws, and Cougar taillights gave the Shelby a totally different look. Scoops replaced the vents above the quarter panel scoops for interior ventilation.

With production moving to Michigan for 1968, the 1967 GT350s and GT500s would be the last Shelbys built at the Shelby American facility in Los Angeles.

The 1967 Shelby GT500 was a torque monster with its dual-quad 428 big-block engine in place of the regular Mustang's 390. *Source Interlink Media*

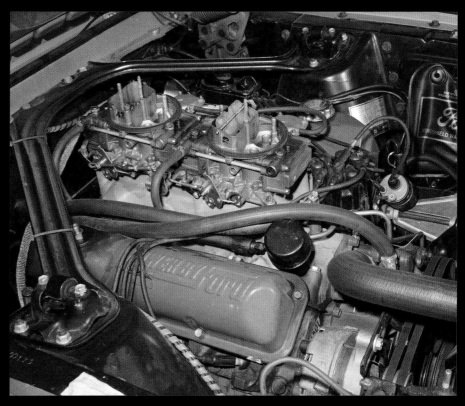

Dual Holley four-barrel carburetors sat on top of the 1967 Shelby GT500's 428 engine. This early prototype doesn't include the finned aluminum Cobra valve covers. *Source Interlink Media*

"Only Mustang Makes It Happen!" said the 1968 Mustang's advertising campaign that starred "Sidney" as the hero: "Sidney spent Sundays sea shelling at the seashore. Then Sidney started digging the 1968 Mustang. Now Sidney's making waves all over." *Ford Motor Company*

seat belts, collapsible steering wheels, and increased dash padding, all of which became standard equipment in the 1967 Mustang.

The revised 1967 Mustang was improved in many ways, including ride and handling. The manual three-speed transmission became fully synchronized, while the automatic was upgraded to the SelectShift Cruise-O-Matic, which allowed manual shifting. New options included a Tilt-Away steering column (borrowed from the Thunderbird, it not only tilted but also swung out of the way for easier driver entry and exit), speed control, roof console with map lights, and a folding glass rear window for the convertible. In addition to better performance and handling, the Mustang was also becoming more of a luxury car.

When the GT Equipment Group was ordered with an automatic transmission, it became the GTA—GT-Automatic—for 1967 only. As a spring sales promotion, the Sprint returned as a package that included the louvered hood with recessed turn signal indicators, wheel covers, and available "Sprint time" pastel exterior colors. More than 100,000 were sold.

The big-block was the newsmaker, yet less than 1 percent of 1967 Mustangs were ordered with the 390 option. The huge majority were equipped with one of the base engines, either the 200-cubic-inch six or the two-barrel 289. The four-barrel 289s, including the solid-lifter 289 High Performance, remained on the option list for one final year.

Following 1960s tradition, the second year of the second-generation Mustang was mildly updated. The 1968 GT option added grille-mounted fog lamps, C stripes instead of body side stripes, and new styled steel wheels. *Ford Motor Company*

Mustang sales topped two million during the 1968 model year, an occasion marked by a photo op with Lee Iacocca as the ceremonial two millionth Mustang hardtop left the inspection area at the Dearborn assembly plant. *Ford Motor Company*

For 1968, the Mustang received a mild facelift with a cleaner front grille, simplified ornamentation for the rear quarter panel scoop, and side marker lights as mandated by new government safety standards. Safety played a large part in the interior revisions, which included a new padded steering wheel and fold-down door handles.

At the beginning of the 1968 model year, Mustang drivetrain selection remained similar to 1967 with the exception of the 289 High Performance, which was discontinued after Hi-Po sales dropped to under 500 in 1967, likely due to the 390's availability. The 289 two-barrel remained the base V-8, but a 230-horsepower four-barrel 302 replaced the four-barrel 289. This new displacement would become a Mustang mainstay for the next 25 years.

For 1968, Ford became more involved in the Shelby, changing the appearance with a new fiberglass front end, hood with forward-placed scoops, and rear end with sequential 1965 Thunderbird taillights. Production moved to the A. O. Smith Company in Livonia, Michigan, as Carroll Shelby shut down his Los Angeles facility at the end of 1967. Both the GT350 and GT500 continued, but the 1968 models were less performance and more luxury, including the first Shelby convertible. Instead of the previous 306 horsepower from the Cobra 289 High Performance, the GT350 was emasculated with the four-barrel 302 with 250 horsepower, making it the lowest-performance Shelby ever. Instead of the prior year's dual-quad 428, a single four-barrel 428 Police Interceptor rated at a questionable 360 horsepower powered the GT500.

The springtime Sprint sales worked so well in 1966 and 1967 that the promotion returned as a "See the Light Sale" in the spring of 1968. Ford upped the ante by offering two versions: Sprint Package A with C stripes, wheel covers, and pop-open gas cap, and Package B for V-8s only with components from Package A but replacing the wheel covers with styled steel wheels and adding foglights. More than 30,000 Sprints were sold, most with the less expensive Package A. *Donald Farr*

*Continued on page 61*

# COBRA JET

When Ford dealer Bob Tasca expressed dissatisfaction with Ford's performance offerings in *Hot Rod*, he also took the opportunity to showcase the KR-8, his personal 1967 Mustang hardtop that had been modified by Tasca technician Bill Loomis. When the original 390 expired during a test drive, a 428 Police Interceptor was built with off-the-shelf performance parts, including 406 heads, 390 GTA camshaft, 427 distributor, and Police Interceptor intake with a Holley carburetor. It was capable of 13.39-second elapsed times in the quarter mile.

The 428 Cobra Jet engine first appeared as an option for Mustang GTs in April 1968. The functional scoop and black stripe on the hood set the CJ models apart from standard GTs. *Ford Motor Company*

A teenaged Bob Tasca Jr. launches his father's KR-8 in the Tasca Ford back lot. The 1967 Mustang hardtop, equipped with off-the-shelf Ford performance parts, inspired the Cobra Jet engine package. *Photo courtesy of Bob Tasca Jr.*

According to Tasca's son, Bob Tasca Jr., Ford wanted to inspect the KR-8: "Some Ford people came out to drive the car and they talked my father into taking it to Detroit to convince the big shots that he could build a better performance car than Ford." The 15-year-old Tasca was with his father for the drive from Rhode Island to Dearborn, where the KR-8's engine was removed and inspected at Ford's experimental garage.

The Cobra Jet name appeared for the first time on the flanks of the Super Stock racing Mustangs. Ford had purchased the rights to the Cobra name from Carroll Shelby, so it was the ideal time to take advantage of the performance image. As for the word "Jet," it was dig at Chevrolet's Turbo Jet.

Reports of the Cobra Jet's success at the Winternationals were just hitting the automotive magazines when the 428 Cobra Jet engine arrived as an option for 1968 Mustang GTs on April 1, 1968. Underrated at 335 horsepower, the CJ was basically a passenger car 428 with many of Tasca's modifications—427-style heads, 390 GT cam, and Holley 735-cfm four-barrel carburetor. Available for the Mustang GT in all body styles, the CJ package added a functional hood scoop and black hood stripe. With its late introduction, only 2,870 were sold. Shelby immediately adopted the 335-horsepower Cobra Jet for the Shelby GT500. To differentiate the CJ-powered GT500s from earlier versions, Carroll Shelby stole a name from Chevrolet. "I heard that Corvette was coming out with a King of the Road," Shelby once revealed. "So I called my trade-dress lawyer and said, 'I want to know if King of the Road has been copyrighted.' He called back and said it wasn't taken. I said, 'You better be there at eight o'clock in the morning to take it.' He did. I called 3M to make the decals, GT500KR."

Rated at 335 horsepower, the 428 Cobra Jet utilized many of Tasca Ford's KR-8 modifications. For the first time, the hood scoop was functional thanks to a special air cleaner with a vacuum-operated flap that allowed cooler outside air into the carburetor under full throttle. *Ford Motor Company*

When the 428 Cobra Jet joined the Mustang engine lineup in the spring of 1968, it was immediately incorporated into the Shelby GT500, which took on a new name—GT500KR, for "King of the Road." *Ford Motor Company*

Bred first...to be first.'67 Mustang.

¦ '67 Mustang

The 1967 advertising drove home the point that the Mustang was the original pony car. By displaying all three body styles, the ad campaign subtly boasted that Mustang offered a 2+2 Fastback, unlike the Camaro or Firebird. *Ford Motor Company*

Although production of 1968 GT350s and GT500s had moved to the A. O. Smith Company near Detroit, Carroll Shelby was more than happy to pose with the latest Shelby Mustangs, which featured new front and rear treatments. *Shelby American*

A convertible with roll bar was added to the Shelby lineup for the first time in 1968. *Ford Motor Company*

*Continued from page 57*

With the passenger-car 390 as the only muscle powerplant in the arsenal, the Mustang continued to lose ground to the Camaro SS396 and Z/28, Firebird HO, and even the Barracuda S.

That would change on April Fool's Day 1968, when Ford introduced a street version of the 428 Cobra Jet Mustangs that had debuted in, and won, the Super Stock class at the NHRA Winternationals in January.

In addition to the usual springtime Sprint model, which was offered in A and B packages, the 1968 Mustang triggered a number of special editions, many produced by regional sales districts or even individual dealerships. The California Ford dealers took their California Special beyond unique colors and bolt-ons, adding Shelby side scoops and rear-end, grille-mounted fog lights, and GT/CS decals. Colorado dealers picked up on the promotion with a similar hardtop called the High Country Special.

Ford originally designed the GT/SC hardtop as a nationwide special edition with a Shelby rear treatment and side scoops. Eventually, California Ford dealers took it as their own, calling it the California Special, or GT/CS. *Ford Motor Company*

## POWER AND LUXURY

Two things were apparent when "The Going Things" 1969 Mustangs arrived in showrooms on August 28, 1968. First, the latest Mustang was once again larger and much different than the previous model, although still based on the same chassis. And two new models—the Mach 1 and Grandé—were added to the hardtop, convertible, and Fastback, now identified

*Continued on page 64*

# THINK BOSS!

By 1968, Ford's Total Performance campaign was in full swing. Having won Le Mans in 1966 and 1967 with Shelby American's full-on GT40 assault, attention had turned to domestic competition, primarily NASCAR stock car racing and the SCCA's Trans-Am, a road-race series that was growing in popularity thanks to the competition, both on the track and in the showrooms, between America's new pony cars.

To maintain sanity, NASCAR and SCCA enforced rules requiring manufacturers to use equipment on the race cars that was available to the general public on street cars. This homologation requirement was often skirted by offering special engines and other equipment, like spoilers, as optional equipment or limited-edition models, resulting in anomalies like the Dodge Charger Daytona with its pointy nose and tall rear wing.

To compete against Chrysler's 426 Hemi engine, legalized for NASCAR as an option in Dodge and Plymouth production cars, Ford developed hemispherical heads for the 385 series 429. Instead of installation in Torinos, as raced in NASCAR, Knudsen wanted to shove the engine into the 1969 Mustang SportsRoof, a feat that required widening the engine compartment with narrower shock towers. Deemed too complicated for the regular assembly line, Ford contracted Kar Kraft in nearby Brighton to modify the Mustangs and install the engines. Internally, Ford identified the engine as the 429 Blue Crescent; in the Mustang, it was known as the Boss 429.

Ford rated the Boss 429 at 375 horsepower, but by detuning for the street, the race-bred engine lost some of its punch. The relatively small 735-cfm Holley carburetor and mild camshaft profile helped with low-end drivability but choked the large-port heads at higher rpm.

Compared to other muscle cars of the era, the Boss 429 was tame in appearance. Offered in five colors for 1969, it looked more like a base six-cylinder SportsRoof except for Magnum 500 wheels, a large functional hood scoop, and chin spoiler. Identification was limited to small Boss 429 decals on the front fenders. By design, the Boss 429 was a limited-production car. Ford built 859 for 1969 and 500 for 1970.

Like NASCAR, the SCCA enforced a homologation rule that required Ford to build at least 1,000 Mustangs with the Boss 302 engine, which incorporated canted-valve heads from the 351 Cleveland engine among other performance enhancements. The Boss 302 Mustang would also provide sales competition for the Camaro Z/28, which had a three-year head start in showrooms.

Ford never built yellow cars with red interiors, but the effect in this promotional image dramatized Larry Shinoda's wild graphics for the midyear 1969 model. Bright Yellow was one of four 1969 Boss 302 colors, along with Calypso Coral (orange), Acapulco Blue, and Wimbledon White. *Ford Motor Company*

Kar Kraft workers celebrated the first specially modified Boss 429 as it rolled off their assembly line on January 15, 1969. *Ford Motor Company*

For the Boss 302, Knudsen demanded "the best-handling street car, bar none!" Longtime Mustang suspension specialist Matt Donner used a 1968 Mustang hardtop to develop a suspension based on Goodyear's new F60x15 Polyglas tires, which dictated heavier-duty spindles and a metal brace around the shock towers to keep them intact over rough road surfaces.

Stylist Larry Shinoda came on board too late to influence the design of the 1969 Mustang, but for the midyear Boss 302 he was able to eliminate the SportsRoof's fake side scoops and add C-shaped side stripes, along with blackout treatment for the hood, rear panel, and headlight doors.

The Boss 429's hemispherical cylinder heads were much wider than regular 429s, so Kar Kraft enlarged the Mustang engine compartment with modified shock towers before lowering the engines into the cars. *Ford Motor Company*

Inspired by the SCCA Trans-Am series, the 1969 Boss 302 was engineered as the "best-handling street car—bar none!" per Bunkie Knudsen's demand. *Ford Motor Company*

The 1969 Mustang, and especially the newly named "SportsRoof" body style, reflected the muscle car influence on American automobile design. The GT package, seen here with its hood scoop and side stripes, would succumb to the popularity of the new Mach 1. In 1969, Ford sold 6,694 GT Mustangs in all body styles compared to 72,458 Mach 1s. *Ford Motor Company*

*Continued from page 61*

as the SportsRoof. New Ford president Bunkie Knudsen's February 1968 arrival had been too late to influence the 1969 Mustang, but his demands for more performance would emerge by midyear.

The 1969 Mustang was lower and longer than previous Mustangs, primarily due to sheetmetal changes. At the front, quad headlights made their only appearance in a Mustang and the faux rear brake scoop—a Mustang styling staple since the beginning—was reduced to an ornament on hardtops and convertibles. The SportsRoof received the most dramatic change, adding a nonfunctional scoop in the rear quarter panel, a built-in ducktail rear spoiler, and three-lens taillights in a concave rear panel.

Like the exterior, the new Mustang's interior received its most extensive overhaul to date. Notably, the instrument panel featured twin pods for more of a cockpit feel. Bucket seats remained standard, with optional bench, but new federal safety requirements mandated headrests for both. Shoulder belts were also added to the safety equipment for hardtops and SportsRoofs.

The 1969 engine lineup was the largest ever for the Mustang. In addition to carrying over the previous year's 200-cubic-inch six-cylinder, the 390, and 428 Cobra Jet, a 250-cubic-inch six debuted along with a new 302 two-barrel to replace the old 289 and a mid-displacement 351 as an alternative to Chevrolet's new 350. When the Boss 302 and Boss 429 engines arrived at midyear, there were 10 engines available for 1969 Mustangs, including the 428 Cobra Jet in two forms, either the standard Q-code or the Ram-Air R-code with functional Shaker hood scoop. Both were rated at 335 horsepower. For all-out Cobra Jet performance, there was also a Drag Pack option. Available with 3:91 or 4:30 gearing, the package added an engine oil cooler and tougher engine internals. Ford called it the 428 Super Cobra Jet.

Finally, the Mustang got its much-needed performance image with the 1969 Mach 1, a packaged model based on the SportsRoof. Using a name that was first seen on a two-seater show car in 1966, the Mach 1 added a blacked-out hood with racing-style click pins and scoop, reflective side stripes, chrome-styled steel wheels with wide-oval tires, and competition suspension, along with a deluxe interior with special seat upholstery, molded door panels, and new Rim-Blow steering wheel. Although available with both 351s and the 390, the Mach 1 was tailor-made for the 428 Cobra Jet, especially when equipped with the optional Shaker hood scoop. The Mach 1 was good for Mustang's performance image and dealer sales—nearly 25 percent of all 1969 Mustangs were Mach 1s.

There was even more good news for performance fans at midyear 1969 when Ford revealed a pair of Boss Mustangs, a 429 to homologate a hemi-headed engine for NASCAR and a 302 for Trans-Am as a direct competitor to the Z/28 Camaro. Both cars were limited production, but their existence stirred up excitement.

The Grandé hardtop was the first Mustang packaged as a luxury model with Deluxe interior with woodgrain trim and cloth bucket seats, electric clock, console, Rim-Blow steering wheel, soft-ride suspension, special insulation, and wire wheel covers. By adding other options—air conditioning, speed control, and AM/FM stereo radio—the Grandé became a mini-Lincoln.

Like 1968, the 1969 Shelby was built at the A. O. Smith Company in SportsRoof and convertible body styles. GT350s gained some respect over 1968 by using the 290-horsepower 351 four-barrel while GT500s continued with the 335-horsepower 428 Cobra Jet from the 1968 GT500KR. But with the Mustang's major bodystyle change for 1969, the latest Shelby needed its own makeover. Looking for less Shelby and more Ford, designers in Dearborn utilized fiberglass for the front fenders, hood, trunk, and tail panel to completely

*Continued on page 68*

The shaker hood scoop became synonymous with both the Mach 1 and 428 Cobra Jet, although it was part of the R-code 428 engine option for all Mustang body styles. *Source Interlink Media*

Luxury items had been part of the Mustang's option list from the start, but the 1969 Grandé was the first to group them in a package. *Ford Motor Company*

## SHINODA: STRIPES AND SPOILERS AND SLATS

Three months after Bunkie Knudsen joined Ford as president, he hired Larry Shinoda away from General Motors as director of Ford's special projects design office. Born in Los Angeles, Shinoda loved both cars and art, studying engineering at Pasadena City College before graduating from the Art Center College of Design. At 16, he was racing on the dry lakes of southern California with Vic Edelbrock and other pioneers of the hot rod industry.

At GM, Shinoda created Chevrolet show cars like the Sting Ray, Mako Shark, and Monza GT. He favored the use of functional aerodynamic improvements, having designed the Camaro Z28's rear spoiler and cowl induction hood.

As one of his first assignments at Ford, Shinoda created the look for the Trans-Am Mustang. His front spoiler was standard on the Boss 302 because it was needed for the race cars, while his rear spoiler and window slats became popular add-ons for the Boss 302 and other Mustang SportsRoofs.

Shinoda also suggested the Boss name, knowing that "boss" was a teenager description for something that was neat or cool. "They [Ford] were going to call it the SR-2, which stood for Sedan Racing, Group II, which I thought was a dumb name," explained Shinoda. "So I suggested they call it 'Boss.'"

Larry Shinoda's graphics and styling tricks, including rear window louvers for the Boss 302, were considered outlandish by some Ford executives, but they proved popular with performance enthusiasts. Shinoda had first used the louvers on a Monza Spider show car while working at GM. "When the Ford people first saw them for the Mustang, they about seized up," said Shinoda. *Ford Motor Company*

Using more fiberglass than before, the 1969 Shelby looked much different than the standard Mustang. *Ford Motor Company*

Ford set up this studio photo to demonstrate the use of fiberglass panels for the 1969 Shelby. *Ford Motor Company*

More than 130,000 SportsRoofs were sold in 1969, more than all 2+2 Fastbacks in 1967 and 1968 combined. Over half were Mach 1s, the SportsRoof that packaged luxury, function, and styling to create an all-around performance Mustang. *Ford Motor Company*

A fiberglass deck lid, rear panel, and quarter panel caps gave the 1969 Shelby its own look, along with Thunderbird taillights and a center-mounted exhaust port. *Ford Motor Company*

For 1970, the Mustang lost some of its muscular looks thanks to a front and rear makeover. In particular, the front end lost the quad headlights from 1969 and the outside lamps were replaced by a pair of scoops on each side. *Ford Motor Company*

*Continued from page 65*

change the appearance and separate the Shelby model from the Mustang more than ever before. The full-width grille previewed the 1971 Mustang, as did the NASA-style scoops, although the Shelby used five— two for underhood cooling, two for hot air extraction, and one in the center for functional Ram-Air into the engine.

At the rear, the Shelby incorporated Thunderbird taillights along with a unique center-mounted exhaust port under the bumper. It was an attention-getter, and even provided the Shelby with a special exhaust tone, but communications from the field reported rear-end fires caused when backfires from the Holley-equipped 428 Cobra Jet engine ignited fuel vapors from the gas filler located right above the exhaust port. Ford eventually recalled 1969 GT500s to add a revised vent tube and install a nonvented fuel filler cap.

All of the 1969 models, including the Boss 302 and 429, returned for 1970 with minor styling updates to battle a pair of new competitors from Chrysler—the Plymouth Barracuda and Dodge Challenger. For 1970, a pair of scoops replaced 1969's outboard headlights for a more European appearance. The concave rear panel became flat and the SportsRoof lost its fake quarter panel scoops, something that stylist Larry Shinoda, hired away from GM by Knudsen, had eliminated on the midyear 1969 Boss 302. Like all 1970 Fords, the ignition switch moved to the steering column to operate a new antitheft mechanism that locked the steering wheel and shifter.

Underneath, the 1970 Boss 302 was unchanged. The exterior was another matter. While paint choices were opened up to include all Mustang colors, it was Shinoda's graphics that grabbed the attention. A pair of black stripes ran the entire length of the SportsRoof body, starting at the leading edge of the hood before branching out over the fenders near the cowl and sweeping back to the rear bumper, interrupted only by a Boss 302 graphic on the front fenders.

The understated Boss 429 also returned with the Mustang's updated styling changes and additional exterior color choices, including the new Grabber shades.

The Grandé continued into 1970 with few changes. The Mach 1, however, was updated with aluminum rocker panel inserts, rectangular fog lights in the grille, new hood striping, and a black honeycomb rear panel. Performance-oriented options, such as Shinoda's rear spoiler and rear window slats from the Boss 302, were popular for 1970 SportsRoofs.

Ford considered replacing the 1970 Mustang's FE big-block with the new canted-valve 429, which debuted in the 1970 Torino. However, although the 390 disappeared, the 428 made its swan song appearance in the 1970 Mustang as one of two versions of the Cobra Jet, either Q- or R-code with Ram-Air Shaker hood scoop. Super Cobra Jet status was once again available by checking off the Drag Pack option on the order sheet. The 1970 Mustang also ushered in a new midsize engine era as the short-lived 351 Windsor four-barrel was replaced by a four-barrel version of the canted-valve 351 Cleveland.

As model year 1970 came to a close, it was apparent that new insurance regulations and upcoming emissions requirements were combining to strangle the muscle car. Ford pulled out of racing in August 1970, ending the need to homologate engines such as the Boss 302 and Boss 429. The Mach 1 and Cobra Jet names would continue into the foreseeable future, but the Boss would survive only one more year.

Likewise, Carroll Shelby read the writing on the wall and pulled the plug on the Shelby Mustang program in the summer of 1969. With parts still in the pipeline, 1969 Shelbys were updated as 1970 models by adding hood stripes and a front spoiler. The Shelby Mustang era was over—at least for the foreseeable future.

High-back bucket seats became standard equipment in all 1970 Mustangs. Houndstooth cloth inserts and woodgrain trim were part of the Grandé package. *Ford Motor Company*

The 1970 Boss 302's stripe package was as daring as it got during the wild muscle car era. Ford sold 8,642 Boss 302s during its two-year run, 1,628 in 1969 and 7,014 for 1970. *Ford Motor Company*

The appearance of the 1970 Mach 1 was tamed with aluminum rocker panel inserts, narrowed black-out on the hood, and small grille-mounted fog lamps. New stylist Larry Shinoda eliminated the fake quarter panel scoops on all SportsRoofs. *Ford Motor Company*

The muscle car era had been good for Mustang sales. Although models with Boss and Cobra Jet engines represented barely half a percent of 1969–1970 Mustang production, the halo effect led to an uptick in SportsRoof sales. More than 42 percent of Mustangs built during the two-year period were the muscular-looking fastbacks, compared to barely more than 10 percent for the previous four model years.

## BUNKIE'S BABY

Shortly after taking over as Ford president in February 1968, Bunkie Knudsen viewed a prototype of the proposed 1971 Mustang. Designer Gale Halderman remembered the response: "He approved that 1971 right in the studio. We asked if he wanted to take it outside and look it over, and he said, 'No, I like it right here.' "

Staring into their crystal ball in the late 1960s, Ford product planners looked ahead to 1971 with visions of ever-larger engines and unbridled performance potential, a trend that Knudsen also embraced. The 428 was on the way for the Mustang and plans were in place for a new 429, possibly as early as 1970. There was even talk of 500 cubic inches for the future. To accommodate the larger engines, the first 1971 Mustang clay models were huge compared to the 1968 Mustang. On the other side of the equation, planners

## '70 Mach 1-quickest pony of them all!

Mach I. Just one model—the fastback with built-in spoiler. You don't need any more, and neither did Mickey Thompson when he boomed the prototype across the endless Bonneville Salt Flats to shatter an armload of Class B and C records.

Obviously the big hit with the Mustang Mach I has always been the great choice of power, and that's just the way we're going to keep things. To start off, there's the standard 351 2V job . . . and for street work it's a bushy-tailed mill indeed. Then come the options. Exhibit A: one brand-new 351 4V V-8. This is the all-new Cleveland engine. It has huge (2.19" intakes, 1.71" exhausts), canted valves and a walloping 11.0:1 compression ratio. Power? Three hundred big, strong, born-and-bred-in-America horses.

Not bad for the first option . . . right? Next is the 428 4V Cobra. This puts 440 foot-pounds of torque where it will do the most good. If you really want to shake up the troops you can have your Mach I with a 428 Cobra Jet. This giant jewel of an engine features the functional "Shaker" hood scoop. It shakes and so does the competition. Nice thing about the people who build the Mach I . . . they don't do half the job and then lay down their tools. No matter which engine you pick—and we know it's a tough decision—you get the competition suspension. This includes extra heavy-duty front and rear springs, extra heavy-duty shock absorbers, and front and rear stabilizer bars. Also you get fiberglass belted wide-tread tires. All the power you need, plus a suspension that lets you get it to the road. That's what makes the Mach I a complete package. And for '70, the Mach I looks as good as it goes. There's a unique black grille with driving lamps, black or white hood paint, wide aluminum rocker panel trim, high-back buckets in knitted vinyl, full instrumentation, wood-toned applique on panel and console, sweep-hand electric clock, and more. Get yourself a Mach I 428 and really "shake up" the troops.

*From its Cobra Jet 428 Shaker scoop to lowered Sport State option and supertires, Mach I is Number One.*

*Put one of these under your local Christmas Tree. Specially prepared Mach I drags in Super Stock . . . wins in Super Stock.*

These two pages tell you all about the 1970 Mach I. They are part of Ford's 16-page '70 Performance Buyer's Digest. It includes detailed specifications and options on all the great 1970 performance Fords . . . Cobra, Torino GT, Boss 302, and Mach I. There are also sections on Ford performance fun vehicles and Ford Muscle Parts. The Digest wraps it all up for you. For a copy just write to:

FORD PERFORMANCE DIGEST, Dept. HR-3.
Box 747, Dearborn, Michigan 48121

MUSTANG Ford

*Boss 429. An earth-shaking combination of big-bore engine and Trans-Am Body. Limited production, coax your dealer.*

As evidenced by this Mach 1 spread, colorful artwork with racing backgrounds dominated Mustang advertising in 1970. The Boss 429 was added at the bottom: "An earth-shattering combination of big-bore engine and Trans-Am body. Limited production, coax your dealer." *Donald Farr*

For the spring of 1970, Ford took advantage of the Boss 302's popularity by applying C stripes, similar to the 1969 Boss 302, and blackout rear panel to create the Grabber. Painted in the Grabber colors, the SportsRoof-only model resembled the Boss but most came with 302 or 351 two-barrel engines and automatic transmission. *Ford Motor Company*

viewed the next-generation Mustang as more luxurious with a softer suspension, roomier interior, and quieter ride.

They never saw the looming insurance restrictions and tighter emissions. Further down the road, an oil embargo would add fuel economy to the concerns.

The Mustang's creator, Lee Iacocca, disagreed with the Mustang's growing heft. "If we hadn't gone nuts and put the big Boss 429 in, the car never would have grown in size," he said later. "That was what triggered it out of the small-car world—performance, performance, performance!"

In a year that saw Ford introduce a new Pinto economy car to join the previous year's Maverick compact, the 1971 Mustang grew two inches wider, two inches longer, and 600 pounds heavier than its 1970 predecessor. All five body styles returned—hardtop, convertible, SportsRoof, Mach 1, and Grandé, plus a new Boss 351 SportsRoof to replace the Boss 302.

Because Ford dealers wanted to see a new car in their showrooms, 789 leftover 1969 Shelbys were updated as 1970 models with black hood stripes and front spoiler. *Ford Motor Company*

The larger dimensions provided a more spacious interior for passengers, while a much revised suspension added a comfortable LTD-like ride to the Grandé and base models. Updates included concealed windshield wipers, flush door handles, variable ratio power steering, and a mini console as standard equipment. Power windows were available for the first time.

Thanks to the added weight, the 200-cubic-inch six-cylinder was retired, leaving the 250 cubic-inch six as the base engine and progressing through the 302 two-barrel and a pair of Cleveland 351s, two-barrel and four-barrel. Taking advantage of the wider engine compartment, a 429 Cobra Jet, based on Ford's new 385 engine series, replaced the 428 FE. The 429 was available as either a regular CJ or CJ-R with functional Ram-Air via a pair of NASA scoops in the hood. Both were rated at 370 horsepower. With the Drag Pack option for cars with 3.91 or 4.11 gears, the 429 CJ became the 375-horsepower Super Cobra Jet with external oil cooler, four-bolt main bearings, solid-lifter cam, and 780-cfm Holley four-barrel.

As late as August 1970, Ford considered continuing the Boss 302 into 1971. But because the special small-block engine was expensive to produce, plus there was no longer a need to homologate for Trans-Am, the Boss 302 went into the history books and was replaced by the 1971 Boss 351 SportsRoof with a 330-horsepower, solid-lifter version of the 351 Cleveland. A worthy competitor to the 330-horsepower and freshly restyled Camaro Z/28, the Boss 351 was a much better street car because the extra cubic inches overcame the low-end torque losses of the large port heads.

Like the 428 Cobra Jet in 1969, the 429 CJ was ideal for the 1971 Mach 1's performance image. The SportsRoof-only body style included a honeycomb grille with driving lamps,

The wider, longer, lower styling of the 1971 Mustang was evident as early as January 1968, when this prototype was photographed in the Ford styling studios. *Ford Motor Company*

With ever-stringent government regulations, testing became more important to reduce emissions, especially on models such as the Mach 1 equipped with the big-block 429. *Ford Motor Company*

While the 1971 Mustang's size and heft were hard to ignore, the SportsRoof's 14-degree, almost flatback, roofline proved the most dramatic change, but not necessarily for the good. "When you look at the rear window through the inside mirror, it appears no larger than a mail slot," commented *Car & Driver. Ford Motor Company*

competition suspension, and a urethane body-color front bumper, a Mustang first. Mach 1 buyers had a choice of hoods, either the standard flat version or one with NASA scoops, which became functional with optional Ram-Air induction for 351s and 429s. Uncharacteristically, base Mach 1 power came from the 210-horsepower 302 two-barrel small-block. An optional Mach 1 Sports interior was the best-looking yet with accent stripes on the seat upholstery, molded door panels, triple gauge package, and woodgrain appliqués. Ford called it "Mach-nificent!"

Despite rumors that 1971 would be the final year for a big-block, the new, larger Mustang did not cure the Mustang's ailing sales figures. Model year production fell to under 150,000, the lowest ever and 40,000 fewer than the 1970 Mustang.

Mach 1 owners were no doubt insulted when Ford added the fog-lamp grille, NASA hood scoops, and side stripes to hardtops for a special spring value option in the spring of 1971. *Ford Motor Company*

# THE BUZZ:
## WHAT THE PRESS HAD TO SAY (THE MUSCLE YEARS)

"With personal cars getting hairier all the time, it seemed likely that Carroll Shelby would do something to keep ahead of the pack. Sure enough, he introduced the Shelby GT500, a car so hairy as to make the others look crew cut by comparison."
—*Motor Trend*, January 1967

"Detroit has cobbled up so many fine designs in the last 20 years that when Ford decided to change the Mustang, everybody held their breath. But it's okay people, everythin's gonna be all right."
—*Hot Rod*, March 1967

"We lived with our 390 for 5,000 miles and could hardly find any faults with its performance. By no stretch of the imagination can the car be considered a bear, but it has great potential."
—*Cars Magazine*, 1967

"The Cobra Jet will be the utter delight of every Ford lover and the bane of all the rest because, quite frankly, it is the fastest running Pure Stock in the history of man."
—*Hot Rod*, March 1968

"In a year when every manufacturer offers hood scoops, Ford outdoes them all with an AA/Fuel dragster-style bug-catcher sticking right through a hole in the hood."
—*Car & Driver*, November 1968

"The original Shelby GT350 was a fire-breather; it would accelerate, brake, and corner with a nimbleness only a Corvette could match. The GT350, 1969-style, is little more than a tough-looking Mustang Grandé, a Thunderbird for Hell's Angels. Certainly not the car of Carroll Shelby's dreams."
—*Car & Driver*, February 1969

"Are you ready for the first great Mustang? One with performance to match its looks, handling to send imported-car fans home mumbling to themselves, and an interior as elegant, and liveable, as a gentleman's club? It's here. The Mustang Mach 1."
—*Car Life*, March 1969

"Ford's not-so-boss Boss 429: A combination of politics and production problems keeps the potent 429 from performing like a super supercar should."
—*Super Stock & Drag Illustrated*, June 1969

"Ford's answer to the Z/28 rates an A. [The Boss 302] is easily the best Mustang yet—and that includes all the Shelbys and Mach 1s."
—*Car & Driver*, June 1969

"The new [1971] Mustang has ballooned another notch closer to an intermediate sedan. From the driver's seat, it seems enormous; you can hardly see the surrounding earth."
—*Car & Driver*, October 1970

"The engineers come off as the real heroes in the development of the Boss 351. It offers drag strip performance that most super cars with 100-cubic-inch or more displacement will envy and generates high lateral cornering forces."
—*Car & Driver*, February 1971

"Our [1973] Mach 1 test vehicle came with the 351-cubic-inch CJ engine, a derivative of the Boss 351 sufficiently de-toxed and de-powered to make the feds happy."
—*Road Test*, July 1973

For the first time in its eight-year history, the Mustang did not undergo a second-year styling update. The 1972 sales brochure even used many of the same photos from 1971. Essentially, the 1972 Mustang was the same as 1971, other than the fact that performance choices like the 429 Cobra Jet, Boss 351, and Drag Pack had fallen prey to the new era of insurance regulations and emissions. The top-of-the-line engine was the 351 four-barrel, listed at 266 horsepower under new, and more realistic, SAE net power ratings. For the first time, horsepower ratings were not mentioned in sales material; instead, literature noted that emissions were reduced by up to 85 percent. All 1972 engines were designed to run on low-octane fuel.

To dress up base hardtops and convertibles, a new Exterior Decor Group option added Mach 1 looks with the honeycomb grille with sportlamps, color-keyed urethane front bumper, and lower bodyside paint, plus the availability of hockey-stick side stripes. For 1972's spring promotion, the Mustang joined the Maverick and Pinto in a patriotic-themed Sprint Decor option for hardtops and convertibles, all white with blue and red graphics along with a U.S.A. emblem on the rear quarter panel. Canadian models got a maple leaf shield.

A last gasp at performance arrived at midyear 1972 with the 351-4V High Output, a 275-horsepower (SAE net) solid-lifter engine that was essentially the same as the previous year's Boss 351. With slightly lower compression and availability in all body styles, the HO package included the four-speed transmission with Hurst shifter and 3.91-geared nine-inch rear end with staggered shocks. Only 398 were built.

Externally, the 1972 Mustang, seen here as a Mach 1, was identical to 1971's version. *Ford Motor Company*

Opposite: The canted-valve 351 Cleveland, in both two- and four-barrel configurations, became the Mustang's workhorse engine in 1971. With the 429 in its final year for the 1971 Mustang, the 351C would become the top engine choice for 1972 and 1973. *Ford Motor Company*

With no need to produce a special Boss 302 engine after pulling out of racing in the summer of 1970, for 1971 Ford offered what was arguably the best of the Bosses. The Boss 351 came with a 330-horsepower 351 Cleveland, four-speed, and 3.91 gears to run solid high 13-second elapsed times in the quarter mile, making it one of the quickest production Mustangs to date. *Source Interlink Media*

Along with Pintos and Mavericks, the 1972 Mustang's Sprint decor option commemorated the USA's 1972 Olympic team with a red, white, and blue theme for hardtops and SportsRoofs. Fifty convertibles were also built for the Cherry Blossom Festival Parade in Washington, D.C. *Ford Motor Company*

A new front-end treatment, complete with energy-absorbing front bumper, set the 1973 Mustang apart. *Ford Motor Company*

By the time Ford dealers took delivery of the first 1973s in September 1972, rumors were already circulating that the Mustang was in the final year of its current configuration. According to the car magazines, the next generation Mustang would be smaller and more fuel efficient, basically returning to its roots as a sporty compact car. The reports also noted that the V-8 engine and convertible—the only one left at Ford—would disappear after 1973.

With one year remaining before the total overhaul, Ford updated the 1973 Mustang with a new front-end appearance, revising the grille with vertical parking lamps and making the color-keyed urethane bumper standard on all models. To meet the government's new five miles-per-hour front impact requirement, the bumper protruded further forward and connected to energy-absorbing rams in the front body structure.

Other than the 351 HO, which quietly disappeared, the engine lineup remained the same as 1972 with a base 250 cubic-inch six and optional 302 and 351 two-barrels and 351 four-barrel V-8s. In a sign of the times, the sales brochure barely mentioned the 351, instead focusing on comfort, convenience, and safety. All engines were equipped with exhaust gas recirculation (EGR) to reduce emissions. Due to a glitch in emission certification testing, the Ram-Air option was oddly available only for the 351 two-barrel engine.

While the Grandé maintained its luxury looks, the Mach 1 changed more than any other 1973 Mustang thanks to new side stripes. Like the previous two years, the Mach 1 failed to reach the speed of sound with its standard 302 two-barrel engine, although both 351s were optionally available. At least the rear spoiler was still available.

For the first time ever, Mustang sales increased without a major restyling effort, up to 134,867 in 1973 compared to 125,093 in 1972. Half of the gain came from convertible sales; word was out that 1973 was the final year for a ragtop.

New side stripes differentiated the 1973 Mach from previous years' models. Hubcaps and trim rings were standard, but many were equipped with new forged aluminum wheels, which were optional for all 1973 Mustangs. *Ford Motor Company*

# 3

# THE
# LITTLE
# JEWEL

ON AUGUST 28, 1973, Ford revealed a totally new Mustang. Much smaller than the previous intermediate-size 1973 model, the 1974 Mustang abandoned V-8 performance by offering only a four-cylinder and optional six-cylinder. Obviously, the Mustang for the 1970s was created to compete against Toyota Celicas and Datsun 240Zs, not Camaro Z/28s and Hemi 'Cudas.

Less than two months after the Mustang II arrived in showrooms, the Organization for Petroleum Exporting Countries (OPEC) ordered an oil embargo in response to the United States' decision to supply weapons to the Israeli military during the Yom Kippur War. Almost immediately, oil prices leaped from $3 to $12 per barrel. Drivers who remembered 25 cents-per-gallon gasoline prices in the 1960s watched in horror as the pump numbers rolled over to 55 cents per gallon almost overnight. In response to the fuel shortage, President Richard Nixon asked gas stations to close on Saturday nights and Sundays, causing long lines on weekdays. Americans accustomed to plentiful fuel at cheap prices were shocked when station pumps ran dry while the nozzle was still in their hand.

Demographics had also changed. The rapidly expanding 25-to-34 age group preferred smaller cars, leading many previous Mustang buyers to defect to the imports. Small cars, including compacts and subcompacts, attracted more than half of all new-car buyers under 35 in the early 1970s. A 1972 national new car buyer study showed that these potential customers wanted sporty, contemporary styling and agility at a good price.

Once again, Lee Iacocca was in the right place at the right time with the right car. Only this time, it was as much luck as marketing research.

After three years of ultra-large Mustangs, the 1974 model returned to its compact roots as the Mustang II. *Ford Motor Company*

Lee Iacocca never cared for the larger post-1966 Mustangs and was happy to compare the 1974 Mustang II with the original. *Ford Motor Company*

## FROM OHIO TO ARIZONA

During the mid- to late 1960s, many of the people involved with the Mustang's success in 1964 climbed the Ford corporate ladder. In January 1965, Iacocca moved into Ford World Headquarters with a promotion to vice president of the corporate car and truck group, which gave him responsibilities for planning, promotion, and marketing for Ford and Lincoln-Mercury. He became less involved with the Mustang and could only watch as others grew the Mustang into the huge 1971 model that was closer in size to a Torino than a Falcon.

In his biography, Iacocca described the 1971–1973 Mustang as "more like a fat pig," blaming Ford president Bunkie Knudsen for pushing big engines, larger body, and weight. "It was no longer the same car," he said. "And our declining sales figures were making the point very clearly."

Complaints about the burgeoning size of the Mustang landed at Ford as early as 1968, when 1965 Mustang owner Anna Muccioli spoke at a Ford stockholder's meeting. Both Iacocca and Henry Ford II were in the room when she announced, "When the Thunderbird came out, it was a beautiful sports car. Then you blew it up to the point where it lost its identity. The same thing has happened to the Mustang. Why can't you leave a small car small?" Her comments drew a hardy round of applause.

By September 1969, Knudsen was out of the picture, unceremoniously fired by Henry Ford II and leaving Iacocca free to further investigate the possibility of downsizing the Mustang to its original dimensions. He wasted little time. At a November Ford management

Responding to the influx of smaller import cars, Ford introduced the Pinto in 1970 as a 1971 model. It would provide the basis for an Arizona concept with more sporty appeal. *Ford Motor Company*

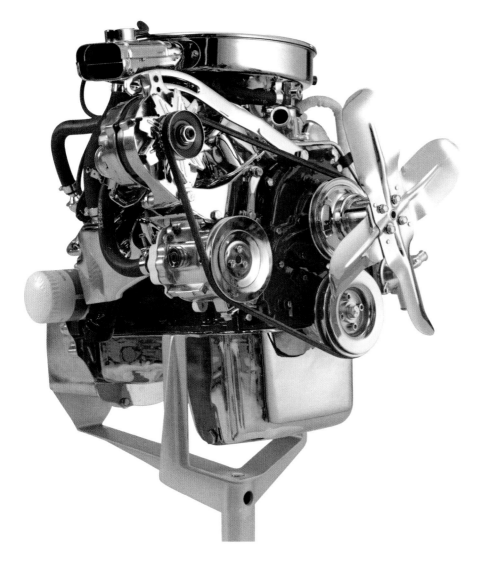

conference, Iacocca expressed his concerns, resulting in plans for a smaller 1974 Mustang, code-named "Ohio" and based on the 1970 Maverick platform. A second "Arizona" program was subsequently launched to explore a separate nameplate based on the Pinto to compete with the 240Z, Celica, Opel GT, and even Lincoln/Mercury's soon-to-be-introduced 1970 Capri.

Advanced product planning manager Nat Adamson was assigned responsibility for the Arizona program. As his team worked on a variety of two-seaters and Pinto variations, market research revealed an emerging interest in sporty subcompacts; surprisingly, potential buyers preferred the Arizona-based concepts over the Ohio project. They also expressed a desire for a fastback with sporty looks and fun driving characteristics.

Unhappy with what his Mustang had become during 1967 to 1971, Iacocca took a personal interest in returning to a smaller Mustang. When Ford purchased controlling interest in Italy's Ghia design studios in November 1970, Iacocca requested concepts for a small, sporty car. He was impressed when Ghia delivered a functioning sample in just 53 days. The Ghia concept not only delivered a new slant on styling, but it also provided a drivable vehicle. "Without our Italian connection, we would have been working on paper and with clay for another year, maybe two," Iacocca said. "But here we had a car with metal and an engine, that we could sit in and roll down the window to see if you

In January 1972, Ford executives Stu Frey, Jack Eby, and Harold McDonald looked over a proposed Mach 1 version of the 1974 Mustang fastback based on the Lincoln-Mercury studio's design competition winner. A nearby 1971 Mach provided perspective of where the Mustang was headed. *Ford Motor Company*

As late as February 1972, Ford was exploring the possibility of a two-seat 1974 Mustang. This short wheelbase drawing was laid over a clay model for comparison. *Ford Motor Company*

could reach the beltline, and check to see how close your hat was to the visor. It was a great early boost for the whole program."

In July 1971, Adamson requested formal approval for his Arizona project. It was not only approved, but also the decision was made to abandon to Ohio program and accelerate Adamson's Arizona proposal as the next-generation Mustang. On the day after approval, Adamson was promoted to light car planning manager and given the responsibility to create the next Mustang from his Pinto-based Arizona car. He had exactly two years to get the job done; Job One for the 1974 Mustang was scheduled for July 1973.

For economy purposes, the standard engine was planned as an overhead cam 2.3-liter four-cylinder, but there was still a question about the optional powerplant—traditional inline six or the more compact German-built V-6 from the Capri. Packing the old straight-six into a smaller car proved troublesome. Iacocca was called to the design studio to see for himself. "We told Lee that if we really wanted a smaller car, we had better start with a smaller engine," said design chief Gene Bordinat. "Lee agreed with us."

As with the 1965 Mustang, Iacocca had strong opinions about the new car's mission. "He was planning an entirely new kind of domestic car for a different kind of customer," said Hal Sperlich, who had ridden the Mustang's success to a position as vice president of product planning and research. "He wanted it to look different from other cars on the market, different from the 1971 to 1973 Mustangs, different from the Pinto, and different from the Capri too."

Basically, Iacocca wanted to modernize his original concept for the 1965 Mustang—an elegant car with a *Mona Lisa* look. A Ghia notchback concept satisfied Iacocca, but the idea for a fastback was also on the drawing board. Like 1962, Iacocca requested a design competition among four of the Ford studios—Lincoln-Mercury, Ford, Advanced, and Interior. The designers had three months, as opposed to the three weeks of 1962, to propose their concepts. They produced 150 sketches and 50 clay models, resulting in both practical and far-out creations. In November 1971, six final proposals were displayed in the design center courtyard.

Lincoln-Mercury design office director Al Mueller recalled Iacocca's review: "Mr. Iacocca viewed these cars with Gene Bordinat and Harold McDonald. His procedure at these showings was usually the same. He walks around the cars a few times and listens to the comments from others. Then he says exactly what he thinks—pro or con. He really flipped over our fastback. His cigar must have rolled around three times. We had won!"

Iacocca noted that the fastback from the Lincoln-Mercury studio somehow looked longer and lower. Iacocca added his suggestions, requesting cues to remind people of the original Mustang, including a mouthy grille opening with a horse emblem and side sculpturing to simulate a scoop, something that had disappeared in the 1969–1973 models.

Designer Don DeLaRossa couldn't shake the idea of a hardtop. "Why not capture some of the flavor of the original model of 1965," he said. "That was a notchback. So we got to work on a notchback with that fully integrated front and rear end."

DeLaRossa's notchback scored surprisingly well in research, indicating that there was a market for the classier look. In the spring of 1972, the 1974 Mustang design was approved for both a fastback and hardtop model.

The 1974 Mustang II satisfied Iacocca's desire to return the Mustang to its original form with long hood, short rear deck styling. The Ghia hardtop, shown here with optional sunroof, also fulfilled Iacocca's demand for more luxury. *Ford Motor Company*

Ten years after Iacocca's cover appearance for the 1965 Mustang, Henry Ford II scored a *Newsweek* cover to illustrate American automakers' move toward smaller cars such as the Mustang II. *Donald Farr*

"No one man designed the 1974 Mustang," Mueller said. "The efforts of the Lincoln-Mercury designers resulted in 30 percent of the work needed to sell the car to management. After that, the Ford design office took over for the remaining 70 percent of the job."

Throughout the development process, Iacocca stressed a new level of quality for the next-generation Mustang, going as far as comparing it to Mercedes-Benz. "The 1974 Mustang will have to be one thing," Iacocca demanded. "It will have to be a little jewel."

## NEW CLASS OF MUSTANG: FIRST CLASS

Like 1964, Ford's PR machine churned into action as the introduction of the new Mustang approached. To drive home the difference in the totally revamped 1974 models from previous Mustangs, the public affairs department suggested a revised name: Mustang II. "As the tenth Mustang, the new car is subject to being accepted as just another model year if it's called simply the 1974 Mustang," said one statement. "On the other hand, a name like Mustang II serves to communicate the idea of a new generation of Mustangs."

A small dealer handout described the era: "Today, more people are looking for economy, luxury, and convenience in a small car." The 1974 Mustang II provided that and more with four models: hardtop, Ghia hardtop, three-door 2+2 hatchback, and Mach 1 hatchback. With an 85-horsepower base four-cylinder and optional 105-horsepower V-6 as the only available engines, performance didn't enter into the Mustang II equation. Horsepower ratings weren't even mentioned in the sales brochure.

Still, there was much to brag about. The Mustang was so completely reengineered that the only vestiges of its Pinto heritage were the rear floorpan along with a few drivetrain and chassis components. Significantly, an isolated subframe, to which the front suspension and engine were mounted, soaked up both road shock and the engine vibrations that were common to four-cylinders at the time. Copying Mercedes-Benz, pieces of trim and

Plush roll-and-tuck seat upholstery added to the Ghia's luxury appeal. *Ford Motor Company*

molding used concealed butt-sleeve joints instead of the traditional American overlap joints. Interior screws were either hidden or made from high-luster aluminum.

Other improvements included rack-and-pinion steering (available with power-assist, a first for an American car) and manual front disc brakes as standard equipment. The combination of upgraded sound deadening and improved fit and finish, as engineered by a special task force, produced a more luxury feel. Instead of a convertible, the Mustang II was available with an optional sunroof that opened via sliding glass panels.

Emphasizing the luxury aspect was Ghia, a replacement for the previous Grandé and named for the Italian company that created one of the first Mustang II designs. It was the epitome of Iacocca's vision for the Mustang II—European elegance with touches like pin striping, white sidewall tires, wire-look wheel covers, and plush interior with walnut tone accents, super soft vinyl or cloth bucket seats with a roll-and-tuck appearance, thicker cut-pile carpeting, and a Super Sound package for a quieter ride. In a sign of the times, a Picardy velour cloth interior was optional.

The 1974 Mach 1, however, was a misnomer with its standard V-6 engine, especially when compared to the 428 and 429 Cobra Jet beasts from its namesake's past. For the most part, the hatchback-only Mach 1 was a dress-up package with blacked-out rocker panels, raised white letter tires on 13-inch wheels, and tachometer with gauge package. An available Rallye package for all 1974 Mustang IIs with the V-6 (except Ghia) provided some bite with Traction-Lok differential, competition suspension, leather-wrapped steering wheel, and sport exhaust with twin exhaust tips.

The 1974 Mach 1 continued the name and blackout graphics from the muscle car era, but its 2.8-liter V-6 engine failed to excite performance enthusiasts who remembered big-block Cobra Jet V-8s from three years earlier. *Ford Motor Company*

Magazine road tests didn't find a lot to get excited about with the 1974 Mustang II, even when dressed in Mach 1 trim. "The car in stock form is regrettably underpowered," said the editors at *Car Craft*. "Looking at the Mach 1 from a performance stand-point, Ford will have to lighten up the car or offer a V-8. We predict they will do the latter." *Source Interlink Media*

The Mustang II debuted at the end of August 1973 to a lukewarm reception, not helped by enthusiast magazine complaints about the lack of performance. Stressing the luxury aspect, Ford loaded up dealers with heavily optioned models that retailed for over $4,000. Buyers who came in to see the new Mustang opted for less expensive Mavericks and Pintos instead. The original prediction of 31,000 Mustang II sales in the first month vanished; only 18,000 were sold.

Then the OPEC oil embargo did more for the Mustang II than any amount of Ford advertising or marketing. As pump prices rose and lines formed at gas stations, Americans rushed to dealerships to trade in their old fuel hogs for more efficient small cars. Used car lots filled with 429 Galaxies and Cobra Jet Mustangs as buyers drove away in new Pintos, Mavericks, and, yes, Mustang IIs. Although the OPEC oil crisis ended in March 1974, the American conscience had shifted to smaller, fuel-efficient cars. By the end of the 1974 model year, Ford had sold nearly 386,000 Mustangs, the fourth highest total in Mustang history, and a huge increase over the 134,867 sales in 1973.

While most auto magazines criticized the 1974 Mustang II's lack of a V-8 engine, *Motor Trend* looked beyond performance and bestowed the new generation Mustang with its coveted Car of the Year award. The editors put the era into perspective: "In 1974, in a time of introspection about the function and purpose of the automobile, and in a time when the entire motoring world is being reevaluated and radicalized by an energy

Iacocca's *Mona Lisa* look returned to Mustang advertising for 1974. "The right car at the right time" proved eerily prophetic when the OPEC oil embargo caused rising fuel prices shortly after the Mustang II's introduction. *Donald Farr*

Other than the 302-cubic-inch V-8 option, the 1975 Mustang changed very little. An opera window for the Ghia added a tad more luxury appeal. *Ford Motor Company*

Ford designers experimented with various paint schemes in an attempt to pump some excitement into the Mustang II. This 1975 styling exercise evolved into the 1976 Stallion. *Ford Motor Company*

## COMPARATIVE DIMENSIONS*

|                | 1965 Mustang | 1973 Mustang | 1974 Mustang** |
|----------------|--------------|--------------|----------------|
| Overall Length | 181.6        | 193.8        | 175.0          |
| Overall Width  | 68.2         | 74.1         | 70.2           |
| Overall Height | 51.1         | 50.7         | 49.9           |
| Wheelbase      | 108.0        | 109.0        | 96.2           |

*In inches
**Two-door hardtop

crisis of enormous dimension, the Mustang II, as the advertisements declare, is indeed 'a new class of small car.' "

Securing the 1974 Mustang II's notoriety as the only Mustang without an available V-8 engine, the 1975 Mustang arrived with an optional two-barrel 302 V-8 rated at 129 horsepower and offered only with automatic transmission, power steering, and power brakes. Because Ford failed to predict customer backlash over the lack of a V-8, the Mustang II was not designed for the larger powerplant, so updates included moving the radiator forward by three inches, lengthening the hood, and strengthening the number two crossmember and side rails.

Otherwise, little changed. A revised grille with a larger egg-crate pattern moved forward almost flush with the grille opening, and radial tires became standard equipment, as did electronic ignition for all engines. The Mach 1 regained some of its lost respectability with the available 302 V-8 engine. An opera window and available half vinyl roof added yet more elegance to the Ghia hardtop, which Ford compared to the 1956 Thunderbird. A Silver Luxury Group option transformed the Ghia into a little Lincoln with silver paint, cranberry velour interior, and hood ornament.

At least the Mustang continued. Three pony car competitors—Challenger, Barracuda, and AMC Javelin—were discontinued after 1974, while cousin Cougar became a larger luxury two-door based on the Thunderbird. Only the Camaro and Firebird remained in their traditional configuration. However, the 1974 Mustang II was now designed to compete with Chevrolet's Monza, not the Camaro.

The two-tone Stallion edition for the 1976 Mustang II was shared with the Maverick and Pinto. *Ford Motor Company*

Thanks to the popularity of the Cobra II package, the front spoiler became a no-cost option for 1977 hatchbacks. *Ford Motor Company*

T-tops were the rage in the mid-1970s, so Ford added the popular removable roof panels as an option for 1977 Mustang II hatchbacks, replacing the moonroof, although the sunroof was still available with flip-up and removable glass panel. *Ford Motor Company*

With fuel economy still very much on the minds of American car buyers, Ford introduced a new MPG line of cars in June 1975, including a Mustang II version. With a slightly modified 2.3-liter four-cylinder and 3.18:1 rear gears instead of 3.40, the four-speed Mustang II MPG boasted 34 miles per gallon on the highway, 23 in the city.

The few updates for 1976 included catalytic converters for all models (as used on California cars and MPG models in 1975), windshield wiper controls on the steering column stalk, and an intermittent wiper option. Horsepower for the four-cylinder jumped to 92, but for performance fans the big news was the availability of a four-speed with the 302, now rated at 134 horsepower. A Stallion package, shared with Maverick and Pinto, came with blackout treatment, styled steel wheels, and Stallion decals. However, the surprise of the year was the Shelby-like Cobra II, conceived and built by Motortown Corporation.

# COBRA II

Oddly enough, it was Jim Wangers, best known for his creative marketing for the Pontiac GTO, who put some excitement back into the Mustang. Having departed Pontiac to consult for coach and accessory company Motortown Corporation, Wangers approached Edsel Ford II, then on Ford's board of directors, with an idea for a 1976 Cobra II, built with parts manufactured and installed by Motortown. The cosmetic package included Shelby-like hood and side stripes, nonfunctioning hood scoop, front chin spoiler, a ducktail-style rear spoiler, black-out grille with Cobra snake emblem, louvered panels over the quarter windows, and brushed aluminum dash and door panel inserts. It was available in a trio of color combinations, all reminiscent of the early Shelbys—blue on white, white on blue, or Hertz-like gold on black.

Through graphics and bolt-ons, Jim Wangers's Cobra II package for the 1976 Mustang II brought back memories of the Mustang's Shelby era. *Ford Motor Company*

With gold stripes on black, the 1977 Cobra II resembled the Hertz Shelbys from 1966. *Ford Motor Company*

"Cobra bites man!" exclaimed this 1978 Cobra II magazine ad, which touted the new stripe package with billboard graphics on the side. *Donald Farr*

Although emissions standards continued to choke horsepower, Ford noted the potential in performance image options and added more choices in 1977, including the Cobra II's front chin spoiler at no extra cost for hatchbacks and a new Sports Performance package that came with the 302 V-8, four-speed transmission, power steering and brakes, and radial tires. In fact, all hatchbacks benefitted from a blacked-out grille, sport steering wheel, styled steel wheels with raised white letter tires, and brushed aluminum instrument panel appliqués. With the Sports Performance package, Ghias received a black or tan exterior along with a number of classy upgrades, including chamois trim and luggage rack.

Surprisingly to some at Ford, Motortown had ended up building 26,259 Cobra IIs in 1976. For Motortown, success came at a price because Ford decided to bring the package inhouse as a separate model for 1977. The blue exterior with white stripes was dropped, but green and red stripes became available for white cars. Sales fell to 11,948, not helped by the fact that the Cobra II's base engine was the 2.3-liter four-cylinder with the V-6 and 302 V-8 as options, a lackluster engine choice that encouraged ridicule for the Cobra II as a "sticker car."

As sales slipped during the Mustang II's fourth year, a *Car Facts Bulletin* announced three updates at midyear 1977: a T-top option for the hatchback, a 2+2 Rallye Appearance package with gold and flat-black accents, and a new graphics package for the 1977½

# THE BUZZ:
## WHAT THE PRESS HAD TO SAY (THE TURBULENT 70s)

"Consistent with Detroit's motto of 'The only thing that doesn't change is change itself,' Ford has seen fit to throw its mutated Mustang to the wolves and introduce in its stead a brand-new image-maker—the Mustang II."
—*Car Craft*, September 1973

"The Mustang II is an example of what Detroit technology, specifically Ford in this case, can accomplish when properly motivated. The base car handles very well, rides better than anything in its price range, and gives the owner a very distinct sense of luxury. Ghia simply amplifies the qualities of the bare-back pony. Mach I lets you dream of Riverside and the Nurburgring. Power is short, but then power is short in most sports luxury cars under ten grand. You won't find anything around that has the Mustang II's ride, handling, and certainly the high level of luxury for the price."
—*Motor Trend*, December 1973

"More than anything else, in selecting the Mustang II [as the 1974 Car of the Year], we feel Ford, and perhaps all of Detroit will follow, has placed good taste, function, and handling/performance before frill, flash, and fad."
—*Motor Trend*, February 1974

"With its good suspension, good steering, and good tires, plus the V6 and a well-designed interior, the Mustang II is the best Ford product we've driven in a long time."
—*Hot Rod*, January 1974

"Power in this new [1975 V-8] Mustang is a vast improvement over the 1974 Mustang, enough to generate a lot of excitement into a ride around the course that was painfully absent a year ago. From a standstill, response is good, but not immediate or thunderous the way it was in the original Mustang."
—*Motor Trend*, August 1974

"Visually, the Cobra II gives the impression that maybe the old Shelby has been resurrected, but a quick return to the government-imposed realities of the 1970s tells you that it just couldn't be."
—*Car Craft*, August 1976

"For the young or the young at heart, a Mustang II T-top optioned like our test car makes a prideful and pleasing piece of transportation."
—*Motor Trend*, February 1977

"The King Cobra option, besides trying to look like a quasi-Trans-Am with a garish hood decal and non-functioning hood scoop, is meant to look like a road racer. That's performance today."
—*Cars Magazine*, August 1978

## KING COBRA

If lots of decals were good, then more decals must be better. That seemed to be the thinking when Ford introduced the 1978 King Cobra, basically a Cobra II on steroids with a huge Cobra snake decal on the hood and large air dam under the front bumper. The King Cobra was Ford's answer to the Trans Am Firebird, which prominently featured a screaming chicken hood decal as Pontiac, like Ford, scrambled to maintain a performance image with less horsepower under the hood.

While the Trans Am could still claim a piece of its muscle car heritage with an available 200-horsepower 400-cubic-inch engine, the King Cobra was restricted to the two-barrel 302 with just 134 horsepower. A standard four-speed transmission provided at least some semblance of the Mustang's former muscle car image.

Offered for the hatchback only, the King Cobra package included blackout grille, color-keyed lacy spoke aluminum wheels, and dual exhaust tips. But it was the graphics package that attracted attention, especially the large, cobra snake decal on the hood that spread out around the rear-facing (and nonfunctional) hood scoop. Aerodynamic improvements included an IMSA-like front air dam, flares in front of the rear wheel wells, and the Cobra II's rear spoiler.

Ford sold 4,318 King Cobras, many of them with T-tops that took the sticker price to $5,638, making the well-optioned King Cobra the most expensive Mustang II ever.

If the Pontiac Trans Am could have its chicken hood graphics, then certainly the King Cobra could counter with a huge snake hood decal. *Ford Motor Company*

Cobra II that included wide over-the-top stripes and side decals with huge Cobra lettering on the doors. Only a handful sold at the end of the model year.

The 1977 Mustang II model year was uniquely extended by several weeks when the U.S. Congress recessed before extending 1977 emission rules into 1978. Because Ford could not legally produce and sell 1978 models, 1978 Mustang IIs built from late June to early August were titled as 1977 models.

The Mustang II entered its final year, 1978, with the same body styles as 1974—hardtop, Ghia hardtop, 2+2, and Mach 1—and very minor changes from the previous year, including variable ratio power steering, twin cushions for the rear seat, and an available variable venturi carburetor for the 302. The Cobra II returned with its new billboard graphics, available as red, green, or blue decals on white or gold stripes on black. A Fashion Accessory package was designed to appeal to women buyers with pinstripes, chic cloth seat inserts, lighted visor vanity mirror, interior door pockets, coin tray, and illuminated entry system. Production dropped to 8,009, not helped by the inhouse competition from the bolder and wilder King Cobra model.

Like 1973's final year of the first-generation Mustang, the last year of the Mustang II saw an increase in sales. Ford sold 213,348 Mustangs for 1978 compared to 132,236 for 1977. Once again, the word was out that the Mustang was due for another makeover, one that would soften, or even eliminate, traditional Mustang styling cues and give the original American pony car more of a European flavor.

In July 1978, Henry Ford II fired Lee Iacocca after three years of animosity between the pair of strong-willed executives. The Mustang would enter its third generation without its biggest fan.

Although overshadowed in later years by the Cobra II and King Cobra, the Mach 1 remained as a 2+2 body style throughout the Mustang II generation. An available front spoiler and T-top roof added to the sporty appeal. *Ford Motor Company*

Ford produced more than 1.1 million Mustang IIs from 1974 to 1978, assuring the Mustang's legacy into the 1980s. *Ford Motor Company*

# CODE NAME
# FOX:
# THE NEW BREED

**THE MUSTANG THAT APPEARED** in dealer showrooms in September 1978 was unlike any Mustang that had come before it, and especially unlike the Mustang II that it replaced. Gone were the familiar pony car characteristics—the open grille, side scoop sculpturing, and tri-bar taillights. The running horse emblem was reduced to a modernized round emblem on the hood. The sales brochure described the 1979 perfectly: The New Breed.

Even before the Mustang II's introduction in the fall of 1973, Ford was planning for its replacement with a platform to take the Mustang into the 1980s. Like the Mustang II, the next-generation Mustang would have to adapt to the changing times. Planners gambled that fuel mileage would trump horsepower in a time when tightening fuel supplies had already raised prices at the pump. There were three ways to improve fuel efficiency: smaller engines, less weight, and better aerodynamics. The Mustang of the future would need all three.

Code-named Fox, Ford's next-generation compact chassis was viewed as a world car platform for a totally new family of fuel-efficient vehicles manufactured from lighter weight materials and powered by smaller, fuel-efficient engines. Scheduled for production at Ford plants around the world, the Fox chassis was designed to share components and cut costs as it replaced a variety of European, Australian, and U.S. cars, including the Pinto, Maverick, and Mustang. In December 1973, shortly after the Mustang II went on sale, Ford president Lee Iacocca signed off on the Fox program.

Even though the Fox-body 1979 Mustang erased many of the traditional styling cues, Ford looked to the past to link the latest Mustang to its heritage as a sporty, compact car. It was the start of a new future for the Mustang, with the Indianapolis 500 pace car edition providing a glimpse of what was in store. *Ford Motor Company*

Although the world car concept never materialized as planned, in the United States the rear-wheel-drive Fox platform evolved into a pair of compact family cars—the Ford Fairmont and Mercury Zephyr—and the next-generation Mustang. The Fairmont/Zephyr was scheduled for 1978, a year ahead of the revamped Mustang, but the Fox-body platform was actually tailored around the Mustang's needs as a sporty car with good handling and more European appearance.

## DIFFERENT ON PURPOSE

The 1979 Mustang would be as different from the Mustang II as the Mustang II was from the 1973 Mustang. For the first time, the Mustang was designed from the ground up and not based on a previous car line, although the same platform would be used for other Ford products, including the simultaneously developed Fairmont/Zephyr and, in the not-too-distant future, the Thunderbird and Cougar.

The design for the 1979 Mustang started out boxy, but by the time of this styling studio photo in May 1976, the final shape had been determined. *Ford Motor Company*

Jack Telnack (right) was instrumental in the design of the 1979 Mustang. Here, he and team members Dave Rees and Bob Zokas review a clay model. *Ford Motor Company*

Opposite: As president of Ford and father of the Mustang, Lee Iacocca signed off on the Fox-body platform for the 1979 model year. Just two months before it went on sale, Henry Ford II fired Iacocca. *Ford Motor Company*

The early designs for the 1979 Mustang were boxy, looking very much like its Fairmont cousin. That changed when design executive Jack Telnack returned from Europe to take over as director of Ford's North American light car and truck design department. Utilizing his European experience and knowledge of aerodynamics, Telnack proposed a much different car, one with a slanted grille, lower hood, and a low European-like beltline. There were no styling cues to tie it to previous Mustangs.

"Jack wanted this car to have the impact of the original Mustang," said Fritz Mayhew, the light car design manager who sketched many of the early concepts. "We felt it was time for a change. We had done about as much as we could with those original design cues from 1964."

With widespread use of modern materials such as aluminum and plastic, the unibody Fox Mustang weighed 2,700 pounds,

Ford promoted the 1979 Mustang as "The New Breed" in an advertising campaign that focused on everything new: "new styling, new handling, new turbo, and new options." *Donald Farr*

The 1979 Mustang abandoned the styling cues that had been so prominent on previous Mustangs. Gone were the tri-bar taillights and side-scoop sculpturing, which gave way to a more European look. *Ford Motor Company*

more like the 1965 Mustang and 200 pounds less than the Mustang II, a savings that would contribute to improved fuel mileage. Although the exterior dimensions were similar to the Mustang II, the wheelbase was stretched from 92.2 inches to 100.5 inches, translating into a roomier interior and more cargo space.

Underneath, the Fox Mustang utilized a modified MacPherson strut front suspension with rack-and-pinion steering and front disc brakes. A new 7.5-inch solid rear axle was supported by a four-link rear suspension with coil springs replacing the former leaf springs.

Although the 1979 Mustang looked nothing like the Mustang II, it continued the previous body style offerings of hardtop and three-door hatchback. With the first-time use of high-impact polyurethane bumper covers combined with the laid-back nose, slatted grille, and low hoodline, the Telnack design slipped through the air like no Mustang before it. Using extensive wind-tunnel testing, Ford engineers achieved a drag coefficient of 0.44 for the hatchback and 0.46 for the hardtop—a 25 percent improvement over the 1978 hardtop—making the Mustang one of the most aerodynamic cars on American roads in 1979.

The interior also reflected a European influence with a full set of gauges, along with multipurpose but confusing steering column stalks that combined the functions for the turn signals, headlight dimmer, horn, and windshield wiper/washer. The optional console included a nifty graphic module with warning lights for malfunctioning exterior lights, low fuel, and low washer fluid.

Engine choices reflected the era. The base powerplant was an 88-horsepower 2.3-liter four-cylinder, not quite matching the Mustang's all-time low of 85 horsepower in 1974. However, for the first time engine engineers looked to turbocharging to boost the Mustang's performance. Unfortunately, due to Ford's inexperience with turbocharging and the late decision to pursue exhaust-driven technology, the turbocharged 2.3-liter produced only 130 horsepower.

The 1979 Cobra was promoted as "ready to strike." Optional hood graphics mimicked the 1978 King Cobra's huge snake decal but in a more subtle fashion. Also available was the TRX package with metric aluminum wheels, Michelin tires, and special suspension. *Ford Motor Company*

# DESIGN BY TELNACK

John J. "Jack" Telnack grew up within walking distance of Ford's sprawling Dearborn facilities. As a youngster, he peered over the Ford proving ground walls to sketch the latest models. Shortly after graduating in 1958 from California's Art Center for Design, Telnack landed a job at Ford. Within a few years, he was working for Joe Oros on wheel cover and fastback designs for Ford's new sporty car, the Mustang.

After a stint as chief designer for Ford of Australia, Telnack returned to the United States in 1969 to take charge of the Mustang studio, just in time to influence the 1971 Mustang. Telnack continued his rise through the company by spending two years heading up Ford of Europe's design department, where he worked with the aerodynamic Sierra. He returned to the United States in 1976 as executive director of light car and truck design. Sketches and models for the 1979 Mustang were well under way, most of them similar to the Fairmont, but Telnack's studio produced a design that was radically different. Instead of slab sides with a flat nose, Telnack proposed a more European look. With a few tweaks, it became the 1979 Mustang and the most aerodynamic Mustang produced to date.

With the success of the 1979 Mustang, Telnack was promoted to Ford's global vice president of design in 1980, where he continued to develop his aerodynamic style by producing cars like the 1983 Thunderbird and 1986 Taurus.

Upon his return from Europe to take over as Ford's director of design, Jack Telnack set out to bring a European look to the next Mustang. He was also responsible for the graphics on the Indianapolis 500 pace car. *Ford Motor Company*

The German-built 2.8-liter V-6 was offered as an option at the beginning of 1979, but it was dropped at midyear due to availability problems and replaced by an 85-horsepower 3.3-liter inline six. The 5.0-liter V-8 returned for 1979, but with 140 horsepower, it failed to appeal to enthusiasts, especially when auto magazines reported sluggish quarter mile times in the 17-second range.

The 1979 Mustang was offered with a variety of options and packages. A sport option added a nonfunctional hood scoop, black lower body, and sport-tuned exhaust with twin chrome tips exiting on the passenger side. Borrowed from Ford of Europe's Granada, an available TRX wheel and tire option came with attractive but oddly sized 390-milllimeter (15.4-inch) aluminum wheels and Michelin TRX performance tires. To take advantage of the improved handling characteristics, the package incorporated a suspension with springs and shocks tuned to match the tire capabilities. The auto magazines were unanimous in their praise for the TRX suspension, with *Road & Track* calling it "nothing short of phenomenal."

Fittingly, the TRX tires and wheels were standard equipment on the 1979 Cobra. Available in base form with the turbocharged 2.3-liter or optionally with the 5.0-liter, the Cobra package added sport-tuned exhaust, hood scoop, and blacked-out graphics. The Ghia also returned for buyers seeking a luxury Mustang, only for 1979 it was available in both hardtop and hatchback body styles.

Despite its lack of traditional Mustang characteristics and performance, the 1979 Mustang's sporty European looks and fuel economy attracted nearly 370,000 buyers, nearly as many as the 1974 Mustang II and earning a fifth-place ranking in all-time Mustang production by model year.

A new low for Mustang was the 1980 carriage roof option for the hardtop. It was nothing more than a roof covering made to look like a convertible top. *Ford Motor Company*

For an image improvement, the hatchback-only 1980 Cobra inherited the 1979 pace car's front air dam, hood scoop, and rear spoiler. *Ford Motor Company*

## THE LEAN YEARS

In only the second year of a total makeover, the 1980 Mustang changed little. But just when performance fans thought things couldn't get much worse, the 1980 model arrived with a downsized V-8. In an effort to meet the EPA's increasingly stringent fuel economy standards, the 5.0-liter was debored to 4.2 liters, or 255 cubic inches. Worse, smaller combustion chambers, valves, and oval intake ports resulted in 118 horsepower, a low point in the Mustang's V-8 history.

Otherwise, engine choices for 1980 remained similar to 1979, although word was out about problems with the turbocharged 2.3-liter, including turbo lag, cold stumbling, and insufficient turbocharger lubrication that sometimes resulted in failures and even fires.

The advertising for the 1981 Mustang was more exciting than the car in an era when the turbo four-cylinder was no longer available and the 4.2-liter V-8 produced only 118 horsepower. *Ford Motor Company*

Equipped with a new 157-horsepower 5.0-liter HO, the 1982 GT jump-started a much-needed modern Mustang performance revival. "Jim Clarke was the driving force behind putting the 302 back in the Mustang," engine engineer Hank Lenox told interviewer Alex Gabbard. "He essentially saved the Mustang as an enthusiast car." *Source Interlink Media*

The Mustang's performance slide rolled further downhill for 1981 with the discontinuation of the problematic 2.3-liter turbo engine, which took a 2½-year hiatus so engineers could work on an overhaul. However, there was good news with an available Traction-Lok differential and the addition of a five-speed manual transmission at midyear. The T-top option also returned, this time for both hatchback and hardtop.

Hampered by a recession and the influx of Japanese front-wheel-drive economy cars, Mustang sales declined steadily through 1980 and 1981, dropping to 271,364 and 182,552, respectively. In March 1980, Donald Petersen was named president and CEO of Ford. He had worked on the 1965 Mustang alongside Donald Frey, Joe Oros, and Hal Sperlich and was clearly a performance enthusiast. Something needed to be done about the Mustang's image and reputation; Petersen was just the man to get it done.

## THE BOSS IS BACK

The cover of the September 1981 *Motor Trend* said it all: "The Boss is Back–302 GT Mustang." Perhaps using the old Boss name was a bit of a stretch, but there was no doubt that the 1982 Mustang's revamped 5.0-liter HO engine was a step in the right direction and welcomed by enthusiasts who had lamented the Mustang's pitiful horsepower ratings for the previous nine years. With 157 horsepower, the optional 5.0-liter HO was the most powerful Mustang V-8 since 1973. To aid traction, slapper bars were added to the rear suspension of HO-equipped Mustangs.

Although available in all 1982 Mustangs, the 5.0-liter HO became closely associated with the new GT that revived a popular package from 1965 through 1969. Replacing the

The 1982 GLX was basically a GT without the body modifications and a luxury interior. It was available with all Mustang engines, including the 5.0-liter and T-top roof. *Ford Motor Company*

A more powerful GT with four-barrel 5.0-liter power and the return of the convertible gave Mustang enthusiasts plenty to get excited about in 1983. *Ford Motor Company*

Cobra as the Mustang's top performance model, the GT incorporated a different grille, nonfunctional hood scoop, front air dam and rear spoiler from the 1979 pace car, and foglights. Also available with the 4.2-liter V-8 and automatic, most 1982 GTs were equipped with the 5.0-liter HO and its mandatory manual transmission (four-speed or, later in the year, Borg Warner T-5 five-speed), making it quicker than the 400-pound heavier Camaro and Firebird. With optional TRX suspension and Recaro high-back bucket seats, the 1982 GT was the best all-around Mustang performance package in years.

In addition to the GT, the 1983 Mustangs were available in L, GL, and GLX configurations, differentiated primarily by interior trim, while the Ghia model was dropped. All four Mustang engines, including the 5.0-liter HO, were available in the four Mustang models.

The 1983 Mustang was essentially the same as 1982 with several updates. Visually, revised front and rear treatments provided a fresh look, while the GT's hood scoop flipped to rear-facing. The 5.0-liter HO engine, now standard in the GT, gained a four-barrel carburetor for an 18 horsepower increase, up to 175, with four-speed only. A Turbo GT joined the lineup at midyear, powered by an improved turbocharged 2.3-liter with electronic fuel injection and 145 horsepower.

The big news for 1983 was the return of the Mustang convertible, missing from the lineup for 10 years. Although considered a factory model, Ford provided roofless notchbacks to

To honor Mustang's 20th anniversary on April 17, 1984, Ford produced a special springtime run of 20th anniversary hatchbacks and convertibles. Promotional photographs were shot with the first production Mustang. In a nod to the Mustang's Shelby heritage, the red rocker panel stripes incorporated GT350, which sparked a lawsuit from Carroll Shelby over the use of the Shelby-owned trademark. It would take nearly 25 years to mend the resulting rift between Ford and Shelby. *Ford Motor Company*

# FOX PACE CAR

Mustang enthusiasts finally had something to talk about when the Mustang was selected as the pace car for the 1979 Indianapolis 500. As with the Mustang's 1964 selection, Ford took advantage of the promotional opportunity by offering a replica of the actual pace car. But unlike 1964 replicas that were little more than white paint and lettering for a sales promotion, the 1979 version provided a glimpse of what could be done with the new Fox-body Mustang.

Ford built 10,487 Indy pace cars between April and July 1979, all identical with Pewter Metallic exterior, black lower body side treatment, and orange/red/black graphics. A decal kit with "Official

Pace Car: 63rd Annual Indianapolis 500 Mile Race May 27, 1979" lettering was supplied for dealer or owner installation. The pace car body modifications included a hood with nonfunctional cowl-induction scoop, air dam with Marchal foglights, and rear spoiler, all of which would find their way onto future Mustangs. Best of all, the TRX suspension was part of the package, and Recaro supplied the bucket seats.

The three pace cars built for the Indianapolis 500 were powered by 5.0-liter V-8s built by Roush Racing.

Merchandise such as this Ezra Brooks whiskey decanter was offered as part of the Mustang's selection as the 1979 Indianapolis 500 pace car. A black pace car jacket was popular with the traditional Mustang crowd. *Donald Farr*

However, the street cars came with either the regular-production turbocharged 2.3-liter or 5.0-liter V-8.

Three-time Formula One World Champion Jackie Stewart, who served as a Ford consultant and spokesman, drove the Mustang pace car at the 1979 Indianapolis 500. *Ford Motor Company*

In 1985, an LX model replaced the L, GL, and GLX designations that had been used in previous years. A new front-end treatment differentiated the 1985 model from the 1984. *Ford Motor Company*

The first limited-edition 20th anniversary 1984 Mustang is inspected as it rolls off the Dearborn assembly line in the spring of 1984. The anniversary models were available in hatchback or convertible with turbo four-cylinder or 5.0-liter power. *Ford Motor Company*

nearby Cars and Concepts for conversion into GLX or GT convertibles. Thanks to pent-up demand for a convertible, more than 23,000 were sold in 1983.

Despite the new convertible and Turbo GT, Mustang sales fell to an all-time low of 120,873 for 1983. With five model years under its belt without a major makeover, the rear-wheel-drive Fox body was growing long in the tooth. At Ford, some began suggesting that the traditional rear-wheel-drive Mustang should be replaced by a front-wheel-drive platform to compete against the incoming tide from Japan.

For 1984, the GL and GLX models were dropped in favor of a single LX designation, which added comfort and convenience over the base L model. Convertibles were offered as both LX and GT, while the GT was available as either a Turbo GT with the 145-horsepower 2.3-liter turbo or with the 5.0-liter V-8, either 175 horsepower with the five-speed or 165 with the now-available four-speed automatic overdrive (AOD).

Two new factory models appeared in 1984—the turbocharged SVO and the limited-edition 20th Anniversary. In southern California, racer Steve Saleen started production of his Saleen Mustang, a modern twist on the Shelby from the 1960s. Purposely low volume, the special editions enhanced the Mustang's appeal, leading to sales of less expensive models. In fact, Mustang sales increased by more than 20,000 units, a rare occurrence from one model year to the next without a major makeover.

By 1985, the winds of change were once again starting to sweep over the Mustang. Bolstered by the SVO and 5.0-liter GT, the balance between economy and horsepower began tilting toward the performance side.

All 1985 Mustangs received a new front-end look as a panel with a narrow air slot replaced the previous year's grille. The L designation was dropped in favor of just two models: LX or GT. The LX was available with all engines, including the 2.3-liter four-cylinder, 3.8-liter six-cylinder, and 5.0-liter V-8, which was upgraded to 210 horsepower with a new roller camshaft and tubular headers. The 5.0-powered GT was also revised with variable rate springs, larger sway bars, and blackout trim. Both LX and GT Mustangs with the 5.0 came

*Continued on page 113*

# 5.0-LITER HO

Just like 1968's 428 Cobra Jet, Ford engine engineers dipped into the parts bin to create the 157-horsepower 5.0-liter high-output (HO) V-8 for the 1982 Mustang. After two years of the woefully underpowered 4.2-liter V-8, the 302-cubic-inch small-block was revived with a 351 camshaft, better flowing cylinder heads, 369-cfm two-barrel carburetor on an aluminum intake, and a twin-snorkel air cleaner. Initially, a four-barrel carburetor was planned, but according to engine engineer Jim Clarke, it required a 50,000-mile EPA cycle for certification and the V-8 team had neither the time nor the budget.

The HO took another step forward in 1983 with a four-barrel Holley carburetor and 175 horsepower, available only with the SROD four-speed manual transmission. The rating remained the same for 1984. However, an automatic overdrive (AOD) transmission also became available; with throttle body fuel injection, it generated 165 horsepower.

The 5.0 HO engine made a giant leap for 1985 when a new hydraulic roller camshaft, tubular headers, and dual exhaust (actually a single catalytic converter that branched into a pair of mufflers) contributed to a 35 horsepower increase, up to 210. The AOD-backed 5.0 with throttle body fuel injection produced 165 horsepower; it was upgraded to 180 horsepower at midyear.

With tightening emissions and fuel economy standards, it was only a matter of time before the 5.0's carburetor was replaced by fuel injection. That happened in 1986 when the 5.0 got a sequential electronic multiport system that included Ford's fourth-generation electronic engine control (EEC-IV) processor. Two

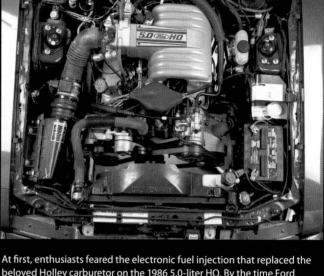

At first, enthusiasts feared the electronic fuel injection that replaced the beloved Holley carburetor on the 1986 5.0-liter HO. By the time Ford added the mass airflow system in 1989, the 5.0 was the hot setup for street and strip. *Ford Motor Company*

more changes basically offset each other: the 5.0-liter's first true dual exhaust was a needed improvement, but regular passenger-car cylinder heads with smaller combustion chambers resulted in 200 horsepower, down 10 from the previous year. The same engine was used for both five-speed and AOD-equipped cars.

By returning to better-breathing open chamber heads, the 1987 5.0-liter produced 225 horsepower, a rating it would retain through 1992. Mass air flow, with a mass air meter in the induction system, was added to California cars in 1988 and expanded to all 5.0s in 1989. For 1993, the horsepower rating was measured differently, lowering the figure to 205, although it was essentially the same engine.

The HO on the air cleaner proclaimed Ford's return to V-8 performance with the 1982 5.0-liter, a two-barrel V-8 with 157 horsepower. The good old days were back again. *Ford Motor Company*

As Ford looked to learn from its profitable European operation in the 1970s, Englishman Walter Hayes moved to the United States as VP of public affairs. Ford had been out of racing since 1970, but by referencing Ford of Europe's successful racing organization, Hayes convinced Henry Ford II that a similar group was needed in the United States. In September 1980, Ford announced its new Special Vehicle Operations (SVO) with three objectives: support private Ford racers, develop a performance parts program, and create high-performance production cars to help fund SVO's other activities. Ford's European director of motorsport, Michael Kranefuss, was recruited to head up the new organization and put together a team of 30 engineers to rebuild Ford's performance image. This time, instead of tire-shredding V-8 torque, Mustang's return to respectability focused on world-class handling, superb braking, and a small displacement engine boosted by turbocharging.

The fruits of SVO's efforts arrived in November 1983 as the 1984 SVO Mustang, built to compete against import sports cars such as the Datsun 280-ZX, Toyota Supra, and Isuzu Impulse. Ford produced a separate sales brochure to tout the SVO's mission as a car "built by driving enthusiasts for driving enthusiasts." With a turbocharged 2.3-liter four-cylinder engine, adjustable suspension, and the Mustang's first four-wheel disc brakes, the SVO hit the market as the best

*Car & Driver* magazine heaped praise on the 1984 Mustang SVO: "This may be the best all-around car for the enthusiast driver ever produced by the U.S. industry." *Ford Motor Company*

all-around performance Mustang ever produced.

After stumbling with its first turbocharged efforts in the late 1970s, Ford found the right combination with the SVO's turbocharged 2.3-liter four-cylinder, which produced 175 horsepower, same as the 5.0-liter, with help from an air-to-air intercooler via a functional hood scoop. However, it was a different kind of power. The SVO's four-cylinder lacked the 5.0's low-speed punch but more than made up for it with the rush of power brought on by the turbocharger's boost. Thanks to EEC-IV technology, the driver could flip a switch to change the engine's ignition timing for regular or premium fuel.

Likewise, adjustable Koni struts and shocks allowed switching between two suspension settings—cross-country and competition. The SVO also utilized a new Quadra Shock rear suspension, consisting of a pair of horizontally mounted shocks to control wheel hop, an innovation that

Aerodynamics played a large role in the SVO's performance and appearance, including the Mustang's first and only dual-plane rear spoiler. *Ford Motor Company*

would eventually replace the slapper bars on 5.0 Mustangs.

Externally, the SVO set itself apart from standard Mustangs with a sleeker front fascia with foglights, hood with off-set scoop, spats at the rear wheel openings, revised taillight lenses, and a distinctive dual-wing rear spoiler. P225/50VR16 Goodyear Eagle NCT performance tires were mounted on unique 16x7-inch aluminum wheels with five lugs as opposed to four lugs like other Mustangs.

Inside, SVO engineers outfitted their namesake car with a monochromatic charcoal interior for comfort and luxury, adding sport seats with inflatable lumbar support, leather-wrapped steering wheel, and standard equipment that included air conditioning, power windows and door locks, and AM/FM stereo with cassette and premium sound. Confirming the SVO's status as a car for driving enthusiasts, the five-speed included a Hurst shifter, a wider brake pedal for heel-and-toe shifting, and a dead pedal foot rest to aid driver bracing during hard cornering.

In spite of the SVO's modern technology and all-around performance, many buyers preferred the torque of the 5.0-liter V-8. Not helped by its $15,500 sticker price, some $2,500 more than the GT, Ford sold less than 10,000 SVOs during its 1984–1986 production run.

The SVO's 2.3-liter engine produced 175 horsepower with a turbocharger and intercooler. The boosted four-cylinder was much improved over Ford's earlier turbocharging efforts. *Donald Farr*

# THE BUZZ:
## WHAT THE PRESS HAD TO SAY

"As admitted in previous reports, Hot Rod Magazine is pretty darn high on the 1979 Ford Mustang. The all-new styling, TRX suspension, and available turbocharger add up to the hottest new-car news of the year."

—*Hot Rod*, 1979

"We spent the better part of three days driving, photographing, thrashing and generally investigating the (1982) GT 302 HO on Ford's Dearborn test track and on the streets nearby. Our opinion is that it's the best-balanced Mustang ever. It exhibits a combination of awesome acceleration, consistently short and powerful stopping, and flat, cat-like handling."
—*Motor Trend*, 1981

"Steve Saleen of Saleen Autosport has taken the additional step to "improve the breed" and make a real thoroughbred racer out of the (1985) Mustang."

—*Hot Rod Mustang*, 1985

"With many technical improvements for 1986, the Mustang out-performs the Camaro by a wide margin and is a serious threat to the Corvette with 6.0-second 0-to-60 times and 14.7 @ 92 mph quarter-mile times."
—*Hot Rod*, 1985

"Ford has hit the jackpot with the (1987) Mustang GT, and as more people discover the lower priced and potentially quicker LX HO sedan, you'll be seeing more two-door Mustangs with 5.0 emblems on the fenders and dual pipes poking out from under the rear bumper."

—*Super Ford*, 1987

"The chassis and suspension changes make the Saleen SSC a stiff piece that never stops reminding you that it's very much a single-purpose car. That purpose being to carve up twisty roads and terrorize fellow motorists at red lights."
—*Car & Driver*, 1989

"A glimmer of hope for Ford fanciers is this year's vitamin-fortified Mustang Cobra. By raiding Ford's voluminous storehouse of parts, tossing away some old-car chaff, and shoveling in more horsepower, the familiar, old steed has been given a new lease on life."

—*Motor Trend*, 1993

*Continued from page 108*

with new 15x7-inch 10-hole aluminum wheels with P225/60VR15 Goodyear Gatorback tires. But the real sleeper for enthusiasts was the lightweight LX hardtop powered by the 5.0-liter.

The 1985 SVO was basically the same as 1984's model except for 3.73:1 gearing replacing the previous 3.41:1 and the addition of a Competition Prep option that deleted the A/C, power windows and locks, and radio. However, at midyear, Ford upgraded the SVO's engine with a new camshaft, reworked intake with larger runners and fuel injectors, split exhaust system, and a one-pound increase in turbocharger boost for 205 horsepower.

## EFI FOX

Through buff books and word-of-mouth, the rumor nearly caused a panic within the Mustang community: the 1986 5.0-liter would lose its familiar Holley four-barrel in favor of electronic fuel injection. "Oh, no!" enthusiasts cried as they feared the unfamiliar technology inside the EEC-IV processor. Most assumed that electronic engine controls would end modifications as they had known them since the 1960s. Nothing could have been further from the truth. As the aftermarket industry caught up, owners learned that modern EFI could be used as a tool—not only for more power, but also for smoother operation and better fuel economy.

Other than the federally mandated addition of a third brake light in the rear window (or as part of the now-standard luggage rack on convertibles), the 1986 Mustang's styling was the same as in 1985. Obviously, economy was out and performance was in. Even though the newly fuel-injected 5.0's horsepower fell by 10, down to 200 thanks to cylinder heads with smaller combustion chambers, there was also exciting news in the form of a Borg-Warner T-5 five-speed, a quicker steering ratio, nitrogen gas struts/shocks, and a stronger 8.8-inch rear end. A true dual exhaust system not only helped horsepower, but the twin mufflers also gave the 5.0-liter Mustang its own distinctive muscle car sound.

On the outside, there were no changes for the 1986 Mustang GT. Underneath, however, the GT was a different car with electronic fuel injection, T-5 five-speed, and 8.8-inch rear end with Traction-Lok differential. *Ford Motor Company*

For a production Mustang right off the assembly line, the 1987 GT was radical with its aero nose, scoops, and louvered taillights. Two-tone exterior colors were also available for the first time. *Ford Motor Company*

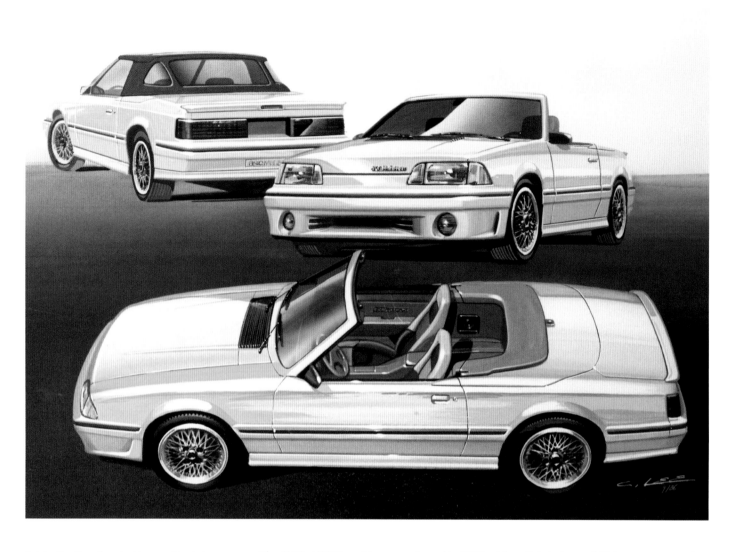

Originally offered on the Mercury Capri, the ASC McLaren two-seater package moved to the Mustang in 1987 when the Capri was discontinued after 1986. With backing from Ford, the ASC McLaren Mustang came with a factory warranty. Sales doubled over the next two years. *Donald Farr*

In early 1987, journalist Jerry Heasley visited Ford's Dearborn test track to inspect the midsized special car development group's *Red Racer*, a 1986 Mustang GT updated to 1987 specs. The GT boasted impressive performance with just a few modifications, many of which would become common as 5.0-liter Mustang owners became more familiar with fuel injection and the Fox-body suspension. *Jerry Heasley*

The SVO's 1985½ revisions continued in 1986 with a slightly lower 200 horsepower rating in what would be the model's final year of production.

With 1986 sales jumping another 70,000 units, up to 224,410, it was obvious that the Mustang's new performance image was a move in the right direction.

Nineteen eighty-seven marked a breakout year for Mustang's performance image. With the return of open-chamber heads, the 5.0 reached its full production potential with 225 horsepower. The base 2.3-liter- four-cylinder was also improved with multiport EFI, giving reason to discontinue the 3.8-liter V-6 and leaving the Mustang with only two engine choices: economy four-banger or performance V-8.

Fresh aero styling updated both the LX and GT. The quad headlights (or four-eye, as identified by enthusiasts) were replaced by dual flush-mount halogen headlights for more aerodynamic looks and improved night visibility. But the LX makeover was mild compared to the GT, which gained a new front end with round foglights, closed grille, scoops in front of the wheel openings, and louvered taillights that enthusiasts either loved or hated. New turbine aluminum wheels were standard on the GT.

The 1987 model set the stage for the Mustang's next seven years. Behind the scenes at Ford, the debate was underway about replacing the Fox-body Mustang with a front-wheel-drive Mazda platform, so there were only minor changes through 1993, including *Continued on page 119*

## FOR SPECIAL SERVICES

During the late 1980s, the view of a Mustang in your rear-view mirror didn't necessarily mean you had the faster car. Many traffic citations were written from the driver's seat of a 5.0-liter Mustang hardtop equipped with Ford's Special Service Package (SSP) for law enforcement.

With the need for quicker pursuit vehicles and improved fuel mileage compared to larger sedans, the California High Patrol ordered the first SSP Mustangs in 1982, followed by Florida in 1983 with other states to follow. Available as a domestic special order (DSO), the SSP Mustangs came with special equipment not available to the general public: engine oil cooler, more durable silicone

At least 34 states utilized SSP Mustangs for pursuit or other official duties, starting in 1982 with the California Highway Patrol. *Ford Motor Company*

Law enforcement officers worked from plain cloth bucket seats in the SSP Mustangs, which were outfitted with equipment that made them more durable for police work. *Ford Motor Company*

coolant hoses, two-piece VASCAR speedometer cable, calibrated speedometer, higher amperage alternator, single-key door and trunk locks, relocated trunk release for quicker access, reinforced floorpans, and full-size spare tire instead of spacesaver. Equipment often varied by state requirements.

For regular patrol duty, the SSP Mustangs received manual transmissions; higher-ranking officers typically got the automatic. Although rumored to have modified engines, the SSP Mustangs came with the same 5.0-liter engine and suspension as production Mustangs. Aside from a handful of hatchbacks produced for the CHP in 1982, all were hardtops.

# SALEEN: POWER IN THE HANDS OF A FEW

Like Carroll Shelby 20 years earlier, Steve Saleen came from a racing background. But unlike Shelby, whose racing career had been sidelined by a heart problem, Saleen was looking for a way to fund his race driving activities by building and selling his own special-edition Mustangs.

While driving a Pontiac in the SCCA Trans-Am, Saleen was exposed to the Mecham Pontiac dealership in Phoenix, where production

Firebirds were converted into Macho T/A editions with more powerful engines, upgraded suspensions, and aerodynamic body components.

When the Mecham racing effort shut down in 1983, Saleen headed home to southern California with an idea to build his own car similar to the Mecham Firebird. Realizing that the newly designed 1982 Camaro/Firebird platform was not as suitable for high-performance modifications, he chose

Ford's Fox-body Mustang GT, which for 1983 came with a 175-horsepower 5.0-liter V-8 and improved suspension.

Soon, Saleen was making the rounds at Ford with an illustration of his proposed Saleen Mustang. His timing couldn't have been better. As Saleen told Brad Bowling, "The four-cylinder SVO had just come out, the GT had generated a lot of excitement, and Ford wanted to show how committed they were to performance.

By 1989, Steve Saleen, with support from his wife, Liz, was annually building hundreds of Saleen Mustangs in both hatchback and convertible body styles.
*Saleen Autosports*

They thought another premium-priced Mustang model would add to that image."

Taking lessons learned from Mecham, Saleen outfitted his prototype's suspension with lowering springs, Bilstein struts and shocks, subframe connectors, 15-inch wheels with Goodyear tires, and tweaked alignment specs. Working on a budget, Saleen chose an existing aftermarket body kit: three-piece front air dam, side skirts, and spats in front of the rear wheel wells. He didn't need the rear spoiler because he planned to use his own design from his Pontiac race car. The spoiler, along with tri-color side stripes, became Saleen staples for years to come.

Saleen established the sticker price at $14,300, right between the

To build his first prototype, Saleen convinced his sister to order a 1984 Mustang GT hatchback to his specifications—no A/C or power accessories—and loan it to Saleen Racing. Robyn Lee Saleen wouldn't get her car back for more than a year. *Brad Bowling*

Mustang GT and SVO, but only sold two for 1984.

However, it was just the beginning for Saleen, who continued to develop his Mustang for 1985 based on a 5.0-liter Mustang LX that boasted 35

In the late 1980s, Saleen converted drop-shipped Mustangs from Ford into Saleen Mustangs at a new 40,000-square-foot production facility in Anaheim, California. The operation and the cars were reminiscent of Shelby in the 1960s. *Saleen Autosports*

more horsepower. With his operation gaining steam, Saleen signed on with a Ford program that introduced the new Merkur line to dealers. This meant leaving southern California to travel the country, but that was exactly what Saleen needed. In the mornings, he would provide driving demonstrations for Merkur dealers and customers. In the afternoons, he traded his driver's suit for a jacket and tie to visit local Ford dealers to pitch his Saleen Mustang.

Through his creative marketing, Saleen added dealers and sales. In 1987, Saleen increased his exposure—and satisfied his own craving for racing—by campaigning Saleen Mustangs in the SCCA Showroom Stock Escort Endurance Series, winning four championships. The Saleen brand was off and running into the future of Mustang performance.

By 1988, owners had discovered the delights of modifying 5.0-liter Mustangs. With just a few basic changes, plus parts from a dedicated performance aftermarket, they were capable of 12-second quarter miles, quicker than even the fabled big-block Mustangs from the 1960s. *Donald Farr*

Aftermarket companies were quick to jump on the 5.0-liter bandwagon to offer turnkey tuner editions. Steeda Autosports introduced its Steeda Mustang in 1988. *Donald Farr*

Performance enthusiasts fell in love with the LX hardtop with 5.0-liter power, seen here as a 1989 model with the 10-hole aluminum wheels. Weighing up to 400 pounds less than the hatchback, the lighter coupe contributed to quicker quarter-mile times. *Ford Motor Company*

*Continued from page 114*

50-state mass air for 1989 and an air bag steering wheel along with the resulting loss of tilt steering for 1990. In 1991, the 2.3-liter received a much-needed horsepower boost, from 86 to 105, with a new twin-plug OHV head and a distributor-less electronic ignition. GTs and 5.0-powered LX models got new 16x7 star five-spoke wheels, while the top-down profile of convertibles was improved with a convertible stack that dropped lower into the rear well area.

Something else began happening in the late 1980s that was better than any Ford marketing program. Enthusiasts began embracing the lightweight and affordable 5.0-liter Mustang as the platform of choice for street performance and drag racing. As owners modified their cars for bragging rights and drag-strip trophies, an industry sprang up with parts manufacturers and race sanctioning bodies. Magazines such as *Muscle Mustangs & Fast Fords* and *Super Ford* covered the scene as Ford Motorsport, which had evolved from Ford SVO, fueled the movement by producing its own line of 5.0-liter performance parts. At the same time, traditional performance aftermarket companies scrambled to produce parts for the growing market.

With few major changes between 1987 and 1993, Ford stirred up interest with special editions but somehow missed the Mustang's 25th anniversary, instead just placing a small "25 Years" dash emblem on Mustangs built between March 27, 1989, and the end of model year 1990. The run of special editions started with a 1990 7-Up convertible, so named because it was initially created for a planned 7-Up Bottling Company contest. When the

Convertibles topped hardtop sales from 1990 to 1993, but they didn't roll off the Dearborn assembly line with their ragtops. Ford sent hardtop Mustangs without roofs to Cars and Concepts near Brighton, Michigan, for installation of the convertible tops. C&C also handled the T-top conversions. *Source Interlink Media*

Ford didn't officially commemorate the Mustang 25th anniversary with a special model, so Saleen did it himself with the 1989 SSC—for Saleen Super Car. Introduced on April 17, 1989, the SSC boasted 290 50-state legal horsepower. Saleen sold 161 at $36,000 each. *Source Interlink Media*

## SVT: POLISHING THE OVAL

By 1990, Neil Ressler had spent over 20 years climbing Ford's corporate ladder to reach the position of vice president of research and vehicle technology. He was also a performance enthusiast, and as such had supported SVO during the 1980s. When the SVO Mustang disappeared after 1986, Ressler felt there was an opportunity to further develop the Mustang GT as a performance car by utilizing components from an SVO-like program.

"There was a designer at special vehicle engineering named Janine Bay," Ressler told Jim McCraw. "We had a Mustang GT that made 225 horsepower. I asked Janine to see if we could improve its performance."

Bay came back with a 265-horsepower prototype that benefitted from a revised suspension, larger brakes, and wider tires. With 40 more horsepower than the production GT, Ressler considered calling it the Mustang GT-40 after the famous Le Mans–winning Fords from the 1960s. Then he learned that Ford would soon lose the rights to the Cobra name, purchased from Carroll Shelby in the 1960s but dormant since 1981. Along with another inhouse performance enthusiast, John Plant, Bay put together a plan to build a low-production, high-performance 1993 Mustang called the Cobra.

By shifting funds from his own budget, Ressler put together a loose-knit group of enthusiasts, all working outside their regular job duties, to develop the new Cobra. "We started calling ourselves the special vehicle team," Ressler said. "About a year later, we formalized the organization with John Plant as the leader."

Introduced at the 1992 Chicago Auto Show, the Cobra lived up to its legendary name with 235 horsepower, 30 more than the 1993 GT, thanks to Ford Motorsport GT-40 heads, a unique intake manifold, and a more aggressive camshaft. To support the extra power, four-wheel disc brakes, a revamped suspension, and Goodyear Eagle P245/45ZR17 tires were added to the package. Visually, the Cobra differed from the GT with a narrow grille opening with small running horse emblem, a rear spoiler, white-face gauges, Cobra snake emblems on the fenders, vane-style 17-inch aluminum wheels, and exterior color choices of Rio Red, Teal, or Black.

Later in 1993, SVT introduced the Cobra R, a turnkey competition version with deleted rear seat, air conditioning, and radio along with adjustable struts/shocks and larger brakes.

Cobra production was limited on purpose. Only 4,993 were built, including 107 Cobra Rs. But SVT wasn't created to set sales records; it was designed to "polish the oval" with cars that showcased SVT's four hallmarks: performance, substance, exclusivity, and value. The mission was accomplished in 1993 with the Cobra, which set the stage for future SVT Mustangs.

The first-generation Fox body went out with a bang with the 1993 SVT Cobra, the first product from Ford's new Special Vehicle Team. *Ford Motor Company*

contest was cancelled, Ford shifted the effort into a special edition with Emerald Green exterior and white interior. Only 4,103 were built.

Late in the 1992 model year, a "summer special" added sizzle to end-of-year sales. Powered by the 5.0-liter, the 1992½ convertible added monochromatic Vibrant Red paint, rear spoiler, and white top; white pearlescent five-spoke wheels; and white leather interior with black piping and first-time use of a convertible headliner.

With compact discs quickly becoming the media of choice for audiophiles, a CD player was added to the 1993 Mustang's option list. Better yet, Ford's new Special Vehicle Team (SVT) applied hot-rodding techniques for a mid-1993 Cobra model. Starting with the 205-horsepower 5.0-liter, improvements were made to the engine's breathing and efficiency to develop 235 horsepower, the highest rating for the production 5.0.

At the end of the Fox-body era, Ford stimulated interest with a pair of 1993 Limited Editions, also called Feature Cars. Similar to the previous year's Summer Special, the 5.0-liter convertibles featured a rear spoiler and monochromatic paint, either Vibrant White with white interior and five-spoke wheels or Chrome Yellow with white or black interior and chrome wheels.

Even with the popularity of the 5.0-liter engine and convertible, the long stretch without a styling change eventually hurt Mustang sales. The Fox-body era started off strong with 369,937 produced in 1979, but by 1991 Mustang sales had fallen under the 100,000 mark for the first time. In 1993, like previous final years before a major revamp, sales rebounded slightly to 114,228.

Inside Ford, a new hero was about to emerge to save the rear-wheel-drive Mustang and move the legendary nameplate into the future.

In 1991, Ford updated 5.0-liter GTs and LXs with 16-inch, five-spoke star wheels, which replaced the previous 15-inch 10-hole (LX) and turbine (GT) wheels. *Ford Motor Company*

With monochromatic paint and rear spoiler, the 1993 limited edition convertibles added interest at the end of the Fox-body era. Just more than 3,000 were sold, split almost evenly between yellow and white. *Ford Motor Company*

# FOX-4:
# SAVE
# THE MUSTANG

IN APRIL 1987, *AutoWeek* confirmed the rumors: Ford intended to replace the rear-wheel-drive Mustang with a front-wheel-drive variation of the Mazda MX6. To Mustang fans, the idea was anti-American. An editorial in *Mustang Monthly* suggested that readers send their complaints to Ford, going so far as to provide an address for president Donald Petersen. Nearly 30,000 letters and postcards flooded Ford World Headquarters demanding "No Mazda Mustang" and raising second thoughts about the Mustang's future.

While development of the front-wheel-drive project pressed forward, Ford vice presidents Alex Trotman and Robert Rewey realized that any plan to continue the Mustang as a rear-wheel-drive vehicle would have to overcome increasingly stringent government safety regulations, including the latest air bag technology and improved side impact protection. The choices came down to investing in the development of an entirely new car or taking a less costly route by reengineering the Fox-body platform. When a 1988 study by small car manager Ken Dabrowski indicated that development of a new platform would prove too expensive, the choices became clearer: rework the existing Mustang into a totally new and modern Mustang or drop the iconic nameplate entirely.

In the summer of 1989, Trotman issued a challenge to save the Mustang. Several directors responded, including Dabrowski. On August 11, Dabrowski called small car engineering design manager O. J. "John" Coletti into his office. Known around Ford as a car guy, Coletti didn't waste time in accepting the challenge of his career. "I'm

Thanks to a dedicated group of Mustang enthusiasts within Ford, the Mustang's heritage as a rear-wheel-drive, V-8 sporty car continued into 1994 and the future. *Ford Motor Company*

When an illustration of the proposed front-wheel-drive Mustang appeared in magazines, loyal Mustang enthusiasts fired off letters of protest to Ford World Headquarters.

Ford's market research determined that customers favored the Schwarzenegger styling exercise, a design that would go into production almost untouched as the 1994 Mustang. *Ford Motor Company*

sure that Ken was thinking I would turn him down," Coletti told writer Bob McClurg. "When he pressed me for an answer, I responded, 'I'd be honored to try to save the Mustang!' "

Within three weeks, Coletti put together a team of managers to represent the functional aspects of vehicle development. Much like Lee Iacocca's Fairlane Committee from the early 1960s, Coletti's group met after working hours. "Saving the Mustang was our objective," Coletti said. "We felt the front-wheel-drive proposals were not Mustangs. They were cars with Mustang badges on them."

For any chance at success, Coletti needed exciting styling to impress senior management along with a business proposition that was too good to pass up.

For the exterior sheet metal, Coletti understood the influence of Mustang enthusiasts, who had rallied around older models with hundreds of clubs and shows. Research included focus groups with 1965–1973 owners and club members. "Owners of classic Mustangs tend to be very opinionated," Coletti explained. "We interviewed scores of them and they were ready for a new Mustang, but they wanted a link to the original 1964½ model."

Coletti's group agreed that the next Mustang should include classic styling cues from 1960s Mustangs. The designers quickly picked up on the long hood/short rear deck proportions, distinctive grille with running horse, side scoop sculpturing, three-lens taillights, and twin-cockpit instrument panel. The team eventually established five objectives: continue building a rear-wheel-drive Mustang at the Dearborn assembly plant, incorporate exterior and interior redesigns with classic styling cues, conform to new safety

# COLETTI IN CHARGE

As a performance enthusiast, John Coletti joined Ford as a product design engineer at precisely the wrong time—1972, right as Ford shifted its focus from Total Performance to fuel mileage and emissions. Coletti soon found himself working on rotary engines and programmed combustion programs, not exactly dream jobs for a gearhead. By the late 1980s, Coletti had escaped fuel economy management to become design manager for the Escort, Tempo, and Mustang. There was one problem: Ford planned to discontinue all three, with the Mustang scheduled for replacement by a front-wheel-drive car in 1993.

Ford executive vice president Alex Trotman wanted to save the Mustang and instructed Coletti to put together a team. Coletti responded, "I figured, 'Why not?' They expected me to fail, so the worst that could happen was that I met their expectations."

However, Coletti more than met expectations. His skunkworks group evolved into Team Mustang to design and develop what became the 1994 Mustang, keeping the Mustang's legacy alive and setting up Coletti to fulfill his go-fast aspirations by overseeing the future creation of SVT and SVE vehicles, some of the most potent Fords ever built.

John Coletti once explained why the Mustang was important to Ford: "If you go to a man in the deepest part of Tennessee and ask him what a Jaguar is, he might tell you it's a cat. But if you ask him what a Mustang is, he'll tell you it's a Ford." *Ron Sessions*

With the approval of the SN95 rear-wheel-drive Mustang, Ford's front-wheel-drive project became the Probe, introduced in 1989 and discontinued after 1997. *Ford Motor Company*

As the first Ford engineering group to be co-located, the new Team Mustang was housed in the Danou Tech Center. "I was used to a process where it took time to get decisions from the program manager," said Coletti. "In this kind of setup, I'd walk around the corner to his office, we'd go over the facts, he'd make a call, and off we went. It was a terrific breath of fresh air." *Ron Sessions*

and emissions requirements, improve quality by 50 percent, and keep the total investment under $500 million.

Sketches from as early as November 1989 laid out the basic proportions. Three months later, Coletti showed Trotman the first full-size clay model of the team's proposed next Mustang. Trotman liked it and even agreed to the possibility that the project may exceed $500 million. But Coletti and others felt the design needed to be bolder with more Mustang flavor. Additional clays were requested, which evolved into three themes with athletic nicknames:

- Bruce Jenner: Named for the Olympic decathlon gold medal winner, the clay featured a round shape and soft features.
- Rambo: An almost sinister-looking design with a jutting, sharp-edged front end and wrap-around taillights. Some said it looked like a Klingon warship.
- Arnold Schwarzenegger: A stronger, more muscular version of the Bruce Jenner with more distinctive Mustang elements yet less aggressive than Rambo.

To gauge customer and enthusiast reaction, the three models were used for research clinics. Rambo was quickly deemed too aggressive, Bruce Jenner too soft. At a focus group held in October 1990, participants overwhelmingly favored the Schwarzenegger model. The Mustang team had its new design, one that would go into production almost unchanged. Focus group participants also approved of the proposed interior with twin cockpit instrument panel and lines that flowed into the console and door panels.

Shortly after research confirmed the Schwarzenegger design, the Ford corporate design committee approved the Mustang program and set a Job One date for late 1993 as a 1994 model. The project also received its codename, SN-95, for "sporty, North American market, version 95."

Coletti had succeeded in saving the rear-wheel-drive Mustang; the front-wheel-drive program evolved into the 1989 Probe. Coletti's group would move on as Team Mustang to develop the 1994 Mustang for production.

## TEAM MUSTANG

With corporate approval in hand, there were two immediate needs for the new Team Mustang: assemble an SN-95 program team and find a suitable location for the 75-member group and its various operations, including design and engineering. Within weeks, Coletti had assigned supervisors, many of them inhouse Mustang enthusiasts. In turn, they were asked to handpick their engineers for prototype builds, body development, vehicle packaging, and powertrain development.

Like proud fathers, director of midsize car design Dave Rees (left) and Mustang design manager Bud Magaldi pose with an early styling clay of the SN-95 Mustang. *Ron Sessions*

The SN-95 Mustang was subjected to extensive testing to meet the goals for ride and handling. This disguised mule was named Cooter after the mechanic in the TV show *Dukes of Hazzard*. *Ron Sessions*

A 3/4-scale version of the SN-95 was used at Lockheed's wind tunnel to fine-tune the final body shape for optimum aerodynamics. *Ford Motor Company*

Then there was the matter of finding a 45,000-square-foot building in or near Dearborn to house a prototype build area, office space, and design departments. After exhausting possibilities on Ford property, Coletti learned that space was available at the Danou Technical Center, a former Montgomery Ward warehouse in Allen Park. Better yet, it was conveniently adjacent to a Roush engineering and prototype facility.

Team Mustang moved into its new home in August 1990. "My office was on the loading dock," Coletti recalled, "right where one of my fellow engineers bought his refrigerator 15 years earlier!"

Working on a tight budget and even tighter schedule, Team Mustang was small but efficient. Housed together in one building, it was the first time a Ford engineering team had been co-located with everyone working in the same area. Team members were dedicated to the SN-95 project and not part of a larger department like styling or accounting.

Team Mustang spent the first year attempting to meet aggressive goals for ride, handling, steering, NVH (noise, vibration, and harshness), braking, powertrain performance, climate control, and comfort. As a result, the old Fox platform was braced, strengthened, and modified so much that it became known as the Fox-4.

By August 1991, Team Mustang had completed its first structural prototype, an actual running vehicle that looked like the upcoming 1994 Mustang. In October, the program received confirmation, a formal approval that secured the Mustang's future. Coletti and program manager Will Boddie used video instead of the usual paperwork to get approval for $700 million to build the next Mustang. They had two years to bring it to market.

## WHAT IT WAS AND MORE

After four years of secretive skunkworks activity and subsequent development as an officially approved SN-95 program, the 1994 Mustang officially debuted on October 9, 1993. As the first major redesign in 15 years and following the "Mazda Mustang" scare of the late 1980s, the 1994 Mustang gave fans much to celebrate as the nameplate approached its 30th anniversary in April 1994.

Outwardly, there was no external resemblance to the 1979–1993 model. In fact, it was tough to believe that the sleek, new Mustang was related to the previous Fox body, even though they shared the same, albeit much reengineered, platform. The hatchback was gone, a victim of Team Mustang's chassis-stiffening goals, leaving only coupe and convertible body styles as either base (without the previous LX designation) or GT models. Unlike previous Fox-body convertibles that were completed at Cars and Concepts, the 1994 version would be assembled on the regular assembly line at the Dearborn assembly plant.

The 1994 Mustang was slightly longer and wider than the 1993 model with a 0.9-inch longer wheelbase. But the big improvement came from the strengthening of the chassis and body structure, a noted weakness in the earlier Fox body. Using computer-aided engineering, the sheetmetal shapes were resistant to twisting and bending. A crossbar beneath the rear seat strengthened the B-pillars, while for GTs engineers added a strut tower brace, a trick borrowed from the performance aftermarket. Impressively, the 1994 Mustang was 44 percent more resistant to flexing, a number that improved to 80 percent for the

Mustang enthusiasts loved everything about the 1994 Mustang's classic design cues except the taillights; they were deemed too Japanese with their horizontal triple lenses instead of vertical ones like the originals in 1965. They would last only two years. *Ford Motor Company*

Dallas Cowboy cheerleaders helped Ross Roberts, Ford Division general manager, introduce the 1994 Mustang on October 9, 1993, during the State Fair of Texas, the first major event after Job One on October 4. *Bob McClurg*

The wedge-shaped body design graced the convertible with a sleeker appearance. Raised rear quarter panels also allowed the lowered convertible top to stack deeper into the body. *Ford Motor Company*

Of the Mustang's 1,850 unique parts, no fewer than 1,330 were all-new for the Fox-4 platform. Ford highlighted many of the changes from the original Fox body with this display showcasing the carryover floorpan in white, modifications in red, and convertible bracing in yellow. *Ford Motor Company*

convertible. To cancel cowl shake in convertibles, engineers borrowed mass dampener technology from Mercedes and BMW to phase out vibrations.

With the need to meet or exceed federal safety requirements, the 1994 Mustang benefitted from tubular steel door beams for side impact, improved front and rear crush zones, and a reinforced roof structure to resist collapse in a rollover. Inside, dual air bags and dual-mode seat belt retractors were standard. All models came with four-wheel disc brakes and five-lug wheels in place of the previous four-lugs. An anti-lock braking system was optional.

The chassis and body improvements also added an extra 200 to 300 pounds, so the barely adequate four-cylinder from 1993 was dropped and replaced by a 145-horsepower 3.8-liter V-6 as the only available powerplant for the base Mustang. Likewise, the GT was available only with the 5.0-liter V-8, rated at the previous year's 215 horsepower even with its lower-profile Thunderbird intake manifold for hood clearance. Both engines were available with the five-speed manual or new fully electronic AOD-E four-speed automatic.

The redesign also provided the opportunity to enhance standard Mustang features, such as an auxiliary power port, an ergonomically positioned radio, a flip-out drink holder in the console, a express-down driver's window, and an update to more environmentally friendly R134a refrigerant for the air conditioning. After hearing a gonzo stereo while sitting in traffic, Coletti asked for a high-powered sound system. He got it in the form of the optional Mach 460 package with digital tuner/cassette/compact disc, subwoofer, door panel tweeters, and additional amplifiers.

Unlike the radically styled 1987–1993 GT, the SN-95's top model differed from the base Mustang with little more than small fog lamps in the front valance, five-spoke 16-inch

# COBRA R: ROUND TWO

With the 1993 Cobra R, SVT proved that it could successfully produce a limited-edition vehicle. To build a better Cobra R based on the SN-95 Mustang, John Coletti, recently transferred to manager of special vehicle engineering after launching the 1994 Mustang, and SVE project engineer Steve Anderson conferred with 1993 Cobra R racers to pinpoint the earlier car's weaknesses. Coletti and Anderson then set out to produce a car to beat the Camaros and Firebirds in the SCCA's World Challenge and IMSA Grand Sport classes.

There was one major obstacle: the GM cars came with a 5.7-liter V-8, putting the 5.0-powered Mustang, even in Cobra trim, at a disadvantage. By convincing the Environmental Protection Agency that the marine 5.8-liter (351-cubic-inch) V-8 came from the same engine family as the 5.0-liter, SVT was able to ride the emissions coattails to drop the larger displacement powerplant into the Cobra R. Roush Racing built the engines, rated at 300 horsepower, then supplied them to the Dearborn assembly plant for installation on the assembly line. From there, the cars were trucked to MascoTech for an upgraded cooling system, 20-gallon fuel cell, and other competition upgrades.

The 1995 Cobra R took the turn-key competition concept to the next level. In addition to the 351, the newest version was equipped with a Tremec five-speed transmission, Eibach springs, Koni double-adjustable struts/shocks, larger disc brakes, and unique 17x9-inch five-spoke wheels with BFGoodrich Comp T/A tires. A number of items not needed for racing were deleted, including the radio, air conditioning, rear seat, and all power accessories except the power mirrors, mainly because the Mustang was not available with manual outside mirrors.

SVT limited production of the 1995 Cobra R to 250 units. All were sold almost immediately at $35,499, plus $2,100 for the IRS's new gas-guzzler tax. As in 1993, collectors grabbed some. However, many were purchased by race teams that used the 1995 Cobra R for its intended purpose of competing against Camaros and Firebirds at racetracks around the country.

Like the earlier 1993 model, the 1995 Cobra R was built for the racetrack. With a 351 engine, a taller cowl-induction fiberglass hood was part of the package. *Source Interlink Media*

The 1994 Mustang's twin-cockpit instrument panel flowed into the door panels on the outside and into the standard console in the center. A new steering wheel design allowed for a new, lightweight air bag assembly that included horn operation. *Ford Motor Company*

Ford advertising promoted the 1994 Mustang as "What it was and more" in reference to the new car's resemblance to the original 1965 Mustang. *Ford Motor Company*

wheels, rear spoiler, exposed dual tailpipes, and small GT Mustang emblems replacing the previous 5.0 emblems on the front fenders. Optional 17-inch wheels for the GT were 1-inch wider with a unique dual three-spoke design.

Conspicuously missing at the 1994 Mustang's introduction was the SVT Cobra, which had debuted in 1993 as the top performance model. However, good things came to those who waited. In early 1994, SVT announced the 1994 Cobra with 240 horsepower—most ever for a production 5.0-liter—thanks to GT-40 heads and earlier-style intake manifold. Offered as coupe or convertible, the Cobra added a bumper cover with round driving lights, the first use of complex reflector clear lens headlights, revised suspension settings, larger disc brake rotors all around, 160-mile-per-hour speedometer (in place of 150 in standard Mustangs), restyled rear spoiler, and Goodyear Eagle GS-C tires on unique five-spoke aluminum wheels.

Typical of the second year after a major redesign, the 1995 Mustang changed very little. For fans of the plain-Jane 5.0-liter LXs from 1987 to 1993, a GTS model came with the GT's 5.0-liter engine but deleted the sport seats, rear spoiler, and foglights. Sales climbed from 137,074 in 1994 to 185,986 in 1995, perhaps because the word was out that 1995 was the final year for the 5.0-liter V-8.

# THIRD R'S THE CHARM

SVT entered model year 2000 with egg on its face after the embarrassment of the under-powered 1999 Cobra. Even worse, it wasn't able to recover in time to offer a 2000 Cobra. The team responded by putting the woes of the 1999 Cobra in the past by making news with its third Cobra R.

For SVT and its occasional Cobra R program, the third time was the charm. Whereas the 1993 Cobra R was essentially a stripped-down Cobra with upgraded performance parts and the 1995 version added a marine 351, the 2000 Cobra R came

with its own special engine, a cast-iron 5.4-liter DOHC tweaked to 385 horsepower and 385 ft-lbs of torque. SVT also looked to the performance aftermarket for Eibach springs, Bassani exhaust, Brembo brakes, and K&N air filter.

The 2000 Cobra R was the fastest factory-built Mustang to date. With a price tag of $55,845, it was also the most expensive. Unlike the 1995 Cobra R, which saw considerable action in Grand Sport classes, the 2000 Cobra R became more of a collector or track-day car.

The 2000 Cobra R's naturally aspirated 5.4-liter produced 385 horsepower, a high point at the time for a Mustang built by Ford. *Ford Motor Company*

With a 5.4-liter V-8 and a wild rear wing, SVT's 2000 Cobra R was a "boy racer" that immediately set a new standard for a production Mustang. *Ford Motor Company*

*Motor Trend* presented Team Mustang with its 1994 Car of the Year award as a reward for their work on the revamped Mustang. *Motor Trend* publisher Lee Kelley (seated at left) presented the award to Mike Zevalkink, Mustang program manager (seated at right). *Ford Motor Company*

Absent at the beginning of the 1994 model year, SVT's 240-horsepower Cobra arrived at midyear, just in time for the convertible to join the 1965 and 1979 models as the only Mustang Indianapolis 500 pace cars. *Ford Motor Company*

## MOD SQUAD

The pushrod Fairlane small-block's 35-year run (except 1974) in the Mustang ended in 1996 as Ford looked to the future by replacing the GT's 5.0-liter with the modern 4.6-liter modular V-8. With a more efficient overhead cam design, the smaller 281-cubic-inch V-8's output was rated the same as the previous 5.0-liter—215 horsepower and 285 lb-ft of torque. Sound engineers even managed to maintain the GT's luscious exhaust note.

Still offered as a base Mustang with the 3.8-liter V-6 (upgraded to 150 horsepower) and GT with V-8, the 1996 model was identified by its new taillights. Mustang fans had expressed their displeasure with the thin horizontal taillights that debuted in 1994, so the 1996's rear panel was updated with vertical tri-bar versions with the first U.S. taillight use of clear lenses with complex reflectors. Other changes included a background in the grille to hide the radiator and a new 17-inch optional wheel for the GT. The transmissions were also improved; the T-5 five-speed was replaced by a stronger T-45 while the AOD-E automatic was upgraded to the latest 4R70W.

While Mustang performance fans were initially skeptical of the GT's new two-valve 4.6-liter, all it took was one test drive in the 1996 SVT Cobra to comprehend the modular V-8's potential. With four valves per cylinder and dual overhead cams, the Cobra's 4.6-liter produced 305 horsepower—most ever for a production Mustang. Although lacking the bottom-end torque of the GT, the Cobra impressed at higher rpm, pulling hard to its 6,800-rpm rev limit. The Cobra's visual cues included embossed Cobra lettering in the rear bumper cover and a hood bubble with a pair of nostrils, but the real thrill came under the hood with the sight of a compartment-filling powerplant that brought back memories of the Boss 429 from 1969 to 1970.

*Continued on page 139*

# GOING MODULAR

Mustang fans realized it was only a matter of time before Ford retired the venerable small-block V-8, which had been used in a variety of displacements for the Mustang since 1964, most notably as a 302-cubic-inch/5.0-liter version since 1968. With the introduction of the modular two-valve V-8 in the 1991 Lincoln Town Car, followed by the four-valve in the 1993 Lincoln Mark VIII, it was inevitable that the traditional pushrod V-8's days were numbered for the Mustang as well.

Identified as modular due to the ability of the engine assembly line to build a variety of displacements without tooling changes, the new 4.6-liter debuted in the 1996 Mustang as a two-valve for the GT and four-valve for the SVT Cobra. The modular engines were built on a cast-iron, deep-skirt block with cross-bolted main bearings, Teflon-coated pistons, and cam chains with random-length links for quiet operation.

For the Mustang GT, Ford engine engineers purposely attempted to match the new 4.6-liter's output and character to the previous 5.0-liter HO. By utilizing less restrictive cylinder heads and a unique composite intake manifold with long runners, the Mustang's first 4.6-liter reached the same 215 horsepower as the 1995 5.0-liter. Unlike the 5.0-liter, it would take the performance aftermarket a couple of years to catch up with the new technology.

While the GT's two-valve 4.6-liter performed similarly to the old 5.0-liter, the SVT Cobra's four-valve, four-cam version showcased the modular engine's potential. Sharing only a few components with the two-valve, the Cobra's bottom end used a lightweight aluminum block with forged crankshaft and powder-metal connecting rods. The game changers at the top were the heads with four valves per cylinder and dual overhead cams for each bank. More aggressive valve timing allowed the engine to sustain torque up to its 6,800-rpm rev limit. With a Cobra-specific multirunner intake with secondary throttle plates, the four-valve 4.6 generated 305 horsepower, qualifying the 1996 Cobra as the most powerful production Mustang to date.

Although enthusiasts were at first skeptical of the modern technology, Ford's engine engineers would prove the modular's value as a performance engine in the coming years. With three-valve technology and supercharging, the 4.6-liter would later set the stage for exciting—and unexpected—Mustang horsepower levels.

Rated at 305 horsepower, the 1996 SVT Cobra's four-valve 4.6-liter set a high-water mark for production Mustang horsepower. *Ford Motor Company*

## BULLITT GT

With the New Edge–styled SN-95 Mustang in its third year with no plans for another styling update before a scheduled makeover in 2005, the Mustang needed a shot of adrenaline to spur interest and sales. Under chief engineer Art Hyde, Team Mustang was searching for a special edition when it fell right into their laps.

"While we were working on finding an appropriate feature car, the auto show efforts were kicking in," said customization manager Scott Hoag. "Unbeknownst to me, Mustang design manager Sean Tant was asked to come up with a Mustang for the L.A. Auto Show and worked to deliver a *Bullitt*-themed Mustang. We had just released a *Bullitt*-like wheel and Sean obviously knew that the 1968 *Bullitt* movie, with actor Steve McQueen in a 1968 Mustang, had been popular. I was sitting in Art Hyde's office when we got a call from someone at the show saying, 'All right, what's going on? We can't keep people away from this green Mustang.' Art and I didn't know what he was talking about, so we called Tant, who said, 'I meant to tell you guys about that.' If there was that much excitement, then there was our feature car."

For the special edition Bullitt GT, Hyde and his team could have simply added Highland Green paint and the vintage-style five-spoke wheels. However, they took the concept much further, tapping into the 1960s vibe with vintage-style instrument graphics and shift ball, racing pedal covers, and brushed aluminum fuel filler cover. Even the C-pillar, quarter panel moldings, and rocker panels were modified to create more of a vintage look.

Unlike previous Mustang feature cars that were primarily appearance packages, the $3,696 Bullitt GT package also added performance enhancements, starting with the 3/4-inch lower suspension with Tokico struts and shocks, unique stabilizer bars, and subframe connectors. Brembo supplied the 13-inch front brake rotors with the first-time use of red calipers visible through the wheel spokes. By utilizing a better flowing aluminum intake manifold with twin-inlet throttle body, high-flow mufflers, and underdrive accessory pulleys, horsepower was increased to at least 270, a 10 horsepower increase over the standard GT.

Offered in Highland Green, True Blue, and Black, the Bullitt GT generated much needed buzz for the Fox-4 Mustang in its twilight years. Production was limited to 6,500 cars, and orders reached that number, but only 5,582 made it through the scheduled production run.

Team Mustang's 2001 Bullitt GT recalled Steve McQueen's popular 1968 movie, *Bullitt*, which starred a Highland Green 1968 Mustang 2+2 Fastback jumping the hills of San Francisco in one of Hollywood's most memorable chase scenes. *Ford Motor Company*

With sharper lines, wraparound headlights, more pronounced fender flares and side sculpturing, angular taillights, and the return of the corral surrounding the grille's running horse emblem, the 1999 Mustang provided a fresh appearance as the Fox-body moved into its third decade. *Ford Motor Company*

The SN-95 body style change provided Steve Saleen with a new canvas for his Saleen Mustang, but he really stepped up with the S351 with a transplanted 351-cubic-inch V-8 from SVT's Lightning pickup. Produced in limited numbers for 1994 and 1995, a Vortech supercharger option boosted output to 480 horsepower. *Source Interlink Media*

To recognize the Mustang's 35th anniversary, 1999 Mustangs came with a special emblem on the front fenders. *Ford Motor Company*

# INDEPENDENT COBRA

The 1999 Cobra marked the Mustang's first use of an independent rear suspension (IRS). Utilizing a Lincoln Mark VIII aluminum differential in a tubular steel subframe, the IRS bolted to existing suspension attachment points in the Mustang's unibody. With its 125-pound weight gain offset somewhat by aluminum engine components, the IRS combined better handling and control with an improved ride, especially on rough roads, compared to the Mustang's traditional live rear axle.

"It's really second to none," said Mustang vehicle engineering manager Paul Giltinan. "It's an upper and lower control arm with a fixed tie rod behind the center of the wheel so you get compliant understeer." Just as important in an upscale car like the Cobra, the IRS dampened the bouncy and jittery nature of the Mustang's live axle. With IRS, the Cobra tracked flat and true with no upsets caused by bumps in the road surface.

A bolder front-end design differentiated the SVT Cobra from the Mustang GT. It was also the first Mustang with an independent rear suspension. *Ford Motor Company*

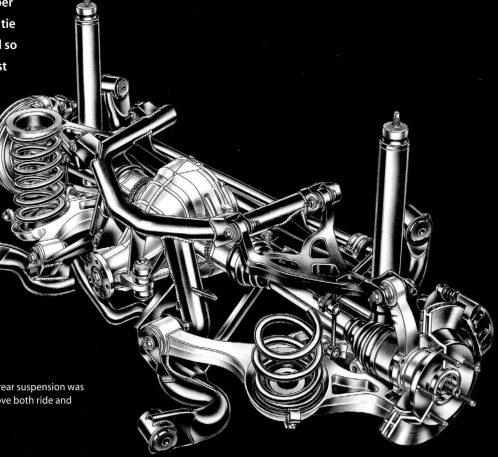

Unique to the SVT Cobra, the independent rear suspension was carried by a tubular steel subframe to improve both ride and handling. *Ford Motor Company*

On September 3, 1998, Ford Vice President and Ford Division President Jim O'Connor and Janine Bay, Mustang chief program engineer, introduced the New Edge–styled 1999 Mustang at the Wildhorse Saloon during the Mustang Club of America's Grand National show. *Ford Motor Company*

*Continued from page 134*

Other than updates to color selection and a standard security system, there were few changes for the 1997 and 1998 Mustangs. A slight enlargement of the 1997's grille opening allowed more air to reach the revised cooling system. Also, the Cobra received new five-spoke wheels for 1998.

## NEW EDGE

To the casual observer, the SN-95's overhaul for 1999 appeared to be little more than a styling update to conform to Ford's latest New Edge styling. But underneath, the 1999 Mustang was a much-improved car with more power for all engines, snappier handling, and better ride quality. Other improvements included a more precise steering gear, tighter turning radius, twin-piston aluminum front brake calipers, wider rear track, less but better-placed insulation, and repositioned front seat tracks to accommodate taller drivers. Borrowing a trick from the aftermarket, the convertible was stiffened considerably with the addition of subframe connectors.

As with prior SN-95 models, the 1999 Mustang was offered as a base car with the 3.8-liter V-6 and GT with the 4.6-liter V-8, both with more power. The V-6 benefitted from a split-port induction system to generate 190 horsepower, more than 1982's 5.0-liter HO. The GT's 4.6-liter output jumped by 35 horsepower to 260, thanks to revamped cylinder heads and longer duration, higher lift camshafts. Behind the engines, Tremec began building the Borg-Warner-designed T45 five-speed manual, and the 4R70W automatic was updated with revised shift strategies to optimize the power increases. In fact, in combination with 3.27 rear gearing, automatic-equipped GTs felt quicker than five-speed models.

Shortly after the introduction of the base and GT 1999 Mustangs, SVT unleashed its latest version of the Cobra. With the same chassis improvements as the regular Mustang line and another 15 horsepower (320 total) from the four-valve 4.6-liter, the SVT Cobra stepped up its game as the top-performing Mustang. Most importantly, the new Cobra came with independent rear suspension, something that buffs books and enthusiasts had been begging for since the first Fox bodies.

In the spring of 1999, a special 35th Anniversary GT package commemorated the Mustang's milestone birthday. Offered in Black, Silver, Crystal White, and a new Performance Red, the limited-edition 35th Anniversary GT coupe or convertible added hood and side scoops, black hood stripe, blackout rear panel, 17-inch five-spoke wheels, rear spoiler, and leather seats with silver inserts. *Ford Motor Company*

The Bullitt GT feature car had barely hit the streets when Team Mustang started working on its second special edition for the aging Fox platform. This time, customization engineer Scott Hoag wanted to bring back the legendary Mach 1 name from the Mustang's past. Noting that Classic Design Concepts offered an aftermarket Shaker hood scoop like the Ram-Air system from 1969–1970, Hoag envisioned the through-the-hood scoop as the perfect styling component for a modern Mach 1 for 2003.

Hoag credits car guys such as Art Hyde and vice president Chris Theodore with pushing the Mach 1 program through. Like the Bullitt GT, it was more than just a visual package. With the 2003 Cobra equipped with a supercharged

The 2003 Mach 1's most distinctive feature was its Shaker hood scoop, a functional Ram-Air unit that recalled the Cobra Jet Mach 1s from 1969 to 1970. *Ford Motor Company*

version of the 4.6-liter DOHC engine, Team Mustang slipped the Mach 1 between the Cobra and the GT by bringing back the naturally aspirated DOHC engine with 305 horsepower. On top was an exact duplicate of the 1969–1970 Shaker scoop but with ducting underneath to funnel cooler outside air into the factory air cleaner assembly. The Mach 1 was available with both five-speed manual and four-speed automatic transmissions, both feeding into 3.55:1 rear gears.

In addition to the Shaker scoop, a number of other styling cues tied the new Mach 1 to the original from 1969, including a black hood and side stripes, chin spoiler, pedestal-mount rear spoiler, and new 17-inch Heritage wheels that resembled vintage Magnum 500s. Suspension mods lowered the Mach by a half inch and subframe connectors stiffened the chassis. Inside, appointments such as ribbed comfort weave vinyl seats, Bullitt-style instrument panel, and aluminum shift ball added to the vintage vibe.

Like with the 2001 Bullitt GT, the Mustang community enthusiastically welcomed the 2003 Mach 1. Even though Ford planned to limit availability to 6,500, nearly 10,000 were sold. The Mach 1 returned the following year and, like most 2004 Mustangs, was a carryover other than new exterior colors.

Members of the press ogle the 2003 Mach 1 at its introduction during the New York Auto Show. *Ford Motor Company*

As engineers and designers worked behind the scenes on the next generation of Mustang for 2005, the final four years of New Edge Mustangs, 2000 through 2004, were destined for few changes for the base and GT models but highlighted by special editions. Other than replacing the 35th anniversary fender emblems with a running horse and a trio of new colors, there were no changes for the 2000 Mustang.

However, in a rare move, the Cobra skipped the entire 2000 model year as SVT sorted out an engine situation that arose when 1999 Cobra owners complained about power output. Independent dynamometer tests confirmed that the new 4.6-liter DOHC was not reaching its advertised 320 horsepower. Embarrassed, Ford discontinued sales of the 1999 Cobra and recalled sold units to replace the intake manifold, engine management computer, and much of the exhaust system. SVT's new chief Tom Scarpello explained, "The only solution to maintain and preserve the integrity of the SVT organization was to fix them. And that's what we did."

The 1998 SVT Cobra was updated with new five-spoke wheels. *Ford Motor Company*

Externally, there was little to differentiate the 1996 Mustang GT and SVT Cobra from the previous 1994–1995 models. Under the hood, it was a different story. The 1996 Cobra was powered by a 305-horsepower version of the four-valve 4.6-liter, while the GT abandoned the outdated 5.0-liter in favor of a 215-horsepower two-valve 4.6. *Source Interlink Media*

With quick acknowledgment of the problem and a sufficient solution, SVT avoided a tarnished reputation, but the situation contributed to delaying the following year's Cobra. However, SVT wasn't completely silent during 2000 as it introduced a third and even more potent rendition of the Cobra R.

The 2001 Mustang continued mostly unchanged with only minor updates, including a new console and standard rear window defroster. Nonfunctional scoops for the GT's hood and rear quarter panels were added to further distinguish it from the base V-6 model, which was available with an optional Sport Appearance Group. Options were greatly simplified by combining them into Standard, Deluxe, and Premium Equipment groups, reducing the number of possible combinations from 2,600 to 50. A midyear Bullitt GT feature car and the return of the SVT Cobra triggered a new round of interest from performance enthusiasts.

Music always played a part in the Mustang soundtrack, but never before did rock and roll sound as good as it did from 2002's optional Mach 1000 sound system, an upgrade

New vintage-style Torq-Thrust wheels were optional for the 2001–2003 GTs. They would inspire a 2001 special edition called the Bullitt GT. Nonfunctional hood and side scoops set the Mustang GT apart from the base model. *Ford Motor Company*

# THE BUZZ:
## WHAT THE PRESS HAD TO SAY
## (MUSTANG MATURES)

Stability and predictability are the new chassis' calling cards. Wander and vagueness can't be found, and just a few minutes behind the wheel and you can tell the [1994] Mustang is going to be an easy ride in the real world."
—*Super Ford*, November 1993

"The 1994 Mustang is a full and legitimate descendant of the car and the excitement spawned in 1964."
—*Motor Trend*, November 1993

"The 1996 Mustang Cobra will be powered by a rapacious four-cam engine that makes the highly revered muscle motors [Boss 302, 351, and 428 Cobra Jet] seem like throwbacks to the steam age."
—*Motor Trend*, September 1995

"The design of the sharply creased sheetmetal on the restyled 1999 Ford Mustang is officially called New Edge. And this designation can be applied to the car's significant improved performance, which is related to a host of mechanical improvements beneath that new skin."
—*Road & Track*, January 1999

"That Saleen has such a real-world car, with blazing power and sophisticated driveability in the same financially obtainable package, is something of a modern miracle. With the S281 in our driveway, the temptation to skip out for a drive was overwhelming."
—*Super Ford*, November 1999

"Only 300 Cobra Rs, all in 'Grabber' orange, will be offered for sale at the turn of the millennium and each will cost between $45,000 and $50,000. Racers seeking the best ever and most expensive iteration of Ford's turnkey platform, put your name on the waiting list now."
—*Automobile magazine*, August 2000

"Should you choose a Bullitt over a standard GT? Of course; if you like the treatment—and we do—by all means buy one. It's clearly muscular styling enhancements are probably reason enough. Or maybe you just want to feel a little bit like Steve [McQueen], and go out and do some Charger hunting once in a while."
—*Motor Trend*, August 2001

"Thanks to the new Mach 1, you can once again look across the hood, nail the throttle, and enjoy that distinctly American muscle car feeling as the engine rocks on its mounts and the hood scoop nods its acknowledgement. Some slices of history are worth repeating."
—*Motor Trend*, December 2002

In 2003, V-6 buyers could step up to a pony package with GT hood, 16-inch polished aluminum wheels, and stampede graphics. *Ford Motor Company*

On November 18, 2003, Ford Motor Company chairman and CEO Bill Ford drove a 2004 40th Anniversary Mustang GT convertible off the Dearborn assembly line as the 300 millionth Ford vehicle. While all 2004 Mustangs got a 40th anniversary fender emblem, the limited-edition 40th anniversary package included dark red metallic paint, gold stripes, and special wheels. *Ford Motor Company*

for the Mach 460 system that added 570 watts of power, a speed-sensitive radio, and a variety of amplifiers, speakers, and subwoofers. The Cobra took another year off as SVT prepared to unleash its supercharged Terminator for 2003.

With General Motors' announcement that the Camaro and Firebird would be discontinued after 2002, the Mustang entered 2003 as the last-standing pony car. Still, with an aging and soon-to-be-replaced platform, Team Mustang wanted to keep the fire burning by offering a number of special editions over the Fox-4's final two years. First up was the 2003 Mach 1, a followup to the 2001 Bullitt that revived a storied name from the Mustang's past. Unlike the Bullitt GT, the Mach 1 and its functional Shaker hood scoop returned for a second year in 2004, when it was joined by a 40th anniversary edition with gold stripes on three available colors, including an exclusive Crimson Red.

The Cobra returned better and stronger than ever for 2003 and 2004 with an Eaton Roots-style supercharger sitting atop the 4.6-liter DOHC engine. Its 390 horsepower topped the previous Cobra's high-water mark by 70 horsepower.

On May 10, 2004, Dearborn assembly plant workers gathered at the end of the line to commemorate the final Mustang assembled at the historic factory. Opened in 1918 to build submarine-chasing Eagle boats for the U.S. government, the plant had built 6.7 million Mustangs since 1964. The final 2004 Mustang off the line not only represented the upcoming move to a newer, more modern assembly plant in nearby Flat Rock, Michigan, but it also signaled the end of the Fox body's 25-year reign as the Mustang platform.

It was time for the Mustang to move into a new era.

Ford staged a special press conference and worker celebration when employee Fred Galicki drove the last Mustang, a 2004 GT convertible, out of the Dearborn assembly plant on May 10, 2004. In the passenger seat was retiree Oscar Hovsepian, who drove the first Mustang off the same assembly line in 1964. *Ford Motor Company*

# THE TERMINATOR

The story is part of Mustang lore. During a 2000 desert run of SVT prototypes, chief engineer John Coletti was not happy with the performance from the naturally aspirated DOHC engine in the proposed 2002 Cobra. As he related to author Frank Moriarty, Coletti told his team during a fuel stop, "I'm going to go in this store and see if they sell Alpo. And I'm going to buy a six-pack and throw it in the back seat because it's a dog."

Coletti then grabbed program manager Tom Bochenek and powertrain engineering supervisor Bill Lane for what became known at SVT as the picnic table performance review. Coletti told the pair, "Guys, that's no Cobra. It's an embarrassment. We ain't doing that car!"

And so it was back to the drawing board. Coletti had made his decision: there would be no 2002 Cobra. But the extra time gave SVT engineers the opportunity to close out the Fox-body era with a new high-water mark for Mustang performance. The 2003 Cobra, or Terminator as it was code-named at SVT, would raise the bar once again.

The 2003 Cobra's makeover started under the hood. Realizing that the 4.6-liter DOHC had reached its practical performance limit as a naturally aspirated engine, Coletti urged his powertrain team to explore supercharging, in particular the Roots-type Model 90 from Eaton Automotive.

The 1970 Boss 429 was the top performance Mustang for 1970, but it was no match for SVT's Terminator. The 2003 SVT Cobra not only set a new performance standard for Mustang, but it also sold well, setting a record for SVT Cobra sales with more than 13,000 sold. *Ford Motor Company*

SVT marketing and sales manager Tom Scarpello (left) and chief engineer John Coletti introduced the 2003 SVT Cobra in a cloud of burnout smoke at the Chicago Auto Show in February 2002. *Ford Motor Company*

Instead, Bill Lane and his group came back with a proposal to use the larger Model 112. Coletti agreed totally, "I'm with you guys!"

While supercharging offered a quick path to Coletti's power goals, it also added stress to the engine. After strenuous dyno testing, the 2003 Cobra's supercharged 4.6 was built on a cast-iron block with stronger Manley H-beam connecting rods, forged pistons, and aluminum flywheel from the 2000 Cobra R program. With revised aluminum heads for improved air flow and a water-to-air intercooler, the supercharged 4.6 produced 390 horsepower at 6,000 rpm and 390 lb-ft of torque at 3,500 rpm.

Taking a cue from the 2000 Cobra R, the 2003 Cobra marked the first use of a six-speed transmission, the Tremec T-56, in a regular production Mustang.

With 70 more horsepower, the 2003 Cobra's suspension was also upgraded, starting with more rubber on the pavement via 275/40ZR-17 Goodyear Eagle F1 performance tires on a new 17x9-inch wheel. Other improvements included higher rate springs all around, upgraded bushings and additional crossbrace for the independent rear suspension, and monotube Bilstein dampers. For the first time, the convertible received its own suspension tuning.

Almost lost in the hoopla over the power increase was the significant change in appearance. While continuing SVT's signature round fog lamps, the 2003 Cobra's front fascia was redesigned, not only for a more aggressive appearance, but to also deliver more air for engine cooling. The new hood, made from

Previous Cobra DOHC engines had been built from regular-production blocks that were final assembled on the niche line at Ford's Romeo engine plant. The special components inside the 2003 short-block forced the first start-to-finish build on the niche line. *Ford Motor Company*

lightweight composite material, included functional, rear-facing scoops to vent warm air from the engine compartment.

With only one more year before a major Mustang makeover, the 2004 SVT Cobra returned mostly unchanged except for a Mystichrome appearance package with DuPont's color-shifting paint. *Ford Motor Company*

# THE REBIRTH

"WHEN YOU'RE DESIGNING A NEW MUSTANG, you're the steward of 40 years of automotive history," said J Mays, Ford's group vice president of design, when describing the all-new 2005 Mustang. "If you don't get it right, you've got eight million Mustang fans to answer to."

After 25 years of Fox-body Mustangs, the time had come to retire the aging platform that had been developed in the early 1970s. After the launch of a new Thunderbird in 1989 and the Lincoln Mark VIII in 1993, the Mustang had become the only Ford car line still using the outdated chassis.

Like the makeover for 1994, the challenge was once again to modernize the Mustang without alienating its fan base. The SN-95's vintage cues had proven popular and successful. Could Team Mustang continue to play the retro card into the new millennium?

As Mustang chief program engineer from April 1998 until May 2002, Art Hyde championed the Mustang through the final years of the SN-95 platform with exciting special editions like the 2001 Bullitt GT and 2003–2004 Mach 1. At the same time, he was overseeing the development of the next-generation Mustang, scheduled as a 2005 model, on a new and modern platform. The majority of design and approval had been completed when Hyde handed over the responsibility of launching the next Mustang to Hau Thai-Tang, a South Vietnamese native who had become smitten by Mustangs when, as a small child, he saw Al Eckstrand's touring military drag-racing Mustangs during their trip to visit American troops. Thai-Tang knew what Mustang enthusiasts expected: "When you have a 40-year family tree, you don't chop it down and plant a new one."

The retro look never looked better than the new 2005 Mustang, which paid homage to the 1967–1968 Mustangs. *Ford Motor Company*

While working on the 2001 Bullitt GT and 2003-2004 Mach 1 programs, Mustang chief engineer Art Hyde was also overseeing the development of a new platform for the 2005 Mustang. Most of the work had been completed when Hyde handed the reins to Hau Thai-Tang in May 2002. *Ford Motor Company*

## THE NEW DEW

Before Team Mustang could worry about side scoops and triple-lens taillights, it had to choose a new platform for the next-generation Mustang. Based on market research from Mustang enthusiasts, keeping the solid rear axle was deemed essential to retaining the Mustang's muscle car character. The perfect starting point was found in Ford's modern DEW98 midsize rear-wheel-drive chassis, as used for the Lincoln LS since 2000 and the retro-styled 2002 Thunderbird.

Many of the 2005 Mustang team members came from the Lincoln and Thunderbird programs. However, by the time they finished adapting the DEW98 platform for the new Mustang, Thai-Tang went so far as to call it all-new, so much so that it became known as the D2C platform, for D-class, 2-door coupe. For the Mustang, the much-changed DEW-based platform took the codename S197.

While the S197 carried over some DEW98 components, like the floorpan and front frame rails, there was little similarity in the suspension, with the Mustang using a modified version of the DEW98's coil-over MacPherson strut front suspension and incorporating reverse L lower control arms for quicker steering response. At the rear, the solid-axle technology progressed into a three-link design with a center-mounted Panhard bar to stabilize the

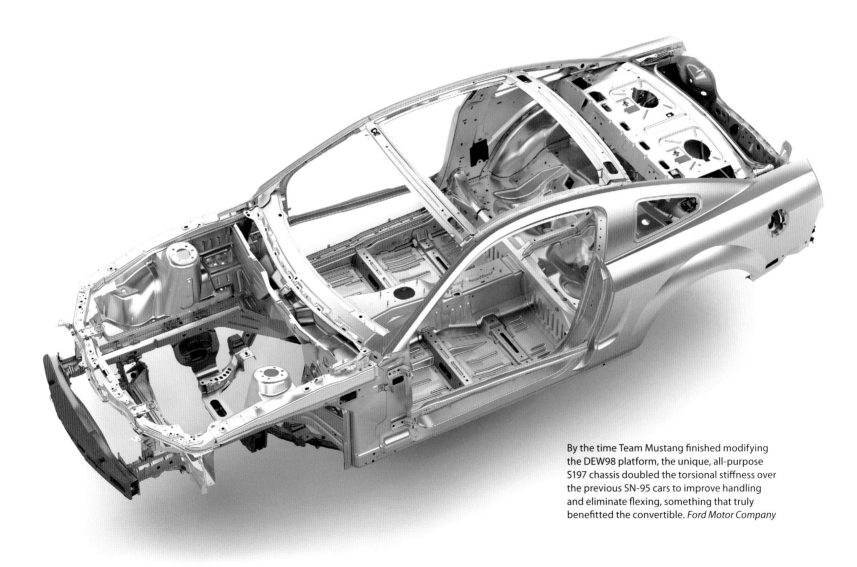

By the time Team Mustang finished modifying the DEW98 platform, the unique, all-purpose S197 chassis doubled the torsional stiffness over the previous SN-95 cars to improve handling and eliminate flexing, something that truly benefitted the convertible. *Ford Motor Company*

Team Mustang found its chassis for the next-generation Mustang underneath the Lincoln LS, but with so many substantial changes, Ford considered it a totally new platform, the D2C, better known as S197. *Ford Motor Company*

Early clay models determined the basic body shape for the S197 Mustang with a fastback-style greenhouse, wide fender flares, and a faint outline of the Mustang's traditional side sculpturing. Front-end experimentation included covered headlights and a smaller grille opening. *Ford Motor Company*

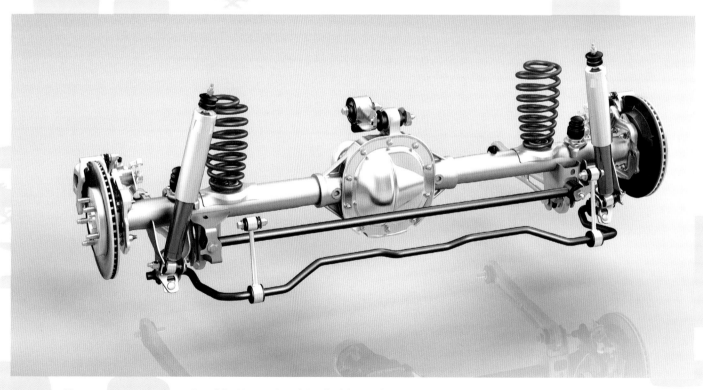

Listening to Mustang enthusiasts who preferred the Mustang's traditional solid rear axle, S197 engineers mounted the rear end with coil springs, computer-optimized lower control arms, single upper control arm, and panhard bar to control side-to-side axle movement. Gone were bandaids such as Quad Shocks, providing the new Mustang with a true handling suspension under its sleek new body. *Ford Motor Company*

Ford president and CEO Jim Padilla and Charlie Hoskins from the United Auto Workers helped celebrate the launch of the 2005 Mustang with employees at AutoAlliance International. *Ford Motor Company*

side-to-side movement of the axle. Engineers were also able to push the wheels to the corners, gaining six inches of wheelbase to better anchor the car to the road while also increasing interior space.

With S197 development underway, the design team understood its parameters for the exterior body. Design VP Mays and designer Doug Gaffka researched previous Mustangs for inspiration. "We laid out a visual photography audit that went from 1964½ to 1970," Mays told Matt DeLorenzo. "We also picked up a little of the Euro-inspired Mustang of 1979 and later, as well as the last two generations of Mustangs."

But in conversations with enthusiasts from within and outside Ford, it became apparent that customers wanted to see a new Mustang based on the first generation. "We kept coming back to the 1967–1968s," said Thai-Tang, "because they were the models that bridged the Mustang's transition from pony car to muscle car."

Mays added, "We knew we wanted to have a '67 Mustang in terms of spirit, but not a literal copy." To assist with the task of creating a modern 1967 Mustang, the design team brought a 1967 fastback into the studio for inspiration.

Early sketches ranged from space-age sleek to retro modern, with some including the Mustang's traditional side sculpturing and the 1967 Mustang's rear-facing hood louvers with turn signal indicators. As the clays evolved, several characteristics emerged that would end up on the final design—a shark-like nose, a mouthy grille with running horse and outboard headlights, three-element taillights, and a faint outline of the side sculptured scoops. The coupe's roofline favored the vintage fastback and eventually included small C-pillar windows,

The S197 design evolved into a roofline with side windows in the C-pillar, similar to the 1966 Shelby, and a rear panel with triple-lens taillights and a faux cap to evoke the center-mounted fuel filler used from 1965 to 1973. *Ford Motor Company*

Obviously, S197 designers were looking ahead as they developed styling ideas for the next-generation Mustang. This clay from April 2002 incorporates prominent side scoops, Shelby-like hood stripes, and a GT500 emblem. *Ford Motor Company*

Interior designers created a totally new look for the S197 Mustang's interior. With twin-eyebrow instrument panel and optional brushed aluminum trim, it was reminiscent of the 1967 Mustang. *Ford Motor Company*

reminiscent of the 1966 Shelby GT350. Unmistakable was the continuation of the long hood, short rear-deck styling from the first-generation Mustang. There was even a fake gas cap at the center of the rear panel and large fog lamps, similar to the 1967 Shelby, in the GT's grille.

Old styling cues notwithstanding, it was obvious that the 2005 Mustang would not be your father's (or grandfather's) Mustang. The new reiteration was much larger—measuring more than four inches longer than both the 1967 and previous 2004 models. The interior included major changes. In place of the SN-95's rounded dual cockpit was a flatter, twin-eyebrow dash pad and instrument panel that was somewhat reminiscent of the 1967 interior, especially when equipped with the optional brushed aluminum trim.

On April 27, 2004, Ford's chief operating officer, Jim Padilla, helped 3,600 AutoAlliance International workers celebrate the opening of the 2005 Mustang assembly line at the high-tech plant in Flat Rock, Michigan, just a few miles south of Dearborn. Ford had invested $700 million in AAI's flexible manufacturing system, which allowed the facility to build up to six different models on two vehicle platforms. AAI also invested $30 million to train employees for the highly skilled manufacturing jobs.

"Mustang is the exclamation point of Ford's product onslaught," Padilla told the gathered workers, dealers, union leaders, and media. "At AutoAlliance, the 2005 model has found a great home. This plant stands as a world-class facility in advanced automotive manufacturing systems and processes."

## BACK TO THE FUTURE

Although the 2005 Mustang coupe wouldn't go on sale until the fall of 2004, Ford wasn't shy about sharing the totally revamped car with the world, releasing photos and details to the media in the spring of 2004. Three new GTs also appeared at the Mustang Club of

# SHELBY'S BACK!

After Carroll Shelby shut down Shelby Automotive in 1969 to end the production of Shelby Mustangs, he spent much of the 1970s in Africa, where he became involved with big-game hunting businesses. In the early 1980s, his old pal Lee Iacocca, having moved to Chrysler, lured Shelby back into the automotive scene to help build a performance image for Dodge. Shelby responded with his pocket rockets, including front-wheel-drive Shelby versions of the Charger and an Omni called the GLH, for "Goes Like Hell." In the 1990s, Shelby began building Cobras again at a new Shelby Automobiles plant in Las Vegas and soon developed a built-from-scratch sports car—the Shelby Series One. It was only a matter of time before he returned to Ford.

Much of the Shelby GT-H appeal came from the fact that the cars were actually touched by Shelby, just like the Mustangs built by Shelby American in the 1960s. *Source Interlink Media*

The lawsuit over Ford's use of the GT350 name for 1984's 20th Anniversary Mustang had created bad blood between Shelby and Ford Motor Company. However, at the 2001 Pebble Beach Concours, Shelby ran into Edsel Ford II, who had lived with Shelby as a teenager during the summer of 1968 while working at Shelby American. The pair decided it was time to smooth over their differences, with Edsel mentioning that Ford wanted to build a modern version of the Ford GT-40. Soon, Shelby was back in Dearborn, not only planning for a new GT500 from SVT, but also collaborating with Ford to build Mustangs at Shelby Automobiles.

In 2003, Shelby met Mattel vice president Amy Boylan when he approached her about manufacturing die-cast Hot Wheels Cobras. He came away impressed with the admitted car girl and hired her to run Shelby Automobiles in 2005. A month later, Shelby's new president was in Dearborn to lay out ideas for Shelby and Ford collaborations, including a deal with Hertz to bring back the Hertz Shelby Mustang rental car. Called the Shelby GT-H, the 2006 model stood out in black paint with Hertz signature gold stripes, like the majority of 1966 GT350Hs, and featured performance modifications from Ford Racing. Like in the 1960s, the Mustangs entered the Shelby facility as new GTs and came out the other side as Shelby GT-Hs. The program created a sensation in the automotive media and among enthusiasts—Shelby was building Mustangs again.

The GT-H was just the beginning. The model returned for 2007 as a convertible, along with the introduction of a Shelby GT and a Super Snake upgrade for the Ford Shelby GT500. More special Shelby Mustangs would follow.

With the 2006 Shelby GT-H, Shelby Automobiles brought back the "Rent-a-Racer" concept of the 1966 Shelby GT350-H for Hertz. It was also the start of a new partnership between Shelby and Ford. *Ford Motor Company*

To build the new and modern 2005 Mustang, Ford moved production from the old Dearborn assembly plant, where Mustangs had been built for 40 years, to the state-of-the-art AutoAlliance International facility in Flat Rock, Michigan. *Ford Motor Company*

America's 40th Mustang anniversary celebration in April 2004, several months before the S197's official on-sale date.

In August, Ford invited members of the press to a special ride and drive across Michigan so journalist reports could coincide with the 2005 Mustang's arrival in showrooms. The journalists who gathered in Ann Arbor for the drive to Gingerman Raceway found a totally new Mustang. Compared to the 2004 model, everything had changed, from the overall appearance right down to the twist-style headlight switch, which replaced the push-pull knob/toggle that had been employed for the past 40 years. Other updates included a separate tilt steering stalk, push-pull power window switches with added auto-up/down function for one-touch operation, and a lower seating position. The door glass sealed better by automatically sliding down about an inch when the door opened, then back up when closed. Round air-conditioning vents were also a big departure from those on previous Mustangs.

Initially offered as a coupe with the convertible delayed until spring 2005, the redesigned Mustang followed recent tradition with two available models—base with V-6 and GT with V-8, both available with Tremec five-speed manual or new 5R55S five-speed automatic. Options like six-way power driver's seat and Shaker 500 stereo were grouped into Deluxe and Premium packages.

The 2005 Mustang gave enthusiasts their favorite styling cues—long hood, short deck, fastback styling, mouthy grille, side-scoop sculpturing, and three-lens taillights. *Ford Motor Company*

For the base model, the previous year's 90-degree pushrod 3.8-liter V-6 was replaced with a modern 60-degree SOHC 4.0-liter sporting 210 horsepower, same as the old carbureted 5.0-liter HO. With improvements such as composite cam covers and liquid-filled engine mounts, the 4.0-liter reduced vibrations compared previous V-6 engines.

Three-valve cylinder head technology and variable cam timing came to the GT's V-8 for 2005, helping the 4.6-liter produce 300 horsepower, up 40 from the previous two-valve version. Utilizing a pair of intake valves in addition to a single exhaust valve, the new heads and revised composite intake manifold with variable runner lengths combined to produce excellent low-end torque and top-end power. With the switch to an aluminum block, the new 4.6-liter reduced front-end weight by 75 pounds.

Electronic throttle control, or drive-by-wire as it was called, was another new innovation introduced to the Mustang for 2005. The elimination of the mechanical linkage frightened some buyers, but the integration of ETC into the Mustang's electronic engine control unit was so seamless that most drivers were unable to tell the difference.

For 40 years, Mustang mufflers had been installed in front of the rear axle. That changed for 2005 with new muffler positioning—

Continued on page 160

Even in base V-6 form, the 2005 Mustang was a sporty-looking vehicle, especially when clad in yellow. *Donald Farr*

Three-valve cylinder heads and variable cam timing were keys to producing 300 horsepower in the 2005 Mustang GT, but there was more first-time modern technology lurking under the hood, including the lightweight aluminum block and drive-by-wire throttle control. *Ford Motor Company*

# MODERN GT500

No one was surprised when SVT failed to deliver a Cobra for 2005. After all, it took time to develop a new performance car from a totally new platform. Behind the scenes, SVT was working on a 2006 Cobra, code-named Condor, with a 5.4-liter V-8. With Carroll Shelby back in good graces at world headquarters, enthusiasts figured it was only a matter of time before Ford and the legendary builder partnered to produce a modern Shelby Mustang. The Condor became the Ford Shelby GT500.

After whetting appetites with a show car at the New York Auto Show, Ford officially announced the 2007 Ford Shelby GT500 in the spring of 2005, noting that both coupes and convertibles would appear in dealer showrooms in the summer of 2006. Not only did the new Shelby GT500 employ a 32-valve 5.4-liter V-8, but it was also supercharged for 500 horsepower, once again raising the bar for production Mustangs. "Our

goal was to build the most powerful, most capable Mustang *ever*," said Hau Thai-Tang, who had moved from Mustang chief engineer to director of SVT.

Noting the collectability of 1960s Shelby Mustangs, SVT described the 2007 Ford Shelby GT500 as an instant collectible, but it was much more than a trailer queen as the engineers also enhanced all-around performance with a six-speed manual transmission,

For the 2007 Ford Shelby GT500, SVT replaced its Cobra model with a name from the Mustang's past. "When it came to designing the GT500, there's no question the 1967–1968 Shelby Mustangs inspired us," admitted Doug Gaffka, SVT design director. *Ford Motor Company*

Just like Shelby American in the 1960s, the parking lot at Shelby Automobiles filled with Mustangs after their conversion into 2007 Shelby GTs. New Mustang GTs were delivered to Shelby Automobiles in Las Vegas for the conversion, which added Ford Racing's power upgrade (for 319 horsepower) and handling pack packages, performance mufflers, and a number of Shelby styling components, including a Cobra-style hood scoop, billet grille insert, side scoops, and silver side and over-the-top striping. *Donald Farr*

race-tuned suspension, and Brembo brakes. Unlike the previous SN-95 Cobra, however, the Shelby GT500 did not come with independent rear suspension, sticking instead with the S197's solid rear axle. "Sure, we could've done it," said Thai-Tang with his prepared response. "We looked at the marginal handling improvement and didn't feel the gain justified the cost."

Externally, the 2007 GT500 combined styling cues from both SVT and Shelby. The sinister-looking front end with prominent upper and lower grille openings was the main visual difference from the Mustang GT. Functional heat extractors in the raised hood dome allowed hot underhood air to escape. The unique rear fascia incorporated lower strakes inspired by the Ford GT sports car's

rear air diffuser and an add-on rear spoiler provided a 1960s look.

Ford sold 10,864 Shelby GT500s for 2007, making it the second best-selling SVT product behind the 2003 Cobra. The GT500 returned in subsequent years with updates to

reflect body style and mechanical improvements in future Mustangs.

In Las Vegas, Shelby Automobiles announced a Super Snake package for 2007 Ford Shelby GT500s. As a post-title package, owners shipped or delivered their GT500s to the Shelby facility for upfitting with a Shelby-designed hood with scoops, black stripes, Ford Racing Handling Pack, free-flowing exhaust, 20-inch wheels and tires, and a number of Shelby exterior and interior accents, including a dash-mounted identification badge with serial number. Most importantly, supercharger and tuning modifications increased the GT500's standard 500 horsepower to either 600 for the base Super Snake or all the way to 725, making it the wildest Shelby Mustang since the original 427-powered Super Snake GT500 from 1967.

Named after a special 427-powered GT500 from 1967, Shelby Automobiles' post-title Super Snake package for the GT500 set new horsepower and performance standards for the Mustang. *Jerry Heasley*

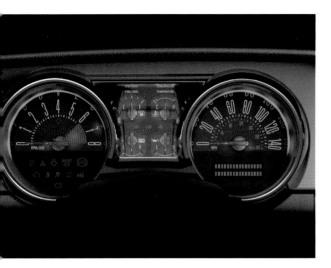

Another new technology was more aesthetic than functional. With the optional MyColor instrument cluster, drivers could personalize their instrument cluster background to any one of 125 colors. *Ford Motor Company*

*Continued from page 157*

single for V-6 and dual for V-8—between the axle and rear fascia. While the new positioning served to reduce drone, Ford's sound engineers used computer programming to make sure the new Mustang, especially the GT, retained its muscular exhaust tone.

At first, it appeared that the SVT Cobra was on hiatus once again, but rumors about Carroll Shelby's presence in the halls of Ford were confirmed when a Shelby Cobra GT500 concept, based on the 2005 Mustang, debuted at the New York Auto Show in March. Ford made no secret that the concept closely resembled an upcoming Shelby GT500 to replace SVT's Cobra.

Delayed until February 2005, the convertible's introduction was treated like a separate launch. It was touted as the best-ever Mustang convertible with a stiffer platform, lighter weight, and less wind buffeting at speed due to the more steeply raked windshield header and modified rear seatback. The fabric top's sealing was also improved to reduce wind noise, and the Z-fold design provided a more finished appearance when lowered.

In typical fashion, Steve Saleen took the resigned S197 Mustang and put his own unique spin on the new body for the Saleen S281, also available as a supercharged SC model. But by 2005, Saleen wasn't the only player in the upgraded Mustang market. Like Saleens, Roush Mustangs were available at select Ford dealerships in one of four models, including the top-of-the-line supercharged Stage 3. Companies such as Steeda Autosports and Kenny Brown Performance built their own brand of S197 Mustangs to appeal to road racers.

Like the rest of the car, the 2005 Mustang's interior was all new. An optional color accent package for GTs added red to the leather seating surfaces, door panels, and floor mats. *Ford Motor Company*

Arriving a few months after the coupe, the 2005 convertible benefitted from the S197's strengthened body structure, which eliminated the earlier Fox-body's cowl shake. *Ford Motor Company*

Sales of the 2005 Mustang almost reached 160,000 for the model year, an increase over 2004 in spite of the convertible's late release.

As typical for the sophomore year of a major redesign, there were few changes for the 2006 Mustang. Updates included an a pony package for the V-6, an 18-inch wheel option for the GT, and a pair of new clearcoat metallic colors, Vista Blue and Tungsten Grey. Perhaps the big surprise was a new Shelby, the GT-H, built by Shelby Automobiles for Hertz Rent-A-Car. All of a sudden, Carroll Shelby was back in the Mustang business.

Year three for the S197 was marked by the midyear GT/CS California Special, along with an optional GT Appearance package, available for both the regular GT and GT/CS, that added a hood scoop, rolled exhaust tips, and engine cover for the 4.6-liter V-8. All 2007 Mustangs were updated with a standard auxiliary audio input jack. New options included heated front seats and SIRIUS satellite radio. SVT finally made its mark on the S197 Mustang with the 2007 Ford Shelby GT500, a replacement for the earlier Cobra model and equipped with a supercharged 5.4-liter V-8 for 500 horsepower along with plenty of styling cues from 1960s Shelby Mustangs.

# IACOCCA EDITION

How do you impress Lee Iacocca? That was the challenge for designer Michael Leone and coachbuilders Gaffoglio Family Metalcrafters when they crafted a true fastback version of the S197 Mustang with hopes that Iacocca would lend his name to the special edition. The fact that Iacocca had never put his name on a car made the task even more daunting.

Leone said the idea for an Iacocca fastback came when he spotted a new Mustang on display at a local mall. He sketched his ideas and took them to Iacocca, who was immediately intrigued. "I liked it so much that I said we'd better build it," Iacocca explained. "It really brings back the fastback."

Fittingly, the father of the Mustang announced the Iacocca Silver 45th Anniversary Edition Mustang on Father's Day 2009. Built on the 2009 Mustang GT, the car added Leone-designed front and rear treatments, hood, fenders, and fastback roof and a special silver paint chosen by Iacocca. Only 45 were built to commemorate the Mustang's 45th anniversary.

Posing with the 2009 Iacocca Silver 45th Anniversary Edition, the image of Lee Iacocca with a Mustang brought back flashes of 1964. It was the first and so far only time that Iacocca's name has appeared on a car. *I Legacy Photo*

In Las Vegas, Shelby Automobiles capitalized on the surprise popularity and even collectability of the 2006 GT-H Hertz rental car program by adapting the package into a 2007 Shelby GT for general public consumption through Ford dealers.

The Mustang rolled into 2008 with few changes other than the addition of standard side airbags, three new colors, and optional HID headlights. But the fourth year of the S197 turned out to be one of the most exciting in Mustang history. Along with the continuation of the V-6 pony package, GT/CS, and Shelby GT500, Ford and Shelby Automobiles conspired to introduce a 540-horsepower 40th anniversary GT500KR inspired by the King of the Road model from 1968. A limited-edition Warriors in Pink Mustang with pink design accents supported Susan G. Komen for the Cure, a breast cancer organization, while, in January 2008, Team Mustang introduced the first of a two-year run of Mustang Bullitts, once again playing off Steve McQueen's 1968 movie. Topping off a wild model year, Shelby Automobiles added a convertible to its Shelby GT line.

Mustang entered its 45th year of production, 2009, with the continuation of the Bullitt, Shelby GT500KR, and Warrior in Pink models, along with a new factory-installed glass roof option for a panoramic overhead view and more interior lighting. Other than new amenities for the premium packages, there were few changes to mark the final year of the original S197. Styling changes were coming for 2010, but that was nothing compared to the surprises coming from engine engineering.

Roush Performance favored the muscle car look for its twist on the S197. The top-of-the-line Stage 3 added a ROUSHcharger supercharger to the new three-valve 4.6-liter for 415 horsepower. *Roush Performance*

Steve Saleen replaced the factory front and rear fascias to achieve a more European look for his Saleen S281s, seen here in SC trim. *Source Interlink Media*

## LEANER AND MEANER

Mustang chief nameplate engineer Paul Randle wasn't shy with his praise for the restyled 2010 Mustang: "The new Mustang is drop-dead gorgeous. This car marks the best efforts of 45 years of passion and enthusiasm among the best designers, engineers, and manufacturing experts in the business."

The S197's complete overhaul of 2005 was only four years old, but with the return of the Dodge Challenger and Chevrolet Camaro in the domestic pony car market, a sheetmetal makeover was deemed necessary for 2010. Designers tapered the front end and narrowed the grille opening for a sleeker appearance, integrating dual parking light lenses that resembled the fender extension scoops in 1970 Mustangs. A power dome in

*Continued on page 168*

Reviving a name from a 1968 special edition, the 2007 GT/CS came with unique front and rear fascias, chin spoiler, side scoops, midlevel side stripes, 18-inch wheels, and black leather-trimmed seats. *Ford Motor Company*

A new Pony Package for the 2006 V-6 added features such as a 1967-like grille bar with small fog lamps, upgraded suspension, rear spoiler, side striping, and a 17-inch wheels/tire package, largest ever for a V-6 Mustang. *Ford Motor Company*

## CHIEF FOR THE BOSS

Dave Pericak couldn't have inherited the Mustang chief engineer duties at a better time. Paul Randle handed over the reins in late 2008, right in the middle of the 2010 redesign and Coyote 5.0-liter development for 2011. Soon, Pericak found himself absorbed in the development and launch of the 2012 Boss 302.

Growing up in a Ford family in Chicago, a young Pericak dreamed of owning a Mustang. His career at Ford began as a manufacturing engineer at a parts plant, where he worked on door panels. Interaction with vehicle chief engineers inspired him to strive for a program leadership position. He never dreamed it would be

Mustang, where he's responsible for engineering, design, manufacturing, quality, and cost—in short, pretty much everything.

# COYOTE 5.0

The chrome 5.0 emblems on the 2011 fenders were similar to the badges that adorned the popular 5.0 Mustangs from the late 1980s, but the 5.0-liter V-8 under the hood of the Mustang GT bore little resemblance to the old pushrod small-block. Thoroughly modern from its oiling system to its finger-follower roller rocker arms, the officially named 5.0 4V TiVCT V-8 produced 412 horsepower to eclipse the 2010 GT's power output by 97. Within Ford, it was code-named Coyote in homage to Ford's Indy four-valve V-8, as used by A. J. Foyt's 1969 IndyCar race team.

With 400-horsepower Challengers already in showrooms and similarly powered Camaros on the horizon, the Mustang's decade-old 4.6-liter, even with three-valve technology, was deemed incapable of keeping up with the competition. In 2007, Ford engine engineers under the supervision of V-8 engine program manager Mike Harrison conceived a new powerplant to replace the aging 4.6-liter. It would be the first time an engine was designed and built specifically for the Mustang and not used in any other Ford car line. The displacement conveniently landed at 5.0 liters, or

302 cubic inches, a pair of numbers that embraced the Mustang's history of Boss 302s and 5.0-liter high outputs.

With 412 horsepower, the Coyote 5.0 not only established a new higher-water mark for a regular production Mustang, but it also set the stage for the future of Mustang performance. Even as engine engineers finalized the new 5.0, they were working on higher performance iterations, including one that would bring back a legendary name from the past.

Starting with the 4.6-liter's modular architecture, engine engineers created the new Coyote 5.0-liter as an all-aluminum V-8 with double-overhead, chain-driven cams and four valves per cylinder. More importantly, new TiVCT (Twin Independent Variable Cam Timing) technology allowed intake and exhaust timing events to work independently of each other for high peak power, a wide power band, and impressive fuel mileage. *Ford Motor Company*

# BOSS IS FINALLY BACK

The retro styling of the 2005 Mustang tempted many within Ford to push forward with a modern iteration of the legendary 1969–1970 Boss 302. But others resisted, noting that it would be difficult to offer a credible Boss 302 with a 4.6-liter (281-cubic-inch) engine.

"The S197 design lent itself really well to any of the iconic products of the 1960s," said Ford Racing's Mickey Matus, who was involved in several Boss proposals. "But despite the obvious opportunity, most were° cognizant of the fact that the Boss was going to be difficult to bring back with integrity and credibility."

Thanks to the Mustang GT's 302-cubic-inch Coyote 5.0, the missing piece of the Boss 302 puzzle fell into place. Working simultaneously with the development of the 5.0-liter, V-8 engine program manager Mike Harrison and his team added CNC-machined heads, lightweight valvetrain components, high-lift camshafts, and—most importantly—a "short-runners-in-the-box" intake to raise the Coyote 5.0's output from 412 to a high-revving 444 horsepower for the Boss 302. In a quest to develop a car that would be at home on both the street and road course, the vehicle dynamics team added manually

A short-runner-in-a-box intake manifold was the key to the Boss 302's high-revving 444 horsepower. *Ford Motor Company*

Ford waited until the time was right to reintroduce the Boss 302. The standard Boss was offered in a variety of colors with black or white stripes and roof. The Laguna Seca stood out on a crowded racetrack with its red stripes and roof on either black or silver exterior. *Ford Motor Company*

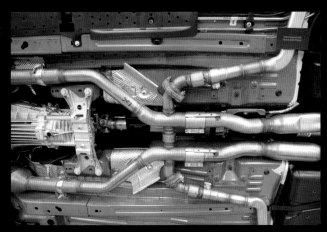

One of the most talked-about aspects of the new Boss 302 was its quad exhaust system. In an effort to enhance the driving experience through sound, the exhaust split off into a second pair of pipes that exited in front of the rear tires. Attenuation discs, actually metal plates with small openings, kept the sound level within legal limits, but they were also easily removable by owners for track-day excursions. *Ford Motor Company*

standard Boss 302's track worthiness with Pirelli PZero Corsa tires, a chassis-stiffening X-brace in place of the rear seat, brake ducts for cooling the front discs, a transmission cooler scoop, pedestal rear spoiler, and a more aggressive front splitter. To make them more visible on racetracks, the Laguna Secas were offered in Black or Ingot Silver with contrasting red stripes, roof panel, and trim.

Because several Boss 302 components were not compatible with assembly plant build procedures, some parts, including the unique side-exiting exhaust and the side stripes, were installed at the nearby mod center, which had been established by vehicle personalization for low-volume builds. Laguna Seca parts that didn't conform to shipping were supplied inside the car for dealer or owner installation.

adjustable dampers, higher rate springs, Pirelli PZero tires, and unique settings for the electric steering, traction control, and stability control.

The challenge for designers was honoring the styling cues of the original Boss 302 without "dusting off 1969," as Mustang product marketing manager Allison Revier put it. Without the iconic 1969 Boss 302 C stripes, it would be difficult to replicate the original Boss, so stripes were part of the package but offered in two colors—black or white—with matching roof. Otherwise, the appearance was functionally modern: front splitter, GT-style grille but with foglight blockoffs, and a small lip rear spoiler that worked better with the front splitter in wind-tunnel testing.

During the Boss 302 development, the Mustang team pushed the envelope to produce the ultimate track car. The group members stretched the limits with larger rear spoilers, wilder front splitters, race-compound tires,

and front brake cooling ducts. But there was only so much they could do with a regular production vehicle, bringing forward the idea of a limited-edition "even more" Boss 302 called the Laguna Seca.

Named after the famous northern California road course where Parnelli Jones's Boss 302 won the 1970 season-opening Trans-Am race, the 2012 Boss 302 Laguna Seca improved on the

To acquaint Boss 302 owners with the capabilities of their vehicles, Ford offered a Track Attack program at Miller Motorsports Park in Utah. Using stock Boss 302s, participants experienced a full day of instruction and track time under the tutelage of Miller instructors. *Jeremy Henrie/Miller Motors Park*

# 662 HORSEPOWER!

Other than a revised grille, new wheels, and quad exhaust tips, SVT's '13 Shelby GT500 didn't look much different from the 2012 version. But in this case, it was what you couldn't see that made the latest GT500 so impressive—arguably the most impressive production Mustang ever.

Needing to counter Chevrolet's 580-horsepower Camaro ZL1, SVT ditched the 5.4-liter engine, as used in the GT500 since 2007, and replaced it with a larger 5.8-liter. With a target of at least 650 horsepower, the all-aluminum V-8 was topped by a higher capacity Twin Vortices Series 2300 supercharger with 14 psi of boost. In dyno testing, the engine made 662 horsepower, not only exceeding the power goal and beating the previous GT500 by 112 horsepower, but also making it the most powerful production V-8 in the world.

To handle the extra power, nearly every system in the GT500 was upgraded, everything "except the back seat," joked SVT chief engineer Jamal Hameedi. For 2013, the Shelby received larger six-piston Brembo front brakes, improved Tremec six-speed transmission with dual-disc clutch, and a one-piece carbon-fiber driveshaft. Because torque also increased to 631 ft-lb, the rear gearing dropped to 3.31:1, contributing to an increase in fuel mileage—15 city, 25 highway, once again keeping the GT500 out of the gas guzzler tax bracket.

During a media day at Atlanta Dragway, *Muscle Mustangs and Fast Fords* editor Evan Smith utilized the 2013 Ford Shelby GT500 launch control to record an 11.81 quarter-mile pass at 122 miles-per-hour on the factory street tires. *Donald Farr*

The goal was 650, but SVT reached a dyno-documented 662 horsepower with the 2013 Ford Shelby GT500's new 5.8-liter engine and a larger supercharger. *Donald Farr*

SVT had another goal for the 2013 GT500—200 miles-per-hour capability for the coupe (the convertible was speed-limited to 155). To drive home the point, the speedometer registered 220 miles per hour. SVT reported that test drivers hit 202 miles-per-hour at the Nardo test facility in Italy.

For drivers who desired to use their GT500 on tracks, a performance package added a Torsen differential, cockpit-adjustable dampers, and unique springs and sway bars while a track package aided cooling for the engine oil, transmission, and differential.

The 2013 Ford Shelby GT500 went down in history as the last Shelby Mustang that Carroll Shelby contributed to at Ford before his death in May 2012. "We worked very closely with him," said Jamal Hameedi, SVT chief. "We wanted to make sure that he agreed with what we were doing, so he was involved in the process from the beginning. It was important to us to get his seal of approval." *Ford Motor Company*

A handshake between Carroll Shelby (left) and Phil Marstens, Ford group vice president for product creation, represented a new partnership for Ford and Shelby. The pair introduced the Shelby Cobra GT500 show car at the New York International Auto Show in March 2005. *Ford Motor Company*

Shelby collaborated with Ford again in 2008 to create the GT500KR, a modern reincarnation of the 1968 "King of the Road." As a pretitle package, the cars started life as standard GT500s before being shipped to Shelby Automobiles for installation of the KR's unique body components (including a carbon-fiber hood with forward-placed scoops like the 1968 Shelby), suspension improvements, and 40 more horsepower. Just more than 1,000 were produced; another 712 were built for the 2009 model year. *Jerry Heasley*

*Continued from page 164*

the hood added a more muscular appearance and the rear end was restyled, although the angled corners were not widely accepted by enthusiasts. Borrowing a trick from the 1968 Shelby, the three-lens taillights became sequential in operation. Smaller updates included a capless fueling system, windshield washer nozzles moved from the hood to the cowl area, and radio antenna on the rear fender. AdvanceTrac Electronic Stability Control became standard to complement the traction control and anti-lock braking system.

To go along with the muscular looks, the 2010 GT incorporated a number of improvements from the 2008–2009 Bullitt, including the cold-air induction system for another 15 horsepower (315 total), reworked suspension calibrations optimized for optional 18- and new 19-inch wheels, and larger 3½-inch exhaust tips. While sound engineers worked to reduce wind noise, they also directed more engine sound to the passenger compartment via an industry-first sound induction tube that ran from the intake tube to the interior.

The base Mustang benefitted from 2010's styling and engineering improvements, but it was still powered by the 210-horsepower 4.0-liter V-6, which was quickly becoming outdated. Ford would address that problem for the following year.

SVT took advantage of the Mustang's sheetmetal changes to update the 2010 Ford Shelby GT500 with new front and rear end styling, revamped suspension tuning, enhancements to the six-speed gearing, 3:55 final drive gearing (up from 3.31), and 19-inch wheels for coupe and 18-inch for convertible with improved Goodyear F1 Supercar tires. Utilizing the GT500KR's cold-air induction system, horsepower from the supercharged and intercooled 5.4-liter 32-valve V-8 increased to 540.

With the end of the GT500KR program in 2009, Shelby Automobiles switched its focus to post-title builds—the GT500 Super Snake, GT500SE, 40th Anniversary GT500, and a Terlingua for six-cylinders. The company also reclaimed its former name, Shelby American, just before president Amy Boylan left and handed the reins to Carroll Shelby's longtime licensing attorney, John Luft.

With fresh sheet metal for 2010, no one expected exterior changes for the 2011 Mustang. Likewise, few outside Ford anticipated the remarkable changes under the hood for both engines—a 412-horsepower 5.0-liter V-8 for the GT and a base 3.7-liter V-6 with a combination of 305 horsepower and 31 miles-per-gallon fuel economy. With 2010's refreshening and 2011's power infusion, the Mustang had become a world-class vehicle capable of competing with higher-priced European and Asian cars.

The more powerful engines were coupled with new six-speed transmissions for both manual and automatic, electric power-assist steering, and suspension upgrades. An available Brembo brake package added 14-inch front discs (from the GT500), 19-inch alloy wheels, and summer performance tires. For the GT, new convenience technology provided a standard message center, MyKey programmable key, and a universal garage door opener. After a one-year absence in 2010, the GT/CS model returned for 2011 with its own front fascia, billet grille, and side stripes.

With huge power improvements for the V-6 and GT models, SVT made some news of its own with the 2011 Ford Shelby GT500 by adding 10 horsepower, up to 550, from a new and 102-pound lighter all-aluminum 5.4-liter V-8. The new engine also offered improved fuel mileage—up to 23 miles-per-gallon highway and 15 in the city—enough that buyers

SVT's Shelby GT500 was powered by a 32-valve 5.4-liter V-8, the largest displacement for a regular production Mustang engine since 1973. Supercharging boosted output to 500 horsepower. *Donald Farr*

As an S197 followup to the popular 2001 Bullitt GT, Ford reprised the special edition for 2008. Based on the Mustang GT Premium and offered in Dark Highland Green or Black, the Mustang Bullitt combined Ford Racing suspension and engine tweaks to increase performance over the standard Mustang GT. *Ford Motor Company*

For 2009, the glass roof option joined the coupe and convertible as a third body style choice. Made from tinted privacy glass, the glass top let the sun shine in at half the cost of a convertible. *Ford Motor Company*

The S197's 2010 styling makeover included a new front-end treatment with narrower grille opening and parking lights integrated into the headlights. The Mustang GT kept its signature fog lights, but the three-valve 4.6-liter V-8 was upgraded to 315 horsepower. *Ford Motor Company*

could avoid the gas guzzler tax. In Las Vegas, Shelby American celebrated the return to its former name by introducing the first Shelby GT350 in 41 years.

Two years into a styling overhaul and one year beyond impressive engine advancements, the 2012 Mustang was basically a carryover from 2011 with no change except selectable steering with three driving modes (Standard, Sport, and Comfort), new Lava Red Metallic paint, and additional sun visor storage. The 2012 Ford Shelby GT500 also took advantage of the selectable steering and added SVT-designed Recaro seats to the option list.

For two years, Mustang team members kept quiet about their 747 project. On August 13, 2010, Ford let the 2012 Boss 302 out of the bag at a Laguna Seca press briefing during the Monterey Historics.

The 2013 Mustang debuted with another mild styling change for the nine-year-old S197 platform, this time updating with a more prominent front grille and a new rear fascia with LED tail lamps plus a black panel designed to soften the appearance of the angular taillights. The latest model also added new features such as HID headlights, heat extractors for the GT hood, SelectShift for automatic transmissions, and hill start assist for manual transmission cars. Pony projection light side mirrors became available to cast an image of the running horse logo onto the ground. The GT's 5.0-liter V-8 took another step forward with 420 horsepower, up eight from 2011, thanks to improvements discovered during

Continued on page 176

Ford rocked the 2010 Mustang's reveal with a drift exhibition by Vaughan Gitten Jr. inside Santa Monica Airport's Barker Hangar. With one Mustang of every year on display outside, the indoor display included a wall of historic racing Mustangs. The event aired live on SPEED TV with feeds to nine Mustang Club of America reveals around the country. *Ford Motor Company*

The 2010 Mustang interior was updated with new materials, genuine aluminum panels, and a one-piece instrument panel that flowed into a center stack for Ford's SYNC communications and entertainment system. *Ford Motor Company*

For the 2010 Ford Shelby GT500, SVT engineers focused on aerodynamic improvements, especially as they related to improved front end air flow for engine cooling. Taking lessons learned from the 2008 GT500KR, the new GT500 offered a combination of power, handling, and braking. *Ford Motor Company*

# THE BUZZ:
## WHAT THE PRESS HAD TO SAY
## (MUSTANG IN THE TWENTY-FIRST CENTURY)

"So strong is the new [2005] car's character that 'Mustang' script appears nowhere, thanks to styling drawing heavily from the Mustang's first generation. While tempting to label the look as retro, once you see this car cruising Main you'll agree this is simply what a Mustang looks like. It certainly won't be mistaken for anything else."
—*Road & Track* web report

"[The 2005 Mustang] feels like far more than the sum of its parts. That is the draw of the Mustang: It makes the most of what it has, doesn't suffer for what it doesn't have, charges you less than you'd expect, and beckons from the showroom until you come and take it home."
—*Car & Driver*, January 2005

"With all due respects to the Mustangs developed and sold by Ford SVT between 1993 and 2004, Cobras are two-seat roadsters built by Shelby American during the 1960s. This is the mindset that underpins the naming—and development— of the first new, legit Shelby Mustang in 35 years. Officially, it's the Ford Shelby GT500. No misapplied Cobra branding in sight."
—*Motor Trend*, May 2005

"On the road or at the track, the Saleen/PJ is arguably the finest execution of any modern Mustang, especially one with a checkered-flag past. It has the looks, and it delivers the goods. It's nostalgic yet innovative."
—*Motor Trend*, March 2007

"The 2008 Mustang Bullitt is well conceived, designed, engineered, and ready to rock. It's crisper, sharper, and a bit quicker than a standard GT. Though not as fast as a GT500, it's better balanced and less expensive. Ford plans 7,000 Bullitts for the U.S. market, and it's likely to be the last special edition dedicated to the movie and the man. Translation: Future collectible."
—*Motor Trend*, January 2008

"What's not an understatement is that the 5.0 is the fiercest and fastest Mustang GT ever. Period. Goodnight."
—*Motor Trend*, June 2010

"The new Mustang V-6 can sprint with musclecars, zigzag with sports cars, and drink with economy cars. The best of all worlds? You could say that."
—*Motor Trend*, June 2010

"There is little in common between the 2011 Mustang GT and the 1993 5.0 Mustang save the name Mustang, the rear-wheel drive/solid axle platform, and the 5.0 badge. Today's 5.0 Mustang is an ultra-modern automobile with a solid platform, great brakes, and a highly optimized, dual-overhead-cam V-8."
—*5.0 Mustang & Super Fords*, August 2010

"The current-gen Mustang body style has cried out for the Boss treatment since its introduction in 2005, and finally Ford has the motor and the interest to do the job."
—*Motor Trend*, November 2010

"Once off the line, you'll need to tighten your grip on the Alcantara-covered steering wheel because the Boss 302 accelerates with zeal, pressing your back into the Recaro seats all the way to its 7,500 rpm redline."
—*Road & Track*, May 2011

"Even with all its newfound power, the 2013 GT500 is more livable and user friendly than it ever was before. Ford has improved its monster Mustang in every way possible—better handling, more technology, increased power, and even a one-mpg improvement in highway fuel economy. This truly is the most potent factory pony car the Blue Oval has ever produced."
—*Motor Trend* web report

Mustang enthusiasts loved the 2010 Mustang's front end but were less enamored with the rear panel treatment that included angled taillights.
*Jim Smart*

Just like the original 1965 GT350, Shelby American's 2011 GT350 was offered in white with blue stripes only. Tuning tweaks were available to take the naturally aspirated version to 450 horsepower; with optional Ford Racing/Whipple supercharger, the GT350 made 525 horsepower.
*Shelby American*

Continued from page 173

Boss 302 development, and an available GT track package that incorporated the Brembo brake package and added 3.73:1 rear axle gearing in a Torsen differential, engine oil cooler, and performance brake pads. First-time options included Recaro seats, new Shaker audio systems, and a 4.2-inch LCD with track apps to enable the driver to measure g-forces along with braking and acceleration times.

While the Boss 302 returned with 1970-like striping for second and final year, the 2013 Ford Shelby GT500 entered truly ground-breaking territory with 662 horsepower from a new 5.8-liter V-8. For the Super Snake package, Shelby American upped the ante with 850 horsepower and introduced a wide-body option to provide room for larger wheels and tires, especially at the rear for increased off-the-line traction.

Throughout its 50-year history, the Mustang evolved with the times—downsizing for the fuel economy needs of the 1970s, responding to enthusiasts' demands for more performance with the 5.0-liter Mustang of the 1980s, and using technology to compete in a twenty-first century market populated by American, European, and Asian competition. By 2012, the word was out: for its 50th anniversary year in 2015, there would be a totally new Mustang, one that would once again advance the storied nameplate and prepare it for the future.

As with the final years of previous generations, the S197 Mustang entered 2014 mostly unchanged with a 305-horsepower V-6 base model, 420-horsepower GT, and 662-horsepower

Roush's spin on the 2010 Mustang GT resulted in the extra-sharp 427R, a carryover from the previous year but with new front valance and hood stripes. A ROUSHcharger supercharger helped produce 435 horsepower. *Donald Farr*

The 2011 Mustang GT may have looked like a continuation of the previous year's model, but the 412-horsepower Coyote 5.0-liter under the hood made it a totally different animal. *Ford Motor Company*

Current Mustang chief engineer Dave Pericak admits he's fortunate to head up the Mustang program: "I'm definitely one of the lucky few. It's an honor to lead the Mustang team. I want to take a great car and make it second to none. Our vision is to make Mustang a world-class sports car." *Ford Motor Company*

In the final styling update for the S197, the 2013 Mustang adopted a more prominent grille, similar to the Shelby GT500. New exterior colors included Gotta Have It Green, seen here on the Mustang Club of America edition. *Ford Motor Company*

Like 1969–1970, the modern Boss 302 was planned as a two-year program. For 2013, the Boss 302 returned on the updated 2013 Mustang with a modern interpretation of former designer Larry Shinoda's reflective hockey-stick stripes. Engineers also tweaked front-end aerodynamics and cooling capabilities, which included a grille with pop-off foglight covers. The Laguna Seca lost its controversial red accents and returned with Sterling Grey stripes on either black or new School Bus Yellow. *Ford Motor Company*

The 2014 Mustang comes at you with base, Shelby GT500, and GT models. *Ford Motor Company*

Shelby GT500 from SVT. Obviously missing was the Boss 302, by design a two-year program like 1969 and 1970. New features for 2014 included revised speedometer/tachometer graphics, additional Oxford White and Ruby Red colors, and appearance packages for V-6 and GT.

Model year 2014 marks the Mustang's 50th continuous year of production, a feat that no other American car line can claim. (Although Corvette debuted in 1953, it skipped the 1983 model year). Mustang will continue to advance into the future while maintaining a link to the past.

Confirming the track capabilities of the 2013 Mustang GT, Boss 302, and Shelby GT500, a 4.2-inch LCD screen in the gauge cluster was available to allow the driver to flip through the available functions such as selectable steering, AdvanceTrac, Track Apps, and Launch Control. *Donald Farr*

# RACING
# TO IMPROVE
# THE BREED

**THE MUSTANG'S ARRIVAL IN 1964** landed it smack in the middle of Ford's Total Performance campaign. "Win on Sunday, Sell on Monday" was the mantra, so along with Fairlanes, Galaxies, and Falcons, the Mustang was groomed for competition, primarily road racing and drag racing. The Mustang was many things to many people, from an economy car for single women to a performance car for young guys, but it was never designed as a race car. So Ford looked outside for assistance, tapping companies such as Shelby American, Holman-Moody, and England's Alan Mann Racing to mold a winning tradition for its new pony car.

In 1964, Ford's Lee Iacocca said, "We will stay in open competition as long as we feel it contributes to better automobiles for the public." Other than the 1970s when Ford sacrificed racing support to pursue fuel economy, Ford bettered the Mustang in competition on road courses and drag strips around the United States and world, many campaigned by performance pioneers such as Jack Roush and Steve Saleen. Independents made contributions as well, including a group of drag racers who established their own grassroots 5.0-liter movement in the 1980s. Today, Mustangs also compete in NASCAR's Nationwide Series and can be found sliding side-by-side against Asia's best in the relatively new sport of drifting.

Over the past 50 years, Mustangs have compiled more than 2,000 professional racing victories in NHRA, Grand Am, IMSA and SCCA competition, among other series.

Jon Gooding was flying high with his second-place finish, behind teammate Tommy Kendall, in the 1997 Trans-Am race at St. Petersburg, Florida. Roush Mustangs won all 13 races during the 1997 Trans-Am season. *Ford Motor Company*

Mustangs made their first competition appearances in European road rallies, this one at the 6,000-kilometer Liege-Sofia-Liege rally through Belgium and Yugoslavia. *Ford Motor Company*

## RALLIES AND ROAD RACING

With its compact size and sports-car looks, the 1965 Mustang was a natural for road racing. Within months of its introduction, Mustang hardtops were competing in European road rallies and winning their class at the 1964 Tour de France Automobile. In the United States, Shelby American got the assignment to convert the 1965 Mustang fastback into a sports car for Sports Car Club of America road racing, resulting in the competition Shelby GT350. This model secured the SCCA's B-Production championship for three years in a row, 1965 with driver Jerry Titus as a Shelby American team effort, followed by 1966 and 1967 championships by independents Walt Hane and Freddy Van Buren.

In 1966, the SCCA created the Trans-Am series, purposely including an over 2.0-liter (305 cubic inches max) class that was ideal for America's new pony cars. Held at professional road-race competitions around the country, including the 24 Hours of Daytona, the Trans-Am promised huge exposure for the manufacturers, especially the company winning the season championship. After Shelby American's 1965 road-racing success with the GT350, Ford looked to Carroll Shelby for help. Starting with hardtops, Shelby applied lessons learned from his R models to build the first Trans-Am Mustangs. During the season, the Mustangs battled the Darts and Barracudas, leading to a final race showdown at Riverside, California, with Ford and Chrysler tied for the manufacturer's points lead. For added insurance, Ford requested Shelby American's assistance, resulting in the entry of a Mustang driven by Jerry

Jerry Titus soaks up the wine, women, and trophy after winning the 1966 Trans-Am championship with his victory at Riverside. *Source Interlink Media*

Shelby American secured Mustang's first Trans-Am championship by sending team driver Jerry Titus and a Shelby-prepared hardtop to the 1966 season's final race at Riverside. Titus won the race and the championship. *Ford Motor Company*

Parnelli Jones chases George Follmer in a Bud Moore Boss 302 tandem during the 1969 Trans-Am race at St. Jovite in Canada. A few laps later, Follmer's No. 16 and both of the Shelby Boss 302s were involved in an accident that practically destroyed all three cars, ending Ford's chances of a Trans-Am championship. *Ford Motor Company*

Titus. The tactic worked. Titus not only grabbed the pole position with a new sedan lap record, but also he won the race and the championship for Ford.

When Camaro, Firebird, and Cougar joined the action for 1967, the Trans-Am series exploded in popularity. Including 1966, Mustang won three of the first five championships before Ford yanked racing support after the 1970 season.

After a disastrous 1968 season with unreliable Tunnel-Port 302 engines and resulting championship for Camaro, Ford doubled its efforts for 1969 with two teams, Shelby and Bud Moore, each with a pair of new Boss 302 Mustangs that, like Camaro's Z/28, were tailor-built to homologate their special engines for Trans-Am. The season began with promising results—Mustangs won three of the first four races. However, the Ford teams were unable to recover from a multicar crash at midseason that essentially wiped out three of the Boss 302s. Mark Donahue's Camaro claimed the championship again.

For 1970, Shelby was out, leaving an experienced Bud Moore team with School Bus Yellow Boss 302s and returning drivers Parnelli Jones and George Follmer. While Chevrolet sorted out its new 1970½ Camaro, the Mustangs ran away with the points lead, nailing down the season championship at the next-to-last race. In the final event of the season, Jones and Follmer put on a two-car show with Jones making a final lap charge for the win. One magazine reported, "The Mustang's domination was so complete that Jones and Follmer only had each other to race with."

Ford pulled out of racing in the summer of 1970, focusing instead on fuel mileage and emissions. Independent Mustang teams soldiered on in Trans-Am (including Bud

*Continued on page 188*

At 1970's Kent 200 in Seattle, Parnelli Jones won the pole and led nearly every lap on his way to his fourth win of the season and claiming the 1970 Trans-Am championship for Ford. *Ford Motor Company*

# FIRST VICTORY

When Ford began building preproduction Mustangs in February 1964, there was more to accomplish than simply final fit and finish. A number of the first cars were destined for special duty, including several hardtops for Ford of Europe. One of the first cars arrived at Alan Mann Racing in England for testing. Mann had experience with Ford Cortinas and Falcons in European rallies; Ford needed Mann's expertise to groom the Mustang into a successful rally car to earn respect in Europe.

In an interview with Wolfgang Kohrn, Mann related that six more Mustangs arrived later for rally preparation, which included replacing the original engines with 289s prepared by Holman-Moody. In the Mustang's first serious competition, two white hardtops entered Belgium's Liege-Sofie-Liege Rallye in August 1964. Both crashed during the 6,000-kilometer race.

The following month, Mann arrived in Lille, France, with four red Mustang hardtops for the Touring class in the Tour de France Automobile rally. Three would compete in the 10-day, 17-stage race, starting in Lille and running through the French towns of Reims, Le Mans, Monza, and Pau. Mann recalled using the fourth car for personal transportation until he had to scavenge parts for the race cars.

At the end of the grueling competition, Mustang codrivers Peter Proctor and Andrew Cowan took the checkered flag with a first-place finish in the Touring class (eighth overall), followed in second by the Mustang driven by Peter Harper/David Pollard.

The 1964 Tour de France victory marked the first professional race win for the Mustang, forever erasing the Mustang's image as a secretary's car in Europe.

Andrew Cowan and Peter Procter celebrate their 1964 Tour de France victory in an Alan Mann Mustang hardtop. It was the first racing victory for Mustang. *Ford Motor Company*

# COMPETITION GT350

Aspiring race driver Jerry Titus was earning a living as technical editor for *Sports Car Graphic* when Carroll Shelby invited him to Willow Springs to observe a test of the first competition 1965 Shelby GT350. Shelby's jack-of-all-trades Ken Miles and driver Bob Bondurant were scheduled to handle the driving duties on that January 1965 day, but Titus test-drove the car as well.

The main reason for Shelby's involvement was racing. Lee Iacocca wanted a performance image for the Mustang and he asked Shelby to supply it through Sports Car Club of America road racing. After all, Shelby had come to Iacocca in 1962 to beg for engines for his Cobra sports car. Shelby quickly proved that he and his band of California hot rodders

could build a winner, so much so that Shelby American inherited the 1965 Ford GT40 program with the goal of beating Ferrari at Le Mans.

Shelby turned to John Bishop, SCCA executive director, to find out what it would take to classify the four-seat Mustang as a sports car. Of prime importance was transforming the Mustang into a two-seater; for his GT350, Shelby met the requirement by replacing the rear seat with a fiberglass shelf that mounted a spare tire. Satisfied, the SCCA placed the GT350 into its B-Production class to battle cars such as the Jaguar XKE, Lotus Elan, Sunbeam Tiger, and Corvette.

Miles and newly hired GT350 project engineer Chuck Cantwell sketched out the specs for the

competition GT350, starting with fastbacks produced at Ford's San Jose assembly plant. Weight savings from the street GT350, such as the fiberglass hood, were also part of the package, but the race version went further with plexiglass side windows, deleted carpet, aluminum door panels, and fiberglass inserts to replace the fastback's heavy C-pillar vent assemblies. The street car's front bumper and valance were replaced by a fiberglass apron for both reduced weight and increased air flow to the radiator. Other modifications included a race-prepared suspension, roll cage, competition gauges, and a larger fuel tank. The 289 High Performance engines were balanced, blueprinted, and hand-assembled for upwards of 360 horsepower.

During Shelby American's test of the first competition GT350 at Willow Springs, *Sports Car Graphic* tech editor Jerry Titus got a chance to test the car. Titus reported in *SCG*, "B-Production should be swamped by it, and any stragglers in A-Production will be quickly gobbled up." *Source Interlink Media*

Miles hauled the prototype competition GT350 to Willow Springs to test its modifications. Titus also got seat time; in just a few laps, he was running lap times within a second of Miles. A few months later, Shelby hired Titus as a Shelby GT350 team driver. During the 1965 season, GT350s won five of the SCCA's six divisional B-Production championships. Titus claimed the Pacific division championship and went on to win the 1965 national championship with a victory at the American Road Race of Champions in Daytona. In 1966, Shelby disbanded the factory team, but independents continued the winning ways.

Shelby American built 36 competition GT350s (later identified as R models by enthusiasts), many of them piloted by top drivers such as Mark Donahue, Dave McDonald, and Dean Gregson from Tasca Ford. Today,

R models are coveted by collectors and vintage racers.

Below: Competition Shelby GT350s dominated the SCCA's B-Production class in 1965. Carroll Shelby tapped Jerry Titus to drive the official Shelby entry. He delivered with the B-Production national championship. *Source Interlink Media*

Above: Other than the R-model front apron, race wheels, and plexiglass rear window with a gap at the top to relieve interior air pressure, there were few external differences between the competition (left) and street Shelby GT350s. The main change was under the hood, where the race-prepared 289 developed between 325 and 360 horsepower, compared to 306 for the street version. *Shelby American*

Although Mustangs didn't compete in NASCAR's top series during the 1970s, they were driver and fan favorites at local bullring tracks on Saturday nights. *Donald Farr*

*Continued from page 184*

Moore in 1970 Boss 302s) and other road-racing series without factory support. Nearly 20 years would pass before a Mustang wore the Trans-Am crown again. From 1976 to 1980, Charlie Kemp competed as an independent with a radical Mustang II in the International Motorsports Association's (IMSA) All-American GT class but faced tough going against the Chevrolet-supported Monzas.

By the early 1980s, IMSA was growing in popularity, bolstered in part by a GTO class that was ideal for large-displacement cars such as the Mustang, Camaro, Corvette, and Ferrari 365GTB4. A Roush-prepared Mustang driven by Willy T. Ribbs and Wally Dallenbach Jr. won the GTO class at the IMSA finale in 1984, igniting the Mustang's rein as the king of GTO for the next two years with consecutive manufacturers' championships and driver

With Mustang IIs in the showroom, enthusiasts such as Danny Rockett turned their attention to earlier Mustang muscle cars for autocross competition. *Donald Farr*

# TERLINGUA RACING TEAM

Even though Shelby American secured the 1966 Trans-Am championship for Mustang, Ford opted to campaign the new Cougar in 1967 with Mercury's NASCAR stalwart Bud Moore. However, Ford sports car manager Ray Geddes wanted to maintain a Mustang presence in Trans-Am, so he borrowed from his own budget to support a Shelby American Mustang for the 1967 Trans-Am. Only it couldn't be an official Ford or Shelby entry. Thus, Shelby's 1967 Trans-Am effort became known as the Terlingua Racing Team.

The name came from the small, abandoned town of Terlingua, Texas. Carroll Shelby's attorney, David Witt, had convinced Shelby to purchase land near the ghost town, so Shelby and his buddies, including longtime friend and artist Bill Neale, *Car & Driver* editor David E. Davis, and Witts, would gather there to escape the daily grind.

Neale was the logical choice to design a coat of arms for a school that Shelby wanted to build for underprivileged boys. Neale designed a logo with a rabbit holding up its paw. "It says, 'Don't put anymore pepper in the chili,'" deadpanned Neale.

Someone printed decals of the Terlingua coat of arms and somehow they found their way onto race cars, including the GT350 R model at its first race. The Terlingua Racing Team started as a joke, so it was the perfect name for Shelby's clandestine 1967 Trans-Am team.

But there was nothing funny about Terlingua Racing Team's performance in the 1967 Trans-Am. With Titus driving a Mustang hardtop painted in a funky shade of yellow—created by Neale and named Godawful Yellow by Carroll Shelby—the Terlingua team won 4 out of the 12 races, outgunning the factory-backed Cougars and Camaros for the season championship and a second straight Trans-Am triumph for Mustang.

Carroll Shelby called the color Godawful Yellow, but there was nothing awful about Jerry Titus' performance in the Terlingua Racing Team Mustang. He won four 1967 races to claim a second consecutive Trans-Am championship for Mustang. *Ford Motor Company Photo/Courtesy Austin Craig*

Mustang began its return to factory-backed racing in 1981 with a Bill Scott Racing Mustang built by Germany's Zakspeed and backed by Ford Motorsport. Klaus Ludwig drove the turbocharged four-cylinder Mustang to a pair of victories during IMSA's Camel GT season. *Ford Motor Company*

While Mustang fans were lamenting no performance in showrooms combined with Ford's hands-off racing policy, Charlie Kemp was campaigning a tube-frame Mustang II in IMSA's All American GT class. Created to compete against factory-backed Chevrolet Monzas, the independent Kemp was never able to finish higher than second in spite of taking a number of pole positions and reaching 212 miles per hour at Daytona. *Charlie Kemp*

titles for John Jones and Scott Pruett. After a brief switch to Merkurs and Cougars for IMSA competition, Mustang made a triumphant return for back-to-back championships in 1993 and 1994 with drivers Tommy Kendall and Joe Pezza.

Mustang began its march back to the top of Trans-Am in 1981 when Tom Gloy notched the first victory since 1970. By 1984, chassis specialist Bob Riley had teamed with Jack Roush, leading to Mustang wins in half of the Trans-Am races during 1985 and 1986. Mustang returned to the top of Trans-Am in the Mustang's 25th anniversary year, 1989, when rookie Dorsey Schroeder won 5 out of the 15 races in a Roush Racing Mustang. In 1996, Roush Mustangs again set the pace as Schroeder won the driver's championship and Tommy Kendall helped secure the manufacturer's title. The following 1997 season was thoroughly dominated by Roush Mustangs, winning all 13 Trans-Am races, including a record 11 straight by Kendall in his All Sport Cobra.

Like Carroll Shelby 20 years earlier, Steve Saleen built street Mustangs as a means to field cars on the racetrack. For 1987's Escort Endurance Showroom Stock series, Saleen drafted Rick Titus, son of former Shelby team driver Jerry Titus, as his codriver along with Lisa Caceres and Desire Wilson for a second car. With 1987 season championships on the line at the final race at Sebring, Saleen showed up with three Showroom Stock Mustangs and eight drivers, including Saleen himself; regulars Rick Titus, Lisa Caceres, and Desire Wilson; plus 1970 Trans-Am champs Parnelli Jones and George Follmer with Pete Halsmer

and Scott Pruett on hand for added insurance. On the final lap, Wilson passed the leading Showroom Stock Porsche to win the race and help secure the team, driver, manufacturer, and tire championships for Saleen.

Ford SVT's 1993 Cobra R was purpose-built for grassroots racers, but there was no factory support for a serious racing effort. That changed for the 1995 Cobra R when Ford contracted Steeda Autosports to develop parts and distribute them to independent Mustang teams for the 1995–1997 IMSA Endurance Championship's Grand Sport class. Steeda also fielded a pair of cars, including the number 20 Cobra R that became the first showroom stock Mustang in 10 years to win an IMSA endurance race.

*Continued on page 195*

Ford was "Racing into the Future" in 1985 when 19-year-old John Jones helped win the IMSA GTO manufacturer's championship in his Roush Mustang. Ford shouted the accomplishment with ad spreads in the popular auto magazines at a time when Mustang performance was making a comeback.

With teammate Lyn St. James, Dorsey Schroeder won the 1989 Trans-Am championship in a Roush Racing Mustang. *Ford Motor Company*

"The Mustang has been the river that runs through my career," said Jack Roush as he stood in front of his collection of Mustangs at one of his many buildings in and around the Detroit area. That statement not only incorporated Mustang automobiles, from the 1965 Mustang he bought new to the NASCAR Nationwide Mustangs campaigned by Roush Fenway Racing, but also his fascination with World War II–era P-51 Mustang fighter planes. Over four decades, Mustangs played a large role in Roush's success as a drag racer, businessman, and one of the most successful road racing team owners of all time.

Roush's relationship with Mustangs started shortly after he graduated from college in 1964. As a reward to himself for landing a job as an engineer in Ford's vehicle assembly and tooling department, he bought a new 1965 Mustang hardtop.

At Ford, Roush drifted toward the company's motorsports activities and was soon involved with fellow employees in a local drag racing club called The Fastbacks, where Roush drove a 1966 Mustang Hi-Po Fastback. In 1970, he turned his love for racing into a career by leaving Ford to form a partnership with Wayne Gapp. The pair won numerous NHRA Pro Stock events and one championship each in NHRA, IHRA, and AHRA with Pintos and Mavericks, along with a Mustang II in 1974. When the Gapp and Roush

Jack Roush likes Mustangs, as evidenced by the collection he keeps at his Michigan museum with everything from a 1965 reminder of his first Mustang to some of Roush Racing's most significant race cars. *Dale Amy*

partnership ended in 1976, Roush formed Jack Roush Performance Engineering, combining his on-track success with engineering savvy to build a thriving company to provide services not only to racers, but also to the Big Three auto manufacturers.

Ford encouraged Roush to return to racing in 1984, only this time it was on road courses for SCCA and IMSA competition. The endeavor paid off with back-to-back IMSA GTO titles for Mustang in 1985 and 1986, followed in 1989 by the Mustang's first Trans-Am championship since 1970. Campaigning Mustangs, Merkurs, and Cougars, Roush went on to claim 24 national championships and titles in the two series, including 12

manufacturer's championships while winning 119 races.

Impressively, Roush captured 10 consecutive IMSA GTO class championships from 1985 to 1994 at the 24 Hours of Daytona, seven of them in Mustangs. Success with racing Mustangs led to the formation of a NASCAR Thunderbird team in 1988 with driver Mark Martin. Later known as Roush Fenway Racing, the team has won five driver championships across NASCAR's top three series, including back-to-back titles in the Nationwide series with a Mustang driven by Ricky Stenhouse Jr.

Roush Industries became a Tier One supplier of engineering and development services to the worldwide automotive industry. In 1995, Roush Performance was formed to develop and market Ford performance parts, along with building a line of high-performance Roush Mustangs.

Roush credits much of his racing and business success to the Mustang: "I've never met a Mustang I didn't like."

Roush returned the Mustang to Trans-Am prominence by winning the 1989 championship in a 25th anniversary Mustang driven by Dorsey Schroeder. *Jerry Winker*

Tommy Kendall dominated the 1997 Trans-Am series in his All Sport Mustang Cobra, taking the checkered flag at 11 of the 13 races in a year that saw Roush Racing Mustangs win all 13 events. *Ford Motor Company*

Steve Saleen bridged Mustang racing history when he selected Rick Titus, son of Carroll Shelby's championship driver Jerry Titus, as his codriver for the 1987 Escort Endurance season. The elder Titus won the 1967 Trans-Am championship in a Terlingua Racing Team Mustang; Rick helped win a 1987 championship for Saleen. *Source Interlink*

In 1995, Steve Saleen partnered with Tim Allen, popular at the time for his hit TV show *Home Improvement*, to form a World Challenge race team. In its second season, the Saleen/Allen Speedlab effort won the manufacturer's championship. *Saleen Autosports*

*Continued from page 191*

Ford Racing started looking to grassroots racers in 1999 with the FR500, a Mustang race car concept based on the 1999 SVT Cobra. In 2005, the idea became reality as the turnkey Boy Racer FR500C. "Mustang hadn't been formerly introduced in road racing in at least a couple of decades," said Ford Racing director Jamie Allison. "We were in Trans-Am, but that morphed into a high-end professional series, compared to what Trans-Am initially started out to be, which was truly racing cars from the factory. That's what we wanted to bring back with the FR500C."

Powered by a 5.0-liter Cammer engine, the FR500C was created for Grand-Am-type racing, complete with roll cage. FR500C Mustangs won the manufacturers title in the Koni Challenge racing series in 2005 and 2008. Later versions included the FR500S for the Mustang Challenge series, created by Ford Racing and Miller Motorsports Park, and the FR500GT for SCCA World Challenge competition. The FR500's ongoing development led to the Boss 302R, a precursor to the production 2012–2013 Boss 302. Competing in the 2010 and later Grand-Am Continental Tire Sports Car Challenge, the Boss 302R teams were not able to deliver a championship over the BMWs, but the stresses of competition led to a number of improvements for the production Boss 302s.

*Continued on page 200*

Ford brought back 1970 Trans-Am champion Parnelli Jones (center) for the introduction of the Boss 302R in 2010. *Ford Motor Company*

*Continued from page 195*

For grassroots racers, Ford Racing offered part number M-FR500-BOSS302S, an entry-level, purpose-built road racing Mustang designed for everything from open-track events to SCCA competition. Equipped with a roll cage, adjustable rear wing, fire system, and other race-ready equipment, the Boss 302S was a capable track performer, as Paul Brown proved by driving one to the SCCA's World Challenge GTS class championship in 2011.

Tiger Racing's Paul Brown proved the track-worthiness of the Boss 302S by claiming the GTS class championship in the 2011 SCCA World Challenge. *Tiger Racing*

In a CJ versus CJ-class final at the 1968 Winternationals, Hubert Platt's red-light start gifted the Super Stock championship to Al Joniec. The outstanding performance by the new 1968 Cobra Jet Mustangs ignited a new performance era for Mustang and Ford. *Source Interlink Media*

## QUARTER MILE AT A TIME

By the time the Mustang arrived in 1964, Ford was well-entrenched in drag racing activities as part of the Total Performance marketing campaign. As early as 1962, the Ford Drag Council had been formed with a group of engineers, supporting Ford dealers, and drivers, including top names Dick Brannon, Bill Lawton, Phil Bonner, Al Joniec, Les Richey, and Gas Ronda. Originally, they were supplied with lightweight 427 Galaxies, then Fairlane Thunderbolts, but it was inevitable that the Mustang would enter the quarter-mile wars. In late 1964, Holman-Moody prepared Mustang Fastbacks for the NHRA's new A and B Factory Experimental (A/FX and B/FX) classes. To compete against Chrysler's Hemi engine, 427s were stuffed between the Mustang fenders, either the 427 high-riser or the new single-overhead-cam (SOHC) 427, which had been developed for NASCAR but eventually banned.

A/FX Mustangs competed in NHRA, AHRA, and match-racing competitions in 1965. Popular driver Gas Ronda won the AHRA World Finals in the Russ Davis Ford Mustang and in the process established a new A/FX record of 10.43 seconds at 134.73 miles per hour. *Source Interlink Media*

But Chrysler had another trick up its sleeve for the 1965 season. By altering the wheelbase of its A/FX cars, they gained a weight transfer advantage off the starting line. A number of the Mustang teams responded by stripping weight, moving engines back, and pushing the front wheels forward so they almost touched the front bumper.

In 1966, the A/FX class transitioned into Experimental Stock. In response to the altered-wheelbase Mopars, Holman-Moody built new Mustangs with tubular frames, straight front axles, and stretched fiberglass front ends, giving the cars their long-nose nickname. More than 1,000 pounds lighter than their 1965 predecessors and powered by fuel-injected 427 SOHCs with up to 1,000 horsepower, the wild Experimental class Mustangs were capable of

*Hot Rod* magazine described the 428 Cobra Jet-powered 1968 Mustang as the "fastest running pure stock in the history of man." Two months later, Ford was running ads with the *Hot Rod* endorsement.

# TASCA FORD

"Win on Sunday, sell on Monday" was a popular slogan during the 1960s. Bob Tasca not only lived it at his Tasca Ford dealership in Rhode Island, but he's credited with coining the phrase.

After climbing from grease monkey to general manager at Sandager Ford, Tasca opened his own Ford dealership in November 1953. He promised "complete customer satisfaction," but also got the jump on Ford's Total Performance campaign by creating a Tasca Ford performance program in 1961.

At first, Tasca sponsored a customer's 406 Ford, then convinced Bill Lawton to swap his 409 Chevrolet for a Tasca team car. For the next 10 years, Lawton drove Tasca's lightweight Galaxies, Thunderbolts, and Mustangs. Tasca's reputation for winning led to increased sales, up to 100 performance cars per month.

For Bob Tasca, performance meant profits, so he was quick to complain about Ford's lackluster offerings in the late 1960s. According to Tasca's calculations, Fords accounted for only 7.5 percent of all 1966 performance car sales. When Tasca's complaints reached Ford World Headquarters via an article in *Hot Rod*, Ford listened, resulting in the 428 Cobra Jet, an engine that would drive Ford's performance program for the next three years.

When Ford's muscle car chapter came to a close in 1970, Tasca moved across the state line into Massachusetts as a Lincoln-Mercury dealer, becoming the world's top dealership by 1986. Bob Tasca passed away at 83 in 2010, leaving today's Tasca Ford-Lincoln in the capable hands of his sons, Bob Jr. and Carl. The family dealership, relocated in Rhode Island, still focuses on fast Fords as an authorized Shelby Mod Shop.

Bob Tasca (left) with his Tasca Ford sales team during a Mustang third birthday promotion. The Mustang at the left is Tasca's personal car that he called the KR-8. *Tasca Ford*

Recognized as a performance dealership since 1961, Tasca Ford supported Ford's racing efforts, including sponsorship of Bill Lawton's A/FX and long-nose Mustangs. *Source Interlink Media*

When the original 390 engine in Bob Tasca's 1967 Mustang hardtop expired, it was replaced by an 428 equipped with off-the-shelf Ford performance parts. Ford would use the engine as a guide to develop the 428 Cobra Jet. *Source Interlink Media*

In response to altered-wheelbase Chryslers, Ford Drag Council leader Dick Brannan asked Holman-Moody to build a Mustang with a longer wheelbase and set-back engine. It is often recognized as the first Funny Car. *Source Interlink Media*

While the factory drag teams basked in the glory, Mustang owners across the country labored in the pits at local drag strips to get their 289s ready for the next round. The owner of this 1966 Shelby GT350 was among the lucky few who picked up sponsorship from a Ford dealer, in this case Burns Ford in Kentucky. *Source Interlink Media*

By 1966, the A/FX class had evolved into Experimental Stock with fiberglass front ends, altered wheelbase, set-back engines, and fuel injection. The front wheels were located 16 inches further forward than stock and the rear axle moved 10 inches closer to the door, providing a final wheelbase measurement of 112 inches. The long-nose Mustang was perfect for Hubert Platt, who was known for his showmanship on the starting line. *Ford Motor Company*

Most A/FX Mustangs were powered by the single overhead cam 427, developed for NASCAR but banned after Chrysler complained that it was not a production engine. For drag racing, the car had a pair of ducts that directed outside air from openings in the radiator support to the dual Holley four-barrel carburetors. *Source Interlink Media*

Although Ford discontinued racing support in 1970, independents soldiered on at local, regional, and national levels. East Detroit's Dave Lyall campaigned a 1970 Mustang SportsRoof in Super Stock with sponsorship from his own speed shop. *Source Interlink Media*

quarter miles in under nine seconds and more than 155 miles per hour. With their altered wheelbases, they were also a handful for the drivers, resulting in loud, bouncing, and swerving passes for the entire quarter mile before a parachute deployed to slow them down. Fans loved it.

The Experimental class continued to evolve in 1967 with most of the drivers campaigning their 1966 Fastbacks instead of switching to the 1967 Mustang. The class became known as Funny Car, a name that Ford's Fran Hernandez coined when he said the following in reference to the 1965 altered wheelbase Chryslers: "We've got to beat those funny cars!"

After a *Hot Rod* article voiced Bob Tasca's complaints about Ford's lack of performance, five white 1968 Mustang fastbacks were unloaded in the pits at the January 1968 NHRA Winternationals in California. Powered by a new 428 Cobra Jet engine and driven by Al Joniec, Hubert Platt, Don Nicholson, Jerry Harvey, and Gas Ronda, the Mustangs impressed

In 1969 and 1970, a pair of Ford drag teams traveled the country with a Cobra Jet Torino and Mustang, either a CJ car for Super Stock or one equipped with a 427 SOHC for match racing. This is the Platt and Payne East Coast team. *Ford Motor Company*

For brand recognition, Ford asked "Ohio George" Montgomery to switch from his 1933 Willys body to a 1967 Mustang. The Malco Gasser became one of the most popular AA/GS cars on the match-race circuit well into the 1970s. *Source Interlink Media*

The Mustang II got in on the drag racing action in 1974 with Billy Meyer's Funny Car. *Source Interlink Media*

right out of the box with four of the five cars reaching the finals for their respective classes. Joniec won his SS/E class by defeating Hubert Platt in a CJ versus CJ matchup, then beat Dave Wren's Hemi-powered Plymouth to claim the overall Super Stock Eliminator championship. Ford used the victory to promote the Cobra Jet as Ford's latest performance powerplant for both the Mustang and Torino.

The following year, 1969, Ford took advantage of the Cobra Jet's success with the Ford Drag Team, a new take on the old Ford Drag Council but with two teams, one for the West Coast and another for the East Coast. Both teams used a Mustang and Torino, with drivers Ed Terry and Dick Wood for the West Coast and Hubert Platt and Randy Payne covering the East Coast. Each team used a pair of Mustangs, one with a 428 Cobra Jet for NHRA Super Stock competition and a second, wilder car with a 427 SOHC for match racing. Between races, the drag teams scheduled visits at nearby Ford dealers to conduct seminars for dealership drag racing teams, a method that not only promoted grassroots Ford drag racing, but also helped sales for the new Muscle Parts program. The program was disbanded when Ford announced its withdrawal from racing in the summer of 1970.

With the lack of factory support, independents carried the Ford banner at drag strips across the United States during the 1970s. Every Saturday night, you could find young men in the pits swapping street tires for drag slicks and opening up headers in hopes of winning a class trophy. In professional racing, former Ford Drag Council member Don Nicholson campaigned a 1970 Mustang in the new Pro Stock class before switching to a Mustang II. In Detroit, Ford engineer Jack Roush teamed with driver Wayne Gapp to form Gapp & Roush, a partnership that would combine for numerous victories, many of them in a Mustang II.

As Ford returned to professional drag racing in the 1980s with Pro Stock Thunderbirds, the production 5.0-liter Mustang emerged as the grassroots racer's weapon of choice. Inexpensive, lightweight, and powerful, the movement started on the street but quickly drifted to the drag strip as owners competed for bragging rights. *Super Stock & Drag Illustrated* editor Steve Collison wrangled a promotional dollar car 5.0-liter Mustang out of

Steve Collison, editor of *Super Stock & Drag Illustrated*, was one of the first to promote the 5.0-liter Mustang's prowess on the drag strip. His articles about "Mean Mr. Mustang," a 1987 LX 5.0 hatchback, educated owners about the best ways to modify their Mustangs. *Francis Butler*

# RETURN OF THE COBRA JET

Until 2008, Oklahoma's Brent Hajek was known for his collection of vintage Ford drag cars. But when Ford announced the 2008 FR500CJ, Hajek recognized the link to the past and bought the first 10, plus the factory prototype. Hajek sent two of the cars to John Calvert, the NHRA's 1991 Stock champion in a 1968 Cobra Jet Mustang. Hajek wanted to debut the new Cobra Jet with Calvert at the wheel during the 2009 NHRA

Winternationals, exactly 41 years after Al Joniec won the Super Stock class in a 1968 Cobra Jet Mustang. The new CJ Mustang was even lettered like 1968 with Rice-Holman Ford and Joniec's name on the doors.

With four former 1968 CJ drag racers watching, Calvert drove the new Cobra Jet to victory in its debut outing, just like in 1968.

Hajek was exuberant: "It's our first national event and we won! This

program was always about paying tribute to the drivers from 1968 who started the legend of the Cobra Jet. Ford Racing did an awesome job building these cars and my guys deserve credit for getting the CJs race-ready in an unbelievably short amount of time."

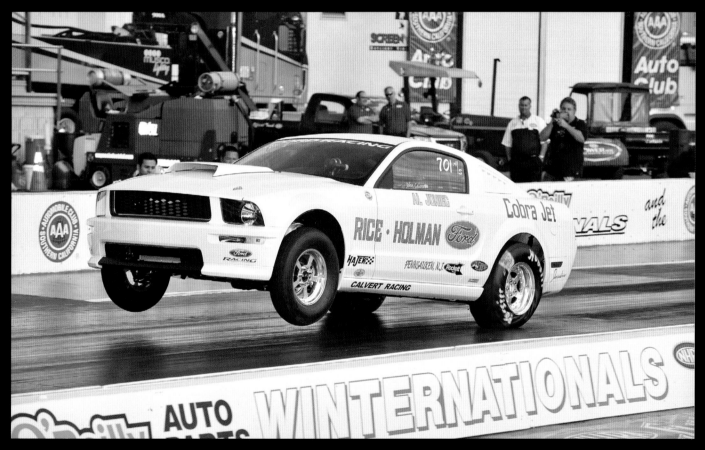

Forty-one years after Al Joniec won the Super Stock championship in a Cobra Jet Mustang at the NHRA Winternationals, John Calvert drove Ford Racing's new Cobra Jet Mustang, dressed to match Joniec's 1968 car, to the Super Stock championship at the 2009 Winternationals. *Ford Motor Company*

Ford in 1987 and helped spread the word about easy but effective modifications with his Mean Mr. Mustang project. Other magazines reported on the burgeoning 5.0-liter scene, featuring the fastest cars and testing the latest parts from Ford Motorsport and aftermarket performance companies. With turbocharging, supercharging, and nitrous oxide, racers such as "Stormin' Norman" Gray, "Nitrous Pete" Misinsky, and Gene Deputy competed in heads-up competitions and became heroes to legions of 5.0-liter fans.

Recognizing the need for organized rules and classes, Bill Alexander and Gary Carter started Fun Ford Sunday in the late 1980s. Events included a car show and drag racing for all Fords, but it quickly became apparent that 5.0-liter racing was the main attraction as the series grew from a single-day event to an expanded nationwide schedule of two-day races known as Fun Ford Weekend. With classes from Street 5.0 to Pro 5.0, the series provided a safe and entertaining venue for Mustang drag racing. Other promoters also jumped on the 5.0-liter bandwagon, including the World Ford Challenge and National Mustang Racers Association.

The Mustang name returned to professional NHRA drag racing in 1997 when Funny Car driver John Force switched from Pontiac to Ford. By winning nine championships in his Castrol-sponsored Mustang, including six straight from 1997 to 2002, Force kept the Mustang name in the drag racing limelight.

After success with the FR500 road racing program, Ford Racing turned its attention to drag racers with the 2008 FR500CJ, a factory-built Mustang drag car with a supercharged, 400-horsepower 5.4-liter engine. NHRA legal for 10-second ETs, the 3,300-pound Mustang came with a unique trim and appearance package, drag wheel and tire combination, and Cobra Jet graphics package. Only 50 were built.

When readers suggested a same-day, same-track competition for 5.0-liter Mustang bragging rights, *Super Ford* magazine responded with the 5.0-liter Mustang Shootout. The first event was held in 1990 at National Trail Raceway, where Ford engineer Brian Wolfe impressed with a naturally aspirated 11.13 ET. Wolfe would climb the Ford ladder to become director of Ford Racing in 2008. *Source Interlink Media*

In 1997, John Force brought the Mustang name to the forefront of Funny Car racing when he switched from Pontiac to Ford. Nine of Force's 15 Funny Car championships came with a Mustang body. *Ford Motor Company*

Bob Tasca's grandson, Bob Tasca III, continues the family's performance legacy by driving the Motorcraft/Quick Lane Shelby Mustang in NHRA Funny Car competition. *Ford Motor Company*

By the mid-1990s, drag racing 5.0-liter Mustangs had progressed from modified street cars to all-out race cars. In 1996, "Racin' Jason" Betwarda campaigned the "World's Fastest 5.0" with hired gun Mike Ragusa behind the wheel and a twin-turbocharged Duttweiler performance engine under the hood. The convertible routinely ran high seven-second ETs at 185 miles per hour. *Donald Farr*

## GET THE DRIFT

After 40 years of Mustangs competing primarily in road and drag racing, Ford jumped tires—first into Formula DRIFT in 2005 by convincing popular driver Ken Gushi to switch from Nissans to Mustangs. Popular with import car fans and, more importantly, a younger, more active audience, drifting showcases power-sliding skills with points awarded by judges for amount of smoke, proximity to the wall, speed, crowd reaction, and other criteria. The 18-year-old Gushi finished the 2005 season in third place after earning the Mustang's first-ever drift win in Houston.

In 2008, Ford shifted its support to Team Falken and driver Vaughan Gitten Jr., who would go on to win the Formula DRIFT championship in 2010. Although still heavily populated with Japanese cars, American cars such as the Mustang continue to gain popularity in drifting competition.

"Our involvement with Formula DRIFT is not new, but we are taking it to the next level," said Jamie Allison, director of Ford Racing. "Enthusiasts can now see great Mustangs on the track with great drivers like Vaughn Gittin Jr. and Justin Pawlak, and they'll get a better chance to interact with our stars and production vehicles through consumer outreach at the events. Formula DRIFT is a major part of our action motorsports program targeting new audiences for Ford."

After switching from Nissan to Ford, Ken Gushi brought the world of drifting to Mustang. *Ford Motor Company*

Since 2008, Vaughan Gitten Jr. has wowed crowds with his drifting talent in a Mustang. He won the Formula DRIFT championship in 2010. *Ford Motor Company*

## NASCAR MUSTANG

Through over four decades, the Mustang had competed in all types of professional racing, except NASCAR. That changed in 2010 when Ford North America Motorsports director Brian Wolfe announced that the Mustang would debut in the Nationwide Series as part of NASCAR's new Car of Tomorrow rollout. "We're excited about Mustang coming to NASCAR," said Wolfe. "It's the most successful product nameplate in racing history and it seems only right that it should be coming to the most popular form of racing in North America."

The update was also part of NASCAR's new muscle car theme for its second-tier series. Like Trans-Am in the 1960s, the new Nationwide lineup pitted the popular pony cars—Mustang, Challenger, and Camaro, although Chevrolet ran an Impala until 2013—against each other instead of front-wheel-drive, four-door sedans. Mustangs replaced the Fusion in four 2010 races before running the entire Nationwide schedule in 2011. Driving for Roush Fenway Racing, Ricky Stenhouse Jr. drove his No. 6 Mustang to back-to-back Nationwide championships in 2011 and 2012.

Although a Mustang in name and body shape only, the Nationwide Series' Mustang put Ford's pony car in the NASCAR spotlight. Ricky Stenhouse Jr. won the 2011 and 2012 championships in a Roush Fenway Mustang. *Ford Motor Company*

# CONCEPTS
# **AND**
# PROTOTYPES

**THROUGHOUT THE MUSTANG'S HISTORY,** Ford teased the car-buying public with concepts and tested new ideas with operating prototypes. Often, concepts stretched the boundaries of Mustang imagination to measure consumer reaction for sometimes wild, always entertaining styling exercises, as with the first Mach 1 concept from 1966 with its low roofline and quad exhaust tips. Others were running prototypes cobbled together to test the viability of new technology. A few were both, such as the original Mustang sports car from 1962 that was created to gauge public perception of a two-seat sports car while also functioning as a drivable experimental car to examine the feasibility of new ideas such as adjustable pedals and pop-up headlights.

But in many cases, futuristic-looking concepts were little more than thinly veiled previews of an upcoming Mustang makeover. For the 1963 Mustang II show car, Ford head stylist Gene Bordinat admitted stealing a trick from General Motors by modifying a 1965 Mustang prototype with sleeker front and rear treatments so it would appear that the future production car had been derived from the concept. In truth, it was the other way around. Ford utilized the clever marketing ploy—and garnering much press attention—several times in the future, including the

Built from an actual 1965 prototype body, the Mustang II was created in 1963 to shift perception away from the Mustang I two-seater to prepare the buying public for the upcoming production Mustang. *Ford Motor Company*

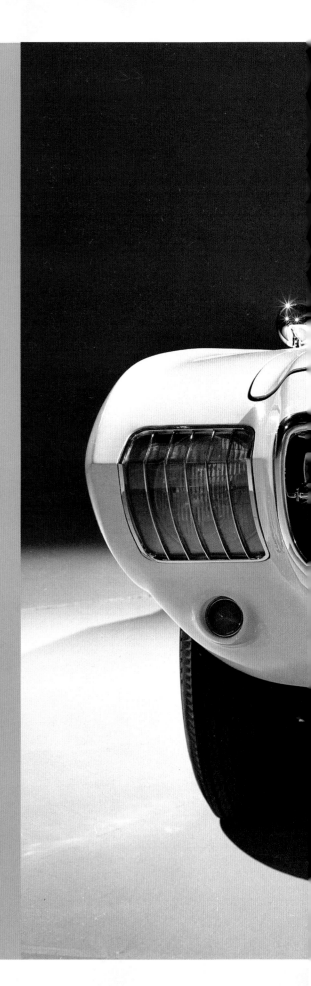

Because Ford had neither the expertise nor the time to build the Mustang I for its debut at the U.S Grand Prix, much of the project was contracted to custom fabricators Troutman and Barnes in California. *Source Interlink Media*

Opposite: The Mustang I was the brainchild of Ford vice presidents Herb Misch and Gene Bordinat. *Ford Motor Company*

two-seater Mach III as a preview of the 1994 Mustang and the GT concept as the forerunner of the 2005 Mustang.

No matter how the concepts and prototypes came together, they provided a glimpse of what the Mustang became or what it could have been. Some of the ideas stuck, such as the original running horse logo. Others, such as adjustable pedals, fell into the engineering trash can.

## MUSTANG I

Although they shared the same name, there was little in common between the Ford Mustang Experimental Sports Car, more commonly known as the Mustang I, and the Mustang that appeared in dealer showrooms in April 1964. It's easy to assume that the two-seat Mustang concept from 1962 led to the production four-seat Mustang. However, other than the name and possibly the idea of rear brake scoops, the only thing that carried over was the running horse and tri-bar emblem, as created by Ford designer Phil Clark.

In fact, development of the production Mustang, then unnamed, was well under way when Ford vice presidents Herb Misch, from engineering and research, and Gene Bordinat, head of styling, commissioned the Mustang I in the summer of 1962. With Total Performance on everyone's mind, the idea was to test the market for a small sports car, similar to the British-built MG or Triumph, and to strengthen Ford's image for engineering excellence and performance.

*Car & Driver* reported on Ford's new concept in the December 1962 issue: "Beyond its obvious purpose as an experimental car to test its components, the Mustang is unique in that it will also function as a show car and a tool for market research."

The Mustang I's interior was as futuristic as the exterior. Seats were fixed, so the steering wheel and pedals adjusted to the driver. *Ford Motor Company*

After air-freighting the Mustang I to Watkins Glen, Ford off-loaded the concept through a crowd into its display tent at the U.S. Grand Prix. *Ford Motor Company*

The Mustang I was a running prototype. As such, the two-seater led the parade laps for the U.S. Grand Prix in October 1962. As seen in this photo, the Mustang I was much smaller than the typical Galaxies of the era. *Ford Motor Company*

Roy Lunn, a designer for Aston Martin before moving to Ford's product study vehicles department, formulated the two-seater's design and function objectives: multitube frame, aluminum body, and a modified version of Ford's V-4 engine from the German-built Cardinal economy car. In a case of one-upsmanship, the Mustang's public introduction was scheduled for the 1962 U.S. Grand Prix at Watkins Glen to spoil Chevrolet's public coming out party for the new Corvair Monza.

Under Bordinat's direction, the body design was sleek and aerodynamic with hideaway headlights, integrated roll bar, and an innovative foldaway front license plate. Because the seats were fixed to the interior, the pedal assembly and steering column were driver adjustable.

Unlike most concepts, the Mustang I was a running, operating vehicle, not only to test new engineering ideas, but also so it could be demonstrated in front of U.S. Grand Prix spectators. At Watkins Glen, race driver Dan Gurney drove the two-seater onto the track for 100-mile-per-hour laps, much to the chagrin of Chevrolet executives who were stuck with their undriveable Corvair Monza concept.

After Watkins Glen, the Mustang I appeared at other races before hitting the international auto show circuit, where it was seen by 1.5 million people. In the spring of 1963, the concept toured colleges to woo engineering students to Ford. Finally, the Mustang I headed off for a yearlong tour of Europe. By the time it returned to Dearborn, Ford had moved on to other projects, including the GT-40 race car, which benefitted more from the Mustang I exercise than the production Mustang.

Typically, concept and prototype cars were destroyed. However, Mustang I engineers and stylists successfully saved their project by hiding it in various locations around Dearborn. In 1975, the Mustang I was officially donated to the Henry Ford Museum, where it can frequently be found on display.

## MUSTANG II

The Mustang I sports car almost backfired on Ford. Suddenly, consumer enthusiasm for a two-seater ramped up, especially from customers who cherished the 1955–1957 Thunderbird. Letters to Ford World Headquarters begged for a real sports car like the Mustang I. But Lee Iacocca was content to leave the small two-seat sports car market to Corvette. He had bigger plans for his four-seat sporty car.

With engineering and design almost complete for the production Mustang, Iacocca had a dilemma: customers were expecting a two-seat sports car. To sway that perception, he requested a four-seat concept car to bridge the gap between the Mustang I and the 1965 Mustang. It would also serve to test consumer reaction to the new car's basic size and styling. Hal Sperlich recalled the process as taking a steel prototype body, making it a convertible, removing the bumpers, restyling the front and rear, and applying cues from the Mustang I, like the white exterior with a thin blue stripe over the top.

Called the Mustang II, the concept was the same size and basic shape as the future production Mustang, right down to the side sculpturing, but the sleek fiberglass nose piece, bumperless rear end, and chopped roofline camouflaged the 1965 Mustang's true appearance. It was concept marketing at its best.

The completed Mustang II was displayed in Ford's styling courtyard on October 10, 1963, shortly before departing for its debut at Watkins Glen. *Ford Motor Company*

With no bumper, the rear-end styling of the Mustang II was totally different from the production Mustang's. The triple lens taillights hinted at what was to come. *Ford Motor Company*

Ford linked the Mustang concept cars to the production versions with this photo of the Mustang I, Mustang II, regular production hardtop, and Shelby GT350. *Ford Motor Company*

The Mustang II was unveiled at Watkins Glen exactly one year after the Mustang I. At a press conference, Iacocca gave away nothing as he told reporters, "The Mustang II is one of a series of recent ideas or show cars Ford Division and Ford Motor Company have built to test public reaction. Showing these vehicles gives us a pretest of likely customer response to styling and mechanical innovations we may be considering for future production models."

Like the Mustang I, the Mustang II toured auto shows over the winter of 1964. It would not be seen in public for another 10 years. The Mustang II was donated to the Detroit Historical Museum in 1975.

## MACH I

With jet aircraft routinely breaking the sound barrier during the 1950s, it's no surprise that Ford originally snatched the Mach 1 name for a Levacar concept vehicle, a one-man "flying car" from 1959. The name returned in 1966 on a concept Mach 1 Mustang to tease the design direction for the 1967 Mustang Fastback. Penned by Pete Stacey and Chuck McHose, who were also involved in the design of the 1967 Shelby, the Mach 1 featured a chopped roof, functional brake cooling scoops, and fixed side windows with toll hatches. The built-in ducktail rear spoiler, center-mounted exhaust ports, and a hatchback third door would appear on later Mustangs, but the swiveling high-back bucket seats never materialized.

An updated version of the Mach 1 returned for the 1968 auto show circuit to reacquaint the public with the Mach 1 name, which was destined for a performance version of the upcoming 1969 Mustang SportsRoof.

## MACH II

Ten years after revising the Thunderbird as a larger four-seat car, Ford was still exploring the feasibility of a true two-seat sports car. Carroll Shelby had filled the gap with the Cobra, but when production ended after 1966 because the little two-seater could not be modified to conform to new safety standards, Ford general manager Don Frey requested the Mach II as a possible Cobra replacement. Roy Lunn, who had been part of the team that created the Mustang I concept in 1962, got the assignment to build the mid-engine two-seater through his special vehicle department with construction taking place at Kar Kraft, a contracted specialty-build company near Dearborn.

Although it looked nothing like a production Mustang when it debuted at the 1967 Chicago Auto Show, the functional and drivable Mach II was built with a number of Mustang components, including a convertible underbody modified to accept a rear-mount 289 small-block, front suspension, and production parts like 1967 Mustang bumpers. The Mach II also incorporated an independent rear suspension, five-speed transaxle, and a Kammback rear end with ducktail spoiler.

Originally built in 1966, the Mach 1 concept returned in 1968 with slight revisions, including covered headlights. *Ford Motor Company*

In addition to the hatchback rear door, the Mach 1 concept teased a number of future Mustang design cues. The built-in rear spoiler would find its way onto the 1969 SportsRoof while the center-mount exhaust port was destined for the 1969 Shelby. *Ford Motor Company*

While *Car & Driver* approved of Ford's two-seat, mid-engine concept, they also realized that the idea was a long way from production, if at all. The magazine noted, "The Mach II embodies too many radical departures from present volume production cars to permit early scheduling."

Stylist Larry Shinoda, who worked on a Mach II-B concept in 1969, admitted that it was Lee Iacocca who pushed for a two-seat sports car. "Unfortunately, by the time we got the clay finished, he had gotten into bed with DeTomaso," Shinoda said. The Ford/DeTomaso relationship resulted in the 1971 Pantera, a two-seat sports car marketed by Lincoln-Mercury.

## MUSTANG MILANO

The Mustang Milano concept, named after the city of Milan in Italy, hit the show car circuit in February 1970 to preview the 1971 Mustang SportsRoof. Truthfully, it gave away little about the next Mustang as it used the front-end shape and NASA-scooped hood of the 1969–1970 Shelby.

Painted Ultra Violet, the Milano also had an interior color-keyed to the exterior and came with luggage made from the same purple leather as the seats. The rear hatch raised electronically, and the laced cast-aluminum wheels provided a glimpse of the lacy-spoked wheels that would be found on mid-1970s Mustang IIs. The taillights attracted the most attention; they glowed green, amber, or red, depending on whether the driver was accelerating, coasting, or braking, a safety innovation that never reached production.

Named after the up-and-coming International Motor Sports Association, the IMSA concept's turbocharged four-cylinder engine hinted toward the Mustang's performance future. The IMSA concept's rear spoiler trimmed rear lift by 10 percent. Even with the wide wheel flares and tires, drag coefficient was down 6.3 percent compared to a stock Mustang. *Ford Motor Company*

# ROUSH'S ANNIVERSARY MUSTANG

Looking toward the Mustang's 25th birthday in 1989, Ford considered several options for an anniversary model, including a special drivetrain. Envisioning more than a paint and stripe job, someone approached Jack Roush about a creating a special car with a special engine.

Roush recalled, "Ford asked us for a powertrain proposal for a 25th anniversary edition. We started with a marine 351 and added a camshaft and fuel injection. We gave it back to Ford and they said the improvement over the regular 5.0-liter wasn't enough. At the same time, we were working on the Thunderbird turbo coupe with the small Borg-Warner turbocharger. So I hung two of them on the 351. Then Ford said it was irresponsible because it was so fast you couldn't keep it in your lane if you stepped on the gas!"

In the end, Roush's proposal was rejected and Ford commemorated the 25th anniversary with a small dash plaque.

To power his 25th Anniversary Mustang, Roush replaced the 5.0-liter with a 351 and bolted on a pair of turbochargers from the Thunderbird turbo coupe. *Source Interlink Media*

Externally, Jack Roush's proposal for a 25th Anniversary Mustang wasn't much different than a standard GT. Under the hood was a different story. *Source Interlink Media*

## QUARTER HORSE BOSS 429

The two Quarter Horse prototypes were just that: 25 percent each of Mustang, Boss 429, Shelby, and Cougar. Built by Kar Kraft, the concept was a proposed replacement for both the Shelby and Boss 429 as the two performance programs wound down in late 1969. Interestingly, the proposal for the Quarter Horse came in September 1969, around the same time that Henry Ford II fired Bunkie Knudsen, the short-term Ford president who had championed the Boss 429 and other performance variants of the Mustang. Even though both Knudsen and the racing program were gone, Ford continued with the horsepower theme to sell Mustangs. The Quarter Horse would have been one of the great Mustang muscle cars if hadn't arrived too late.

Kar Kraft built two prototypes, one in Grabber Blue and another in Candy Apple Red. Both survive today.

## SPORTIVA MUSTANG II

Sticking with the tradition of the earlier Mustang II and Mach II concepts, Ford provided a preview of the upcoming 1974 Mustang II by displaying the Sportiva concept at early 1973 auto shows. But unlike previous concepts, the Sportiva was nearly a spitting image of the 1974 Mustang, except for its semi-convertible body style. A convertible Mustang II was never offered, but the Targa-type roof bar hinted at the T-tops to come.

Like several previous Mustang concepts, the Milano featured hideaway headlights, although no production Mustang ever used the popular styling trend of the era. *Ford Motor Company*

At Ford, the Quarter Horse concept was known as the composite Mustang because it used parts and pieces from several car lines. The formula was simple: take a Mustang SportsRoof and mix in a Cougar instrument panel, hood and front fenders from the Shelby, and Boss 429 engine. *Ford Motor Company*

Ford's Sportiva concept previewed the 1974 Mustang II at car shows and racetracks around the United States. The closest that the Mustang II ever came to the targa-style roof, with removable top, was the T-top option. *Ford Motor Company*

Ford SVO would take the limited-production idea of the McLaren M81 and run with it for the 1984–1986 Mustang SVO. *Ford Motor Company*

Coletti's Boss 429 concept SN-95 Mustang drew a crowd when it showed up one evening for a cruise night at Eddy's Drive-in in Detroit. *Tom Wilson*

## IMSA IDEAS

The Mustang's performance outlook was bleak in 1980. The hottest engine for the production Mustang was the 255-cubic-inch V-8 with cylinder heads and induction designed for emissions and fuel mileage, not horsepower. To show that there was a glimmer of hope for the future, Ford produced the Mustang IMSA concept, a racy Fox body for the auto-show circuit. The race-oriented design elements—pop-riveted flared fenders, 12-inch Gotti wheels, aerodynamic grille-less nose, deep front air dam, and rear-facing Shaker hood scoop—strongly suggested that Ford was thinking about a return to competition for the Mustang.

*Car & Driver* was so impressed it used the IMSA Mustang for the magazine's March 1980 cover. "What Ford has done amounts to a peeling back of the company's mild-mannered, three-piece, pinstripe suit," the report said. "Underneath, for all the world to see, there's Nomex. With 'racing' written all over it."

Working in Ford's special features studio, designer Graham Bell created the IMSA concept with two objectives: fortify the Mustang's appearance and trim aerodynamic drag at the same time. Starting with a base Mustang and pieces borrowed from the 1979 pace car, Bell smoothed and reshaped the body for a wind-cheating design that incorporated a blanked off grille opening and plastic sheeting to seal off turbulence-generating air traps. Inside, thumb switches on the steering wheel controlled the radio and other features, an innovation that was ahead of its time.

Roush Racing built the 604-cubic-inch Boss 429 engine for the Boss SN-95 Mustang. *Tom Wilson*

On the heels of the IMSA concept, Ford introduced a McLaren M81 in late 1980 as a joint effort with McLaren Performance of Formula One racing fame. The McLaren M81 continued the IMSA theme with a turbocharged four-cylinder engine, functional air-extractor hood, and wide BBS wheels. Unlike the IMSA concept, the McLaren M81 was actually scheduled for a limited production of 250 cars. But at $25,000 each, reportedly only 10 were sold, including the prototype.

## CAMARO'S WORST NIGHTMARE

SN-95 program manager John Coletti likes telling the story. In May 1992, he was stuck in Detroit traffic when he heard a radio report about Chevrolet's planned introduction of a new Camaro at the 1993 Detroit Auto Show. With the revamped 1994 Mustang still a year away, Coletti pondered how Team Mustang could spoil the Camaro's debut. Looking up, he spotted a Dodge Viper billboard and found his solution: a Mustang supercar concept. Not only would SN-95 styling cues test consumer reaction for the upcoming Mustang, it would also upstage Chevrolet. His goal: Camaro's worst nightmare.

Arriving home, Coletti began researching Mustang concept car history. In a stack of old magazines, he found reference to the original Mach I and Mach II concepts from the 1960s, which provided him with ideas and a name—Mach III.

With no budget for a concept car, Team Mustang got creative to build a pair of Mach IIIs for the 1993 auto shows, scrounging up scrapped SN-95 prototypes to use as platforms and convincing Lincoln-Mercury to donate 4.6-liter DOHC engines. Team members worked nights and weekends to build the speedsters.

Designed by powertrain development supervisor Tom Johnson and engineer Brad Backer as a drivable vehicle with a powerful yet environmentally friendly engine, the

Ford design manager Bud Magaldi and design executive Darrel Behmer sketched the two-seater Mach III body, making it a speedster design with prominent styling elements that would be found on the upcoming 1994 Mustang. *Ford Motor Company*

four-valve 4.6 was equipped with an Eaton supercharger and an ethyl glycol-cooled intake manifold to reach 360 horsepower on gasoline and 450 horsepower using straight alcohol.

Just six months after Coletti's brainstorm, the Mach III concepts were completed for display at the 1993 Detroit and Los Angeles auto shows, attracting plenty of press attention and upstaging Camaro.

## CRUISING THE BOSS

With his duties as SN-95 program manager completed, Coletti moved to Ford special vehicle engineering. But he wasn't done with Mustangs. When his counterpart at Chevrolet, Jon Moss, dropped a 750-horsepower big-block into a Camaro ZL-1 concept car, Coletti countered by enlisting Roush Performance to install a supercharged 604-cubic-inch Boss 429 into an SN-95 Mustang. To complete the package, the Boss graphics were created by Larry Shinoda, the ex-Ford stylist who had originally recommended the Boss name and designed the stripe packages for the 1969 and 1970 Boss 302s.

In 1994, Coletti and *Super Ford* editor Tom Wilson drove the Boss to one of Detroit's favorite Saturday night cruising spots, Eddie's Drive-In. When the bright orange Mustang rumbled into the parking lot, the crowd "swarmed around us as the Boss hammered away at idle," Wilson reported. "The bodies gathered three deep, the looks on their faces saying they've given up on car building after having this thing in the neighborhood."

In 1999, *Car & Driver* pitted Moss's ZL-1 Camaro against Coletti's Boss 429 for a drag test. At Milan Dragway, the Boss ran a 10.55 at 135.05, beating the Camaro by nearly half a second and seven miles-per-hour in the quarter mile. Coletti beat Camaro again.

"These concepts are thoroughly modern automobiles that point to a bright future for Mustang," said J Mays, Ford design chief, at the public debut of the Mustang GT concepts. *Ford Motor Company*

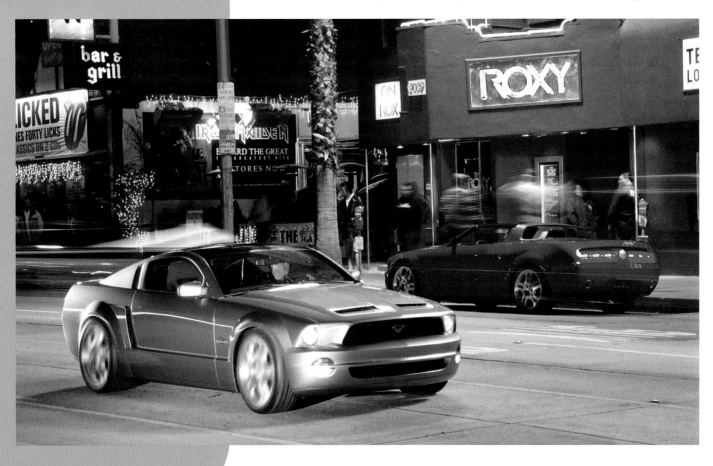

## ULTIMATE PARTS CAR

With a big chunk of its business coming from the sale of performance parts, Ford Racing showcased how its parts could be used for road racing with an FR500 concept. Introduced in 1999 at the ultimate performance parts show, SEMA, the ultimate parts car, as Ford Racing director Dan Davis described it, fulfilled a number of objectives, including the opportunity to broaden Ford Racing's catalog offerings for the Mustang GT's 4.6-liter engine.

Based on the 1999 SVT Cobra, the FR500 concept was loaded with modifications, starting with a 5.0-liter version of the DOHC modular V-8 with 415 horsepower thanks to improved four-valve heads, which were later marketed in the Ford Racing catalog. The FR500's dual-mode mufflers also made it into the catalog.

The FR500 retained the Cobra's independent rear suspension, which was retuned for improved handling, but the front suspension was moved forward to extend the wheelbase by five inches. The exterior used mostly carbon-fiber body panels, including hood and front fenders. Later, Ford Racing expanded on the FR500 concept with a series of turnkey race cars, starting with the FR500C in 2005 and followed by the FR500S, FR500GT, and drag-car FR500CJ.

## SUPER GT

In an unusually candid acknowledgement, the press release admitted, "The Mustang GT concepts are strong indicators of the next generation Mustang's design direction." The remark told Mustang enthusiasts two things: (1) The GT concepts looked a lot like the upcoming 2005 Mustang. And (2) don't believe everything you see.

Introduced at the January 2003 North American International Auto Show, the pair of Mustang GT concepts, a silver coupe and red roadster, were hand-built show cars created to cause a stir at the auto shows while also soliciting feedback from the press and consumers. As everyone would learn in a few months, the press release was correct—many of the GT concept design elements provided hints about the 2005 Mustang.

Mustang fans were relieved to see the prominent 1967-like Mustang front end with mouthy grille opening and running horse, forward placed scoops similar to the 1968 Shelby's, and the traditional side sculpturing with scoops. However, just like the first concept with

"What we're revealing today is a performance parts story wrapped up in a car," said Dan Davis, Ford Racing director, at the debut of the FR500 race car concept. "We saw this as a great opportunity to demonstrate the engineering expertise at Ford Racing Technology and to energize our people by challenging them to show the world what they think would be 'their' best Mustang." *Ford Motor Company*

J Mays, Ford's vice president of design, and chairman/CEO William Clay Ford introduced the Mustang GT convertible concept, a preview of the 2005 Mustang, to journalists and Ford employees on January 5, 2003, at the North American International Auto Show. Exactly a year later, the real 2005 Mustang would debut at the same Detroit show. *Ford Motor Company*

the Mustang name in 1962, the two-seat arrangement would give way to four seats for production. The GT concepts' supercharged 4.6-liter DOHC engine also did not appear in 2005, although a variation would find its way into a future SVT Mustang Cobra.

The GT-R concept from 2004 celebrated the Mustang's 40th anniversary but also pointed toward the Mustang's future in racing. *Ford Motor Company*

## CAMMER GT-R

For the Mustang's 40th anniversary in 2004, Ford signaled that it was on the cusp of a new era of road racing with the Mustang GT-R concept. With bright Valencia Orange paint inspired by the Grabber Orange 1970 Trans-Am Mustangs, Ford vice president Jim O'Connor explained, "The Mustang GT-R shows that Ford is back in road racing in a serious way." The GT-R turned out to be the first volley in a series of road race concepts, leading up to production cars such as Ford Racing's FR500 and the 2012–2013 Boss 302 Laguna Seca.

Designed as a technological showcase, the car still had a number of existing or production-feasible race parts, starting with Ford Racing's 440-horsepower 5.0-liter Cammer crate engine that was already available to grassroots racers. Built at Saleen Special Vehicles, the GT-R retained 85 percent of the production 2005 Mustang body structure. "When a car as good as the 2005 Mustang comes along, we don't need to look much further for a pure race car," said Doug Gaffka, design director for Ford Performance Group.

## THE GIUGIARO CONNECTION

The original Mustang's all-American design didn't always fare well in Europe. So in 1965, as a joint venture between Ford and *Automobile Quarterly*, Giorgetto Giugiaro created an entirely new and much more European body while working as a designer for Italian coachbuilder Bertone. The resulting concept toured the Italian car shows and appeared as part of Ford's Total Performance road show at the 1966 New York International Auto Show, where it took a Best of Show award.

Forty years later, Giorgetto's son, Fabrizio, was smitten by the 2005 Mustang. As styling director for Italdesign–Giugiaro S.P.A., the younger Giugiaro approached Ford's vice president

When Italian father-and-son designers Giorgetto and Fabrizio Giugiaro first saw the 2005 Mustang, they envisioned an exotic look for the new body style. The Giugiaro Mustang concept debuted at the 2006 Los Angeles Auto Show. *Ford Motor Company*

of design J Mays with the idea of putting an Italian twist on the 2005 model. "When we saw the new Mustang, we knew two things: it was the best we'd seen since the original and we had to get our hands on one," Fabrizio said.

Mays liked the idea. "It seemed only fitting," Mays explained. "This design study reinforces the global appeal of Mustang, so when design icon Giorgetto Giugiaro offered to work his magic alongside his son, it underscores the timeless allure of Ford's most iconic car."

Built as a running, operating vehicle, Ford supplied the new Mustang chassis along with a Ford Racing suspension and supercharged 4.6-liter V-8. With electronically operated scissor doors and retractable headlights, Fabrizio was quick to state that the concept was not a peek at future Mustang design, although a production version of the all-glass roof would be added as a Mustang body style for 2010.

In 1965 while working for coachbuilder Bertone, Giorgetto Giugiaro totally reworked the original Mustang to create the Bertone Mustang in collaboration with *Automobile Quarterly. Ford Motor Company*

## TWIN-TURBO CONCEPT

With Ford looking to EcoBoost turbocharging technology as a solution for both fuel efficiency and performance in regular production vehicles, Ford Racing chose turbocharging for its Twin-Turbo concept based on the Mustang FR500CJ. "Ford has embraced turbocharging technology and a lot of our production engineers are working with the technology on a daily basis, so we have a lot of knowledge," said Ford Racing powertrain engineer Rob Deneweth during the CJ concept's introduction at the 2012 SEMA Show. "We decided to apply that knowledge to the Mustang Cobra Jet to showcase what our engineers and suppliers know how to do."

Based on the FR500CJ race car that debuted in 2008, the Twin-Turbo concept added a pair of Borg Warner turbos from the Focus ST. Bolted to a 5.0-liter engine, the smaller, more efficient turbos reduced turbo lag while electronically controlled wastegates from production EcoBoost engines kept the titanium aluminide turbines spinning to maintain boost pressure for lower ETs. Dressed in Ford Racing's new global livery with offset black and blue over-the-top stripes, the FR500CJ twin-turbo possibly provides a glimpse of how Mustangs, both street and race, will make power in the future.

Based on the FR500CJ, Ford Racing's Mustang Cobra Jet Twin-Turbo Concept may provide a glimpse of Ford's racing future with smaller displacement and forced induction. *Ford Motor Company*

# 9

# POPULAR
# CULTURE

**BY 1966, MUSTANGS WERE EVERYWHERE.** With more than a million on American highways, if you didn't own a Mustang, you knew someone who did—friend, relative, or neighbor. Unlike other compact cars, which were viewed as little more than basic transportation, the Mustang transformed its owners into local celebrities. In rural South Carolina, Guy and Mary Ruth Vanderford's 1960 Falcon blended in with the Galaxies, Impalas, and Valiants on their local highways. When they traded the white four-door for a Signal Flare Red 1966 Mustang GT, the 50-something grandparents were suddenly celebrities in their small town.

Mustang's impact on America stretched far beyond the streets and highways. At the end of 1964, a Wimbledon White Mustang convertible played an iconic role in *Goldfinger*, the third film in the popular James Bond series. In 1966, soul singer Wilson Pickett released "Mustang Sally," a chart-topping single about a girl who finds her freedom in a brand-new 1965 Mustang. In the 1970s, Mustangs appeared in many of the era's popular television shows, including *The Mary Tyler Moore Show* and *Charlie's Angels*.

According to Ford, Mustangs have appeared in more than 500 movies and hundreds of television shows. "Mustang has had the most roles of any Ford vehicle and there are no competing cars that come close," said Bob Witter from Ford Global Brand Entertainment, the office in Beverly Hills that works to put Ford-branded vehicles in movies, television, and other entertainment media. "From a product placement perspective, Mustang is the gift that keeps giving and giving."

Actor Steve McQueen performed many of the driving stunts in *Bullitt*, a 1968 movie that secured the Mustang's place in popular culture during the film's nearly 10-minute chase scene with a black Dodge Charger. *Alamy*

In 1999, the Mustang celebrated its 35th birthday alongside another American cultural icon, the Barbie doll, which was turning 40. *Ford Motor Company*

The Mustang has become so ingrained in American culture that it was selected for a U.S. Post Office "Celebrate the Century" stamp in 1999 as part of a 15-stamp series with other 1960s icons such as a man walking on the moon, Woodstock music festival, and the Beatles. *Ford Motor Company*

# MUSTANG IN THE MOVIES

Over the past 50 years, the Mustang has become a staple of American movie culture. With the car's sporty exterior and powerful engines, movie producers and directors have featured the Mustang in numerous films. In some of them, the Mustang was the star. Actors such as Steve McQueen, Will Smith, Jack Nicholson, Sean Connery, and Nicolas Cage have all saddled up in Mustangs. In fact, many of them liked the car so much that, when filming was over, they opted to add a Mustang to their garage.

"When you were driving a Mustang, you were special," said Witter. "You were noticed. You stood out."

**Here are some of more notable Mustang appearances in popular films:**

- *Goldfinger* (1964): Released in December 1964, the film was the first to show off Ford's new Mustang, a white 1964½ convertible driven by a beautiful female assassin (Tania Mallet). To end a chase in the Swiss Alps, Bond (Sean Connery) utilizes his Aston Martin's tire-shredder wheel spinners, just one of his many 007 gadgets, to rip open the Mustang's rear tire.

- *Good Times* (1967). "King of the Kustomizers" George Barris built a pair of wild his-and-her Mustang convertibles for Sonny and Cher's groovy movie.

- *Bullitt* (1968): In one of the most memorable chase scenes in movie history, detective Frank Bullitt (Steve McQueen) drives a Highland Green 1968 Mustang Fastback to chase and be chased by a black Dodge Charger, jumping and bouncing over the hills of San Francisco.

- *Diamonds Are Forever* (1971): Reprising his role as James Bond, Sean Connery eludes police in a red 1971 Mach I, driving it on two wheels to squeeze through a narrow alley in downtown Las Vegas. In one of the great cinematic bloopers, the Mustang enters the alley on its passenger-side wheels and exits on the driver's side.

- *Gone in 60 Seconds* (1974): In the Mustang's original starring role as *Eleanor*, producer, director, and stunt driver H. B. Halicki leads police on a wild 40-minute chase scene in a 1973 Mustang SportsRoof, wrecking 93 cars in the process.

- *Bull Durham* (1988): Kevin Costner plays "Crash" Davis, an aging ballplayer in this sports comedy love triangle. Since Davis once tasted glory in the major league, it's only fitting that he picked up a 1968 Shelby GT350 convertible along the way.

- *True Crime* (1999): Steve Everett (Clint Eastwood) drives a high-mileage 1987 Mustang, a well-worn convertible that matches his character.

- *Gone in 60 Seconds* (2000): In a remake of the original from 1974, retired car thief Randall Raines (Nicolas Cage) must steal 50 cars in 24 hours. This time, *Eleanor* is a silver and black 1967

# SONNY AND CHER KUSTOMS

Well-known for reworking cars for Hollywood stars, southern California's "King of the Kustomizers" George Barris also built special vehicles for movies and TV shows. Sonny and Cher were at the height of their popularity as pop singers in their hippy clothing, and for their 1967 movie *Good Times*, the couple needed vehicles to match their image. Barris was the logical choice to build the cars.

"I wanted him to use Mustangs because I liked the lines of the car," Sonny Bono told *Mustang Monthly*.

"We were pretty hot back then and Sonny and Cher had matching everything. All our clothes were kind of unisex, so George Barris came up with the idea to make matching cars."

Externally, the 1966 Mustang convertibles were identical with split grilles, hood vents, modified taillight panels, and wire-spoke wheels. Custom paint differentiated the his-and-her convertibles, with Sonny's painted in two-tone gold, Cher's in two-tone pink. To match the singers'

fur boots, the interior incorporated fur floor covering and seat inserts. The cars were built as a joint venture between Barris, Sonny and Cher, Columbia Pictures, Ford Motor Company, and AMT, which produced a 1/25-scale plastic model kit.

After touring the World of Wheels circuit, the Sonny and Cher Mustangs were stored until purchased by Mustang collector Don Chambers in 1982. More recently, the cars sold as a pair at the 2010 Barrett-Jackson Collector Car Auction.

"King of the Kustomizers" George Barris built a pair of his and her Mustang convertibles for Sonny and Cher's 1966 movie *Good Times. Source Interlink Media*

One of the Mustang's first entries into American popular culture when Tania Mallett drove a white 1964½ Mustang convertible in the 1964 James Bond film *Goldfinger*. *UA/Photofest*

Mustang styled by the studio as a modified Shelby GT500.

- *The Princess Diaries* (2001): Anne Hathaway stars as Mia, an awkward 15-year-old who gets her 1966 Mustang fixed up in time for her 16th birthday.

- *Hollywood Homicide* (2003): Detectives K. C. Calden (Josh Hartnett) and Joe Gavilin (Harrison Ford) drive a 2003 Saleen S351 in this action dramedy.

- *A Cinderella Story* (2004): Unpopular Sam Montgomery (Hillary Duff) drives a blue 1966 Mustang convertible in the romantic comedy.

- *I Am Legend* (2007): A red and white Ford Shelby GT500 costars with Will Smith, the sole survivor of a New York City plague that kills most of humanity and transforms the rest into monsters.

- *Bucket List* (2007): When blue-collar worker Carter Chambers (Morgan Freeman) and billionaire Edward Cole (Jack Nicholson) meet in the hospital after both were diagnosed with lung cancer, the unlikely pair commit to checking off the things they'd like to do before kicking the bucket. On Chambers's list: drive a Shelby Mustang.

- *Trouble with the Curve*: (2012): Clint Eastwood, who plays aging baseball scout Abe Lobel, spent a lot of time behind the wheel of a 1966 Mustang convertible while filming this sports drama.

# BULLITT

When Steve McQueen drove a Highland Green Mustang Fastback in the 1968 film Bullitt, the car became the star as it bounded over the hills of San Francisco in what is still considered one of the greatest chase scenes of all time. During the nearly 10-minute segment, McQueen's character, Lt. Frank Bullitt, pursues the villains in their black Dodge Charger.

The Mustang's selection for the movie probably had more to do with Ford's product-placement agreement with Warner Brothers than with any specific need or request, although stunt driver Bud Elkins once said that the Mustang Fastback was a fitting vehicle for a gritty cop like Lt. Bullitt. Two 1968 Mustang Fastbacks, both equipped with 390 engines, were acquired through Ford for the film. Race car builder Max Balchowsky

prepared the Mustangs for their high-flying jumps by reinforcing the shock towers, adding crossmembers, and modifying the engines. "Steve liked the sound of the car and he wanted

Taking advantage of the Bullitt Mustang's popularity, Ford introduced a Bullitt GT special edition in 2001. Steve McQueen's son, Chad, posed for publicity photos with the new Highland Green Mustang and a 1968 Bullitt replica owned by Dave Kunz. *Ford Motor Company*

mags," Balchowsky told interviewer Susan Encinas. "We hopped it up because Steve wanted the car hopped up. He was still a kid."

Because the primary stunt Mustang was damaged during filming, it was sent to a salvage yard and eventually destroyed. According to Bullitt Mustang historian Brad Bowling, a Warner Brothers' employee bought the second car. The Fastback survives today in the possession of an **anonymous owner.**

Few movie automobiles are more well known and recognized than the 1968 Mustang 2+2 Fastback from Steve McQueen's 1968 film *Bullitt. Courtesy Everett Collection*

When southern California entrepreneur H. B. Halicki visited a movie set after investing in a film, he said to himself, "I could do this." Combining his love of cars and skill as a stunt driver, Halicki conceived, wrote, produced, directed, and starred in the 1974 film *Gone in 60 Seconds*, which featured a 1973 Mustang SportsRoof as Eleanor. The movie attracted a cult following with its 40-minute chase and crash scene that wrecked 93 cars. Halicki became known as the "Car Crash King" and promoted the film by displaying Eleanor, crumpled and dented, in front of movie theaters. He grossed $40 million with his independently produced film.

When Halicki was killed during a freak accident while filming *Gone in 60 Seconds 2* in 1989, his widow, Denice, inherited the rights to the

No other movie Mustang was copied as much as *Eleanor* from the 2000 remake of *Gone in 60 Seconds*. *Source Interlink Media*

movie. In 2000, she worked with Touchstone Pictures and producer Jerry Bruckheimer to remake her husband's *Gone in 60 Seconds* with Nicolas Cage, Angelina Jolie, and Robert Duvall. The film was an

immediate success, grossing over $25 million on its first weekend and creating another Mustang movie icon with its reprised Eleanor, a modified 1967 Mustang fastback.

Creator, writer, producer, and director H. B. Halicki performed most of the stunt driving in the original *Gone in 60 Seconds*, including this 128-foot jump in *Eleanor* at the conclusion of the 40-minute chase scene. He suffered compressed discs in his spine from the landing. *Photo courtesy of Denice Halicki*

## MUSTANGS IN MUSIC

Dean Hillestad combined his love of Mustangs and music into the unique hobby of collecting songs with Mustangs in the title or part of the lyrics. Hillestad's obsession started when he stumbled across the vintage album *Mustang!* by the Zip-Codes at a Shelby American Automobile Club convention. With song titles such as "Fancy Filly from Detroit City" and "Super Fine 289," Hillestad was intrigued enough to pay $50 for a mono version of the album, which featured a cover with photos of a Poppy Red 1965 Mustang hardtop. "Most of the songs are pretty hokey," he admits.

With the emergence of radio in the 1950s, rock and roll became the soundtrack to teenagers across America as they cruised suburbia in their Chevys and Fords. A few years later, and just two months before the Mustang's introduction in 1964, the Beatles changed the course of popular music forever. The first sounds to vibrate the tiny dash speaker in many 1965 Mustangs were Beatles tunes, which dominated American airwaves during the mid-1960s.

Mustangs also became the subject for songwriters. Wilson Pickett's "Mustang Sally" from 1966 is the most famous and still a popular dance song. Hillestad has collected nearly 20 professionally recorded covers of the tune, many of them by popular artists such as the Young Rascals, Buddy Guy, and Herbie Mann. The Beach Boys' Brian Wilson cowrote "Move Out Little Mustang" for Jan and Dean's 1964 album, *Little Old Lady from Pasadena*. Other writers incorporated Mustangs into the story line, such as Delbert McClinton and his "When Rita Leaves," where the singer laments the fact that Rita left with his "sky blue Mustang ragtop" and "burned that pony to the ground." In 1990, rapper Vanilla Ice referred to the 5.0 Mustang in his summer hit "Ice Ice Baby": "Rollin in my five-point-oh; With my ragtop down so my hair can blow."

Dean Hillestad began collecting Mustang music when he found a copy of *Mustang!* by the Zip-Codes. *Donald Farr*

A 2007 Ford Shelby GT500 was Will Smith's ride in the 2007 postapocalyptic science fiction horror film *I Am Legend*. *Ford Motor Company*

When country singer Keith Urban (center) needed a Mustang for his music video for his 2009 record *Sweet Thing*, Nashville Mustang owners Ken and Nish Peters came to the rescue with their black 1969 SportsRoof. *Photo courtesy of Ken Peters*

With the advent of music videos, the Mustang became a visual element for the MTV generation, although Martha Reeves and the Vandellas filmed one of the first music videos much earlier, in 1965, for "Nowhere to Run" while cavorting in Mustangs on the Dearborn assembly line. Mustangs old and new have appeared in more recent videos, including a starring role for the 1969 Mustang SportsRoof in Keith Urban's 2008 hit "Sweet Thing."

## SMALL SCREEN

Just like the movies, Mustangs have been popular in television series as transportation for main characters or part of episode plots. In fact, ABC made a leasing deal with Ford in 1973 to guarantee the on-screen appearance of Ford vehicles on many of Aaron Spelling's popular productions of the time, including *Charlie's Angels*. While Kelly (Jacklyn Smith) landed a Mustang II Ghia and Sabrina (Kate Jackson) was saddled with an orange Pinto, Jill (Farrah Fawcett, and later Cheryl Ladd as sister Kris) scored big with the sporty Cobra II. During the show's first season in 1976, the Cobra II's popularity skyrocketed thanks to the TV exposure.

With prominent Ford sponsorship, Mustangs have received plenty of screen time on *American Idol*, America's most-watched television series since 2003. As the season four winner, Carrie Underwood took home a 2005 Mustang convertible. *Ford Motor Company*

# MUSTANG SALLY

Sir Mack Rice, a little known Detroit-based R&B singer/songwriter in the 1960s, was captivated by a friend's interest in Ford's new Mustang and decided to write a song about it. His original title was "Mustang Mama," but he eventually changed it to "Mustang Sally" at the insistence of friend and fellow singer Aretha Franklin. Rice recorded the song in 1965 and it reached number 15 on the R&B charts. But it wasn't until Wilson Pickett chose Rice's tune for his 1966 recording that it became one of the most popular dance songs in history. Pickett's version reached number four on Billboard's Top 100 chart. It remains one of the most recorded and most requested dance and DJ songs of all time.

Think you better slow your Mustang down . . .

Songwriter Sir Mack Rice still performs "Mustang Sally." He appeared at Ford World Headquarters during the Mustang's 40-city tour in 2005. *Ford Motor Company*

Sir Mack Rice originally recorded "Mustang Sally" in 1965, but it was Wilson Pickett's version, released as a single in 1966, that made the song an American cultural icon. *Donald Farr*

In addition to appearing on-screen, Mustang convertibles were popular parade vehicles for television and movie personalities. Joe Flynn from *McHale's Navy* caught a ride in a 1966 Mustang GT during the Riverside 500 parade in January 1966. *Source Interlink Media*

# MUSTANG SONGS

Dean Hillestad's collection of Mustang songs includes the well-known and the unknown. Here's a sampling:

## MUSTANG IN THE TITLE

| Song | Artist |
|------|--------|
| "Run, Little Mustang" (1964) | The Zip-Codes |
| "Mustang" (1964) | Link Wray and his Ray Men |
| "Wild, Wild Mustang" (1964) | Dick Del and the Del-Tones |
| "Mustang Sally" (1966) | Wilson Pickett |
| "Mustang Sally" (1966) | Young Rascals |
| "My Mustang Ford" (1966) | Chuck Berry |
| "Drive My Mustang" (1966) | The Persons |
| "Move Out Little Mustang" (1967) | Jan and Dean |
| "Cherry Red Mustang" (2004) | Dusty Wright |
| "1965 Mustang" (2006) | Five for Fighting |
| "Plain Jane in a Mustang" (2010) | Lisa Best with Lonnie Mack |

## MUSTANG IN THE LYRICS

| Song | Artist |
|------|--------|
| Ice Ice Baby (1989) | Vanilla Ice |
| Kiss Me in the Car (1993) | John Berry |
| High Water (2001) | Bob Dylan |
| Steve McQueen (2002) | Sheryl Crow |
| When Rita Leaves (2004) | Delbert McClinton |
| Whiskey Girl (2004) | Toby Keith |
| Sixgun (2005) | Reckless Kelly |
| Ain't No Woman Like You (2006) | Trace Adkins |
| Red Staggerwing (2006) | Mark Knopfler |
| Crazy Ex-Girlfriend (2007) | Miranda Lambert |
| Five-O Ford (2008) | Rev. Horton Heat |
| Sweet Thing (2008) | Keith Urban |

Known for its surfing and cruising records by artists such as the Ventures and Jan and Dean, Liberty Records released *Mustang!* by the Zip-Codes in 1964. *Donald Farr*

During the 1970 to 1977 run of the *Mary Tyler Moore Show*, main character Mary Richards (Mary Tyler Moore) drove a variety of Mustangs, most notably a white 1970 hardtop in the opening credits. In the third season's finale (March 1973), Mary stresses over the money needed to buy a new 1973 Mustang convertible. In the popular *Beverly Hills 90210* from 1990 to 2000, Brandon Walsh (Jason Priestly) drove Mustang convertibles, either a 1965 model or a 1995 GT. In real life, Priestly drove a 1995 Cobra R in IMSA Grand Sport competition.

While Mustangs were seen often in *Charlie's Angels* and *The Mary Tyler Moore Show*, Ford's sporty pony car was also featured prominently in plots for single episodes of many other TV series. Mustangs played a frequent role in the popular *Married with Children* (1987–1997). In season one's episode five, "Have You Driven a Ford Lately," Al Bundy (Ed O'Neill) and neighbor Steve Rhoades (David Garrison) bond by restoring a 1965 Mustang convertible, only it turns out to be a stolen car. Toward the end of the series' run, Al bought a 1996 Mustang "Testica 2000" to replace his Plymouth Duster.

Perhaps most importantly, the only car to beat General Lee in an overland race in *The Dukes of Hazzard* was a 1968 Mustang GT Fastback.

Today's Mustang has also seen its fair share of starring TV roles. In 2008, a Shelby GT500KR reprised the role as KITT for a TV series based on 1982's *Knight Rider*, which starred David Hasselhoff in the original KITT, a tricked out Pontiac Trans Am. In *Alcatraz*, Detective Rebecca Madsen (Sarah Jones) drives a *Bullitt*-like 1968 Mustang Fastback on the streets of San Francisco. In 2012, with Madsen wearing a familiar blue turtleneck sweater, the show re-created the 1968 *Bullitt* chase scene using a 2013 Mustang GT.

For 2008's remake of *Knight Rider*, Justin Bruening played the role of main character Mike Tracer while a 2008 Shelby GT500KR became the new KITT, replacing the Pontiac Trans Am from the original series. *Ford Motor Company*

In 2012, the TV series *Alcatraz* re-created Steve McQueen's 1968 *Bullitt* chase scene using a 2013 Mustang GT. *Ford Motor Company*

# MUSTANG
# COMMUNITY

**IN ONE OF THE IMMUTABLE LAWS** of human nature, people like to share their interests with others. So it was only natural that Mustang owners have always sought out other Mustang owners for fun, camaraderie, and the sharing of information about accessories, performance enhancements, and repairs.

Organized clubs grew out of Mustang owners' desire to communicate and socialize with each other. Since 1964, clubs have formed the backbone of an ever-growing Mustang community that includes shows, races, parts manufacturers, magazines, and website forums. Many are affiliated with national organizations such as the Mustang Club of America or Special Vehicle Team Owners Association. Some are specific to a city or area, while others focus on a special edition, a certain generation, or even a color, such as the Yellow Mustang Registry. Many are not officially clubs or tightly organized; technically, the Boss 302 Registry isn't a club, yet it serves as the official Internet gathering spot and organizes infrequent Boss reunions.

For many, club involvement not only provides a large pool of available information from other members, but it's also a social activity with monthly meetings, organized cruises, and holiday parties. Although only a small percentage of Mustang owners, even those who would describe themselves as enthusiasts, belong to a club, these active organizations drive the Mustang community. For many years, clubs revolved around the 1965–1973 models. Today, many clubs embrace all Mustangs. It's not unusual for members to drive a new Mustang while stashing an older model in the garage for shows and weekend enjoyment.

Main Street in Steamboat Springs, Colorado, shuts down for the Rocky Mountain Mustang Roundup. Hosted each June by a number of Colorado Mustang and Shelby clubs, the event provides something for every Mustanger with a show, cruise, and autocross. *Photo courtesy of Rocky Mountain Mustang Roundup*

The Boss 302 Registry website serves as a gathering place for owners of 1969–1970 and 2012–2013 Boss 302 Mustangs. In 2012, Ford hosted the group during a Boss reunion at the AutoAlliance assembly plant where the new Boss 302s were built. *Ford Motor Company*

It's hard to miss the cars owned by Yellow Mustang Registry members when they park together at the Ford Nationals in Carlisle, Pennsylvania. *Donald Farr*

## NATIONAL COUNCIL OF MUSTANG CLUBS

The first Mustang club was organized as an outgrowth of the Ford-supported National Council of Falcon Clubs. With the Mustang's arrival, the overwhelming enthusiasm for the sporty new car soon overshadowed interest in the Falcon. In April 1964, Ford incorporated the Mustang into the NCFC, renaming it as the National Council of Falcon/Mustang Clubs. Soon, Falcon was dropped entirely as the organization evolved into the National Council of Mustang Clubs (NCMC). In fact, many of the club's early members traded their Falcons for Mustangs.

By the late 1960s, the NCMC had grown to represent more than 500 dealer-sponsored Mustang clubs around the United States and the world. Activities and involvement varied by dealership. Some hosted monthly meetings while others staged slaloms and road rallies. On the weekend nearest the Mustang's April 17 anniversary, a regional NCMC club hosted Mustang Rallye Day U.S.A., a national event with proceeds benefitting a charity.

By 1970, the National Council of Mustang Clubs had grown to more than 200,000 members. However, interest and participation waned when Ford merged the NCMC with the Ford Drag Team in the early 1970s to create the Ford Motorsport Association. With fuel prices rising and Ford out of racing since the summer of 1970, interest quickly declined and by 1974 the FMA was discontinued.

## MUSTANG CLUB OF AMERICA

Although Ford's active involvement with Mustang clubs ended with the discontinuation of the Ford Motorsport Association in 1974, Mustang owners weren't ready to give up their social interaction. Coincidentally, the FMA's demise coincided with the arrival of the Mustang II, which was not well received by fans of earlier Mustangs. Instead of trading

For the 45th Mustang anniversary celebration in Birmingham, Michigan, Kathy Miller organized a gathering of owners who still possessed their 1964½ Mustangs. Ten of them brought their Mustangs to the anniversary show for the first-ever gathering of 1964½ original owners. *Donald Farr*

# ANNIVERSARY SHOWS

In 1994, Ford and the Mustang Club of America teamed up to produce the first major Mustang anniversary show at Charlotte Motor Speedway. Held over the April 15–17 weekend, the 30th Mustang anniversary celebration attracted more than 2,800 Mustangs and an estimated 60,000 people for the three-day event with manufacturer midway and open track. The gathering attracted national attention when President Bill Clinton visited the show and drove his personal 1967 convertible down pit road.

Subsequent anniversary events were held at five-year milestones: 35th in Charlotte, 40th in Nashville, and 45th in Birmingham, with a pair of 50th anniversary celebrations planned for April 17–20, 2014, at Charlotte Motor Speedway and Las Vegas Motor Speedway.

Ford sponsors the Mustang Club of America's anniversary shows, held every five years. At 1999's 35th anniversary celebration in Charlotte, Jim O'Connor, former Ford Division president, unveiled the 35th Anniversary Edition 1999 Mustang while Tom Scarpello, SVT marketing manager, pulled the wraps off a prototype of the 2000 SVT Cobra R. *Ford Motor Company*

As the owner of a 1967 Mustang convertible, President Bill Clinton attended the Mustang 30th anniversary celebration. He toured the show field during the event at Charlotte Motor Speedway, taking time to share a laugh with Bob and Rochelle McNeal, owners of a Playmate Pink 1967 convertible. *Ford Motor Company*

More than 3,000 Mustangs and 70,000 Mustang fans crammed into Nashville Superspeedway in April 2004 for the Mustang 40th anniversary celebration. *Josh Bolger*

As early as May 1966, the National Council of Mustang Clubs was attracting over a thousand Mustangs—all 1965 or 1966 models—to its dealership-sponsored meets around the country. *Sports Car Graphic* magazine reported more than 1,300 Mustangs at this event sponsored by the Southern California Dealer Association. *Source Interlink Media*

for a new Mustang, enthusiasts held on to their first-generation Mustangs or acquired preowned models that were suddenly plentiful and cheap on used car lots as owners traded them for more fuel-efficient cars. Within a few years, the 1965–1973 Mustangs found new popularity as collector cars.

In March 1976, four Georgia enthusiasts met to discuss the formation of a national Mustang club. On April 11, 1976, Stan Jones, George White, Gary Goddard, and Tom Taylor established the Mustang Club of America (MCA), a national organization "dedicated to the preservation, care, history, and enjoyment of 1965–1973 Mustangs."

Word spread quickly. Just four months later, more than 100 Mustangs from 20 states participated in the MCA's first Grand National show, held at Stone Mountain Park near Atlanta. The MCA quickly began recruiting chapters in other parts of the country, starting with the First Tennessee Regional Group. With concours judging playing a large role in shows, the MCA created the Mustang's first judging criteria and format for originality, similar

Road rallies were a big part of the early National Council of Mustang Clubs meets. *Source Interlink Media*

On April 21 to 28, 1968, the Southern Arizona Mustang Club participated in the National Mustang Roundup in San Francisco. An outgrowth of Holmes Tuttle Ford's Falcon Owners Club, the Southern Arizona Mustang Club survives to this day, making it the world's oldest Mustang club. *Ford Motor Company*

to what had happened for Model As and Thunderbirds. For the first 10 years, the MCA was dedicated solely to the 1965–1973 Mustangs. However, as newer Mustangs gained popularity as 5.0-liter and SVO models, owners of 1974 to current Mustangs were welcomed in 1986. The move also led to a closer relationship with Ford, which joins forces with the MCA to produce memorable Mustang anniversary events every five years.

Today, the Mustang Club of America has more than 11,000 members and more than 100 regional groups around the United States and the world. The MCA regional clubs are responsible for the majority of Mustang meetings, shows, open track events, and other activities. Many contribute to local and national charities for assistance with causes from cancer research to animal protection.

## SHELBY AND COBRA CAMARADERIE

The cars from Carroll Shelby were tailor-made for enthusiasts with their racing heritage, performance, and unique appearance. Perhaps most importantly, they had been touched by the charismatic magic of Carroll Shelby. Owners felt a certain kinship with each other, so it was natural that they enjoyed getting together to compare notes.

Each year, Mustang Club of America regional clubs host five national shows at venues around the country, including the Grand National on Labor Day weekend. *Donald Farr*

As a nonprofit organization dedicated to the preservation, care, history, and enjoyment of all Mustangs, the Mustang Club of America has established criteria and a rulebook for concours judging. *Donald Farr*

In the *Shelby Registry*, Rick Kopec explained the attraction: "Back in those days, seeing another Shelby or Cobra on the road was a much more exciting—and personal—experience than today. If you passed a Shelby or Cobra going in the opposite direction, it wasn't uncommon to turn around and chase the other car down to introduce yourself and talk to the owner."

Shelby American's public relations department created the first Shelby club—Cobra Owners Club of America—in 1965, but as the name implied, it was for Cobra sports cars only. In 1972, the Shelby Owners Association was formed to incorporate both Shelby Cobras and Mustangs. By 1975, the SOA had grown to 1,500 members with an annual national convention that attracted 500 participants and 329 cars in 1974. However, many members were not satisfied with the club's operation, so four SOA members—Austin Craig, Rick Kopec, Royal Krieger, and Ken Eber—split off to form their own Shelby organization, the Shelby American Automobile Club (SAAC).

With renewed enthusiasm and a bimonthly publication called *The Marque*, SAAC gained a following. Club conventions became annual pilgrimages for the Shelby faithful, starting in 1976 with SAAC-1 in Oakland, California, an event that drew 700 attendees from the club's 2,000 members. For SAAC-6, the club set the stage for future events by taking over the Laguna Seca road course in California. Open track events became a staple of future SAAC conventions.

In addition to keeping the Shelby name alive, SAAC also maintains the integrity of the

Jim Osborn (left), seen here with Jack Yeager, was a driving force during the early days of the Mustang Club of America. Osborn served as president on multiple occasions and chaired the first anniversary celebration show in 1994. *Donald Farr*

Open track and vintage races are a large part of Shelby American Automobile Club event activities. SAAC's Oklahoma region takes over Tulsa and the Hallett Motor Racing Circuit every June for the Mid America Ford and Shelby Nationals. *Donald Farr*

The Shelby American Automobile Club national conventions are known by their numbers. SAAC-4 was held in Downingtown, Pennsylvania, in 1979. *Donald Farr*

cars from Shelby American, which was particularly important as values climbed in the 1980s. During a 1984 visit to Carroll Shelby's offices, SAAC director Rick Kopec stumbled across boxes of Shelby American production records in an attic. Using the data to add to information already gathered by SAAC registrars, Kopec oversaw the publication of the *Shelby American World Registry*. The fourth edition, published in 2011, was split into three volumes. With 1,300 pages, the first volume for 1965–1967 Shelby Mustangs weighed nearly six pounds.

In 2000, SVT created its own Special Vehicle Team Owners Association with the motto "Drive Safe and Have Fun" as a way to enhance the SVT ownership experience, which included the SVT Cobras. When a Ford restructuring left the SVTOA in limbo, Ford Racing stepped in to reenergize the SVTOA as an independent national club dedicated to "the enjoyment, care, and history of SVT vehicles."

After Shelby Mustang production started again in 2006, Shelby Automobiles saw the need for an organization dedicated to the new breed of Shelbys. Since SAAC concentrated on pre-1970 Shelbys, Team Shelby was created in 2007 for owners of 2006 and later Shelby vehicles. Carroll Shelby saw it as the opportunity to link owners of newer Shelbys into a dream garage populated by 2007 and later GT500s, Super Snakes, Shelby GTs, GT-Hs, even Series 1 and Shelby Dodge vehicles. To run the club, Shelby Automobiles brought in Robert Lane and Sharon Elliott, who operated the website-based S197 Shelby Owners Association. Recognizing the power of the web, Shelby Automobiles wanted its club to offer the immediacy of a website with a forum based on member-generated knowledge and comments.

"We didn't want to form and operate a club on our own," said then-Shelby Automobiles president Amy Boylan. "So we looked for a partner who was a true enthusiast and capable of creating an organization that would give members real value."

## FORD NATIONALS

When Chip and Bill Miller (unrelated) expanded their spring, summer, and fall Carlisle swap meets to include a Ford event, their All-Ford Nationals quickly grew into one of the world's largest annual gatherings of Mustangs and Fords. Currently known as the Ford Nationals, the three-day weekend combines the famous Carlisle swap meet with a car show, special displays, burnout and beauty contests, and a manufacturer's midway. With sponsorship from Ford, participants can test-drive new Mustangs and have performance parts installed at a Ford Racing garage.

The 82-acre Carlisle Fairgrounds fills with Mustangs, Fords, and fans during the annual Ford Nationals each June. *Donald Farr*

Part of Carlisle's appeal is its swap meet, where attendees can shop for everything from Mustang belt buckles to parts cars. *Donald Farr*

To kick off its bash, Team Shelby members cruise from Los Angeles to Las Vegas for their annual spring get-together at Shelby American headquarters. *Jerry Heasley*

## COLLECTORS

Amassing a collection was not on the minds of enthusiasts who purchased several Mustangs for personal enjoyment in the 1960s. Escalating values and potential profits never entered the equation; these owners simply loved Mustangs and couldn't turn down the opportunity to buy one of interest, even if it meant stashing their beloved cars behind a barn or in a shed. When early Mustang values dropped during the 1970s, many Mustang fans gobbled them up. The classifieds in a 1977 issue of the Shelby American Automobile Club's *The Marque* list a 1966 Mustang GT convertible for $2,000, a 1970 Boss 302 for $3,000, and a 1968 Shelby GT500KR convertible for $4,000.

True collector status for the Mustang began in the 1980s when values began to climb alongside other desirable cars from the 1960s, especially muscle cars. For those with the

Restorer and collector Bob Perkins specializes in low-mileage Mustangs, particularly the Boss models from 1969 to 1971. *Donald Farr*

means to purchase, this provided the chance to not only enjoy the cars, but to also realize a profit in the future. For example, values for the Boss 302 rose from less than $2,000 in the mid-1970s to more than $10,000 in the late 1980s. By 2007, well-documented and restored/original Boss 302s were valued at more than $100,000 before dropping slightly after the economic downturn in 2008. Not a bad return on investment if you bought one in 1979—in most cases, better than the stock market. The same held true for other Mustangs, especially Shelbys and other high-performance models.

Today, Mustang collections vary as much as enthusiasts. Like clubs, many collections focus on a particular year, model, era, or special edition. There are also collectors of Mustang memorabilia, model cars, advertisements, and even oil filters for Mustang engines.

## PARTS INDUSTRY

Much of the Mustang's original appeal came from the ability for owners to make their own modifications, whether it was for performance, convenience, or appearance. Right from the start, Ford promoted accessories, from tissue holders to Cobra six-barrel induction. In the 1960s, Mustang owners acquired parts in one of three ways: from the popular aftermarket performance parts companies, used in salvage yards, and from Ford dealers

New Jersey's Fadi Cherfane focuses on 2006 and later Shelbys in a collection that is often called Shelby East. *Jerry Heasley*

for replacement and repair components. Over time, new companies sprung up around the manufacture of Mustang parts.

As soon as the first 1965 Mustangs hit the street in the spring of 1964, the popular aftermarket companies were ready with accessories and performance parts. The Mustang provided a shot in the arm for manufacturers such as Hurst, Edelbrock, and Hooker, which were among the first to offer shifters, intakes, and headers, respectively. Demand for performance parts soared in the late 1960s as Mustangs joined the muscle car wars, both on the street and drag strip. Owners of base Mustangs flocked to dealer parts counters to order high-performance parts designed for Shelbys and other performance models. In the late 1960s, Ford launched Muscle Parts, a program that sold "staged" speed equipment and provided tech tips through a catalog and a pair of supplements, one with parts interchange information and the other for cars equipped with Boss 302, 351 Cleveland, and 429 Wedge engines. Shelby also issued a catalog each year with accessories and performance parts.

Muscle Parts came to a screeching halt in the early 1970s as Ford focused resources on emissions and fuel mileage. However, the 1965–1973 Mustangs were still popular for modification and customization, especially since they were readily available as used cars.

In the 1960s, most Mustang performance parts came from the established hot rod aftermarket. However, in the late 1980s, the popularity of the 5.0-liter Mustang resulted in a number of startup companies that specialized in performance parts. In south Florida,

Charley Card, better known as "Honest Charley," sold thousands of Mustang speed parts through his Honest Charley Speed Shop catalog in the 1960s. In 1964, he was promoting "hisself" with a new Mustang hardtop. *Source Interlink Media*

sports car enthusiasts Steve Chicasola and Dario Orlando combined their first names to start Steeda Autosports, which not only produced Steeda Mustangs but also evolved into a manufacturer of parts for Fords and other auto manufacturers. Kenny Brown, who had managed the Saleen team that won the Escort Endurance championship in 1987, parlayed his knowledge of Fox-body suspensions into Kenny Brown Performance, which also built Kenny Brown–edition Mustangs.

Other companies offered products for all cars but became closely attached to the Mustang movement. For example, Flowmaster mufflers provided the sound of the 5.0 liter, and K&N Engineering benefited from the popular use of its high-flow air filters for the late-model Mustang market.

Launched in the early 1980s, Ford SVO was quick to jump onto the 5.0-liter bandwagon by using its connection with mainstream Ford engineering to offer parts such as GT-40 heads and intake. SVO was later renamed Ford Motorsports and today does business as Ford Racing Performance Parts, still offering equipment for the older pushrod V-8s but also pioneering new products for the Coyote 5.0 in current Mustangs.

As the original 5.0-liter engine spawned an entire industry for Mustang performance parts in the 1980s, the growing interest in the restoration and collectability of 1965–1973 Mustangs also opened doors for business opportunities in that market. Some businesses, such as California Mustang, were formed in the late 1970s specifically for vintage Mustangs, while others, including National Parts Depot and Larry's Mustang & Thunderbird Parts, branched out from earlier involvement with Thunderbirds.

As replacement parts for 1965–1973 Mustangs became less available from Ford and harder to find at salvage yards, enthusiasts were restoring and repairing Mustangs in record numbers. To satisfy the growing demand for replacement and maintenance parts, reproductions entered the marketplace from a number of sources, including startup companies, existing

Many of today's high-end collectors buy and sell Mustangs at the popular auctions. Enthusiasts enjoy the action from the Barrett-Jackson Collector Car Auction on SPEED TV. *Jerry Heasley*

Mustang collectors covet the Marti Report, a Ford-licensed service from Kevin Marti's Marti Autoworks that documents 1967 and later Mustangs through Ford's production database. *Donald Farr*

Both Ford and Shelby took advantage of the muscle car boom in the late 1960s by offering parts to enhance Mustang performance. Speed components from Ford's Muscle Parts program were available from Ford dealership parts departments. Performance parts for today's Mustangs are available from Ford Racing and Shelby Performance Parts. *Donald Farr*

In the early 1990s, a young Brian Murphy and his brother Ken developed a new multistage EFI intake manifold for 5.0-liter Mustangs. From that first product, they grew their startup company, BBK Performance, and later launched Brothers Performance, one of today's largest speed-shop warehouses. *Source Interlink Media*

parts suppliers, and even individuals specializing in just a few products. Others offered rebuild and restoration services for original parts, such as carburetors, distributors, and four-speed transmissions. Today, with everything from air-cleaner decals to full replacement bodies available, one can almost build a brand-new 1965–1970 Mustang from reproduction parts.

To assure quality from parts that carry Ford trademarked logos, Ford Motor Company initiated a program to license and oversee reproductions. In many cases, licensed companies are supplied with the original drawings and specifications.

## MUSTANG MEDIA

During the Mustang Club of America's first Grand National show in 1976, Larry Dobbs happened to be vacationing in Georgia in his 1966 Mustang convertible. With vendors selling used Mustang parts, the show sparked an idea. Two years later, Dobbs published his first *Mustang Exchange Letter*, a buy-sell-trade publication that quickly became *Mustang Monthly*, the first successful all-Mustang magazine.

Petersen Publishing, home to *Hot Rod* and *Motor Trend*, soon launched *Hot Rod Mustang* as an annual in 1980, then steadily increased the frequency until it became the monthly *Mustang & Fords* in the 1990s. Two more Mustang magazines, *Fabulous Mustangs* from Argus and *Mustang Illustrated* from McMullen Publishing, soon joined the party. In 1988, *Cars Illustrated* editor Steve Collison picked up on the popularity of the 5.0-liter Mustang and tested the waters with *Muscle Mustangs & Fast Fords*, which quickly grew into a monthly magazine for CSK Publishing. Meanwhile, Dobbs Publishing added heavy 5.0-liter content to *Super Ford* magazine.

From mostly original cars in *Mustang Monthly* to all-out drag cars in *Muscle Mustangs & Fast Fords*, the magazines covered the Mustang universe. Not only did they share news and information, but they also served as a means for parts companies to reach customers.

When Scott Drake (left) couldn't find a trunk weatherstrip for his Mustang in the early 1980s, he used high school shop skills to produce a mold and have them manufactured. From humble beginnings with rubber weatherstrip, Drake created additional Mustang reproduction parts to establish Scott Drake Enterprises, which today also produces performance parts for new Mustangs. *Jerry Heasley*

To show what could be done with Dynacorn's replacement body shell, Ford Motor Company commissioned Classic Design Concepts to build an "all-new" 1967 Mustang fastback from Ford-licensed reproduction parts. *Dale Amy*

By 1990, enthusiasts could choose from six Mustang magazines on the newsstands, covering everything from restoration to drag racing. *Donald Farr*

A Mustang man cave isn't complete until it's got a Mustang pool table. *Donald Farr*

Nothing says Mustang lifestyle more than a Mustang as a conversation piece in the living room. At Drew Alcazar's parties, guests mill around a restored 1969 Boss 429. *Photo courtesy of Drew Alcazar*

Mustangs brought them together, so Tracy and Don Buffum got matching Mustang running horse tattoos during their honeymoon. *Donald Farr*

But the world was changing. The fast-growing Internet offered quicker information transfer as sites such as Corral.net and StangNet provided forums for users to share advice, news, and experiences, both good and bad. The established magazines scrambled to establish their own websites. Some didn't make it—*Fabulous Mustangs* and *Mustangs Illustrated* folded in the late 1990s while *Super Ford* merged with *5.0 Mustang*.

Over the years, the Mustang media has played a large role in the Mustang community by sharing news and information, first on the printed page and later by actively engaging enthusiasts through website forums.

## THE MUSTANG LIFESTYLE

Like golfers and fishermen, Mustang enthusiasts enjoy their hobby in many different ways, including shows, cruising, concours competition, racing, restoration, collecting, or just driving to the grocery store on nice days. For many, the Mustang is a lifestyle with social activities revolving around other Mustang owners. Some decorate their homes with Mustang posters, photos, and die-cast models. Garages also serve as a man cave with TV, bar, and easy chairs. It's not uncommon to find Mustang books and photo albums on the living room coffee table. Even wedding parties depart for the reception in a parade of Mustangs.

Those who live the Mustang lifestyle also dress the part to show off their automotive allegiance. Just look around at Mustang shows and you'll see people in Mustang- or Shelby-related T-shirts and caps, some from previously attended events and many from Ford. Mustang and Shelby apparel is even available at major retailers. Vendors such as Henry Rasmussen criss-cross the country to sell Mustang-related apparel at the major shows. Some enthusiasts make it permanent with tattoos, typically a running horse logo or, at the extreme, an ink illustration of their Mustang.

# INDEX